A Guide to Go to God

Or

An Explanation of the Perfect Pattern of Prayer,

The Lord's Prayer

By
William Gouge, Bachelor in Divinity and
Minister of God's Word in BlackFriars

"This is the way, walk in it." Isaiah 30:21

Edited by Dr. Don Kistler

The Northampton Press
. . . for instruction in righteousness . . .

The Northampton Press
A Division of Don Kistler Ministries, Inc.
P.O. Box 781135, Orlando, FL 32878-1135
www.northamptonpress.org

*

A Guide to Go to God was first published in London in 1626.
This Northampton Press edition, in which spelling, grammar,
and formatting changes have been made, is 2020 by
Don Kistler and The Northampton Press.
 Printed in the USA.

*

ISBN 978-0-9826155-2-2

Cover Design by Sam VanGrouw at Architype
In Pompton Plains, NJ

Contents

Foreword By Derek Thomas

Apparently the Puritan William Gouge often professed "that his greatest pleasure in the world was in preaching the gospel."[1] Most, if not all sound (to use Paul's word[2]) preachers, would say the same. There is nothing quite like the experience of preaching the gospel with the Holy Spirit's wind blowing at the sails.

William Gouge maintained Presbyterian convictions, but remained within the Church of England. He spent 45 years at St. Anne Blackfriars, London, first of all as a "lecturer" (1608-1621), and then as rector until his death in 1653. He was still preaching the gospel he loved so much at the age of 78.

Born on November 1, 1575, in Bow, near Stratford in Middlesex County, Gouge received a classical education at schools in London and Felsted. He later transferred to Eton College, near Windsor, and eventually to King's College, Cambridge where he graduated with a Bachelor's Degree in 1598 and a Master's Degree in 1602. He earned a Bachelor of Divinity Degree in 1611 and a doctorate in 1628. Gouge demonstrated remarkable learning when he was appointed a fellow of King's College upon receiving his Master's Degree (he showed particular skill in Hebrew). He also lectured in logic and philosophy, strongly defending Ramism [the teachings of Peter Ramis] and its advocacy of syllogistic reasoning, as his predecessor, William Perkins, did at Christ College, Cambridge.

Shortly after receiving his Master's Degree Gouge's father urged him to visit London where he met Elizabeth Caulton,

---

[1] Benjamin Brook, *The Lives of the Puritans*, 3 vols., vol. 3 (Pittsburgh, PA: Soli Deo Gloria Publications, 1996), 165.

[2] See 1 Tim. 1:10, 6:3; 2 Tim. 1:13, 4:3; Tit. 1:9, 13, 2:1, 2, 8.

who quickly became his wife. Thirteen children were born, eight of whom survived into adulthood. Sadly, in 1625, Elizabeth died giving birth to the thirteenth child. William lived another 28 years.

William Gouge had a reputation for being a great preacher and the church at Blackfriars grew under his ministry. The congregation particularly loved his Wednesday lectures. Among his most notable books are *The Whole Armour of God* (1616), *Of Domestical Duties* (1622), *An Exposition of John's Gospel* (1630), *God's Three Arrows* (1631), *The Saint's Sacrifice* (1632), *A Short Catechism* (1636), and his *Commentary on The Whole Epistle to the Hebrews* (1655).

In 1621, Gouge spent nine weeks in prison at the command the King James I for publishing Sir Henry Finch's writings on the restoration of the Jews, a work deemed to be "threatening." Eleven years later he formed a society that Archbishop Laud viewed as threatening the stability of the Church of England by encouraging Puritan standards within the church. The society was brought to trial and the verdict was confiscation of the funds and banishment of the society members. The banishment was never enforced.[3]

Gouge was also acquainted with sorrow and trial. Benjamin Brook writes:

> In the decline of life, he was much afflicted with an asthma and the stone [i.e.: kidney stones]. Under these painful maladies he often groaned, but never murmured. Labouring under these afflictions, he frequently said, "Soul, be silent; soul, be patient. It is thy God and Father who thus ordereth thy estate: thou art his clay; he may tread and trample on thee as he pleaseth: thou hast deserved much more. It is enough that thou are kept out of hell. Though thy pain be

[3] See, Eric Rivera, *Christ is Yours: The Assurance of Salvation in the Puritan Theology of William Gouge* (Bellingham, WA: Lexham Press, 2019), 22-23.

> grievous, is it tolerable. Thy God affords some intermissions. He will turn it into thy good, and then put an end to all…" Under his greatest pains he used the words of Job: "Shall we receive good at the hands of God, and shall we not receive evil?"[4]

Gouge's piety was apparent to all. He was known as the "father" of the Divines because of his wisdom and willingness to assist fellow ministers. His family attested that they had never seen him angry or impatient. He was especially kind to the poor and had a heart for overseas missions. During his student years he never missed a 5:30 AM group college prayer meeting unless he was away from school, and he kept a monthly fast with some of his friends.

Contrary to the austere Puritan stereotype, Gouge was exceedingly kind and urged Christians to make family a priority. He took great care in conducting family devotions each day.

And as for marriage, "All duties of a married couple were to be performed devotedly, kindly, and cheerfully" he wrote.[5] Along with other Puritans, Gouge emphasized that love was the mutual duty of both husband and wife, indeed, the foundational duty of marriage: "A loving mutual affection must pass betwixt husband and wife, or else no duty will be well performed: this is the ground of all the rest"[6]

An attestation to Gouge's prominence is the fact that he was called upon to preach a formal statement at the reinstatement of a twenty-year old man who had committed apostasy and converted to Islam.[7]

---

[4] Brook, *Puritans,* 168.

[5] William Gouge, *Of Domestical Duties*, reprint of 1622 edition (Grand Rapids, MI: Reformation Heritage Books, 2012), 85

[6] Ibid., 163.

[7] The full story is given by Eric Rivera, *Christ is Yours*, 106-108.

Trained as a cook near Stepney Church, Vincent Jukes found himself on board a ship bound for Genoa, Italy. While at sea, Turkish pirates commandeered the ship. Seven men died and twenty were severely wounded. Jukes was among thirty-three survivors taken and sold into slavery. He served in the court of the King of Algiers, and he was later passed on to the king's brother who in turn sold him to a Muslim man of African descent. Repeatedly beaten, Jukes was forced to renounce Christianity and acknowledge Mohammed as the great Prophet. Circumcised and made to wear Turkish attire and conform to Turkish customs he was later sold again to a Grecian who made him a soldier aboard a Turkish ship. Jukes and three other foreigners aboard the ship conspired to free themselves and, armed with knives, rushed upon the sailors, stabbing them and seizing their muskets.

On Jukes' return to England he was distressed night and day and couldn't sleep. His conscience was troubled by his renunciation of the Christian faith. He confessed his apostasy to the vicar of Stepney church, who informed the Archbishop of Canterbury, William Laud. Due to the severity of the issue a solemn penance was prescribed. At this point the archbishop called on William Gouge to preach at Jukes's reinstatement into the church. Gouge chose the parable of the Prodigal Son in Luke 15 as his text. The sermon was published with the title, "A Recovery from Apostasy."[8] Gouge spoke of the role of the devil in this apostasy and began, as a consequence, a series of almost a hundred sermons on the armor of God in Ephesians 6:10–20, and later published with the title, *The Whole-Armor of God*.[9] This passage contains the apostle's instruction to pray "at

---

[8] *A Recovery from Apostasy* (London: George Miller, 1639. Readers should also consult his similar work, *Treatise of the Sinne against the Holy Spirit* (London: I. Beale, 1639).

[9] *The Whole-Armor of God* (London: I. Beale, 1616).

all times in the Spirit, with all prayer and supplication" (Ephesians 6:18). Prayer was a matter dear to his heart.

In 1643, Gouge was appointed as a delegate to the Westminster Assembly. Unlike many of his fellow delegates, since he lived in London, he did not have to be away from his home and church for several months. He seems to have engaged actively in the various debates. During the debate on the imputation of Christ's righteousness (an issue that not all members of the Assembly agreed upon) Gouge responded to the question, "How can God look upon me as having sinned when I have fulfilled the whole law?" by saying: "God doth not look upon us as having fulfilled the whole law for ourselves, but by our Surety, and therefore it is said 'accounted'."[10]

In the debate on the relationship between law and gospel, an issue of great significance, Gouge considered it "dangerous to place repentance before faith" for fear of legalism.[11] And, in a debate on whether ministers should know Greek and Latin, Gouge responded: "If a deficiency in Latin, how shall they come to read books?"[12]

Gouge on Prayer

Joel R. Beeke and Randall J. Pederson write that in prayer Gouge was "pertinent, judicious, spiritual, seasonable, accompanied with faith and fervor, like a true Son Jacob wrestling with tears and supplications."[13] In 1626 Gouge wrote, *A Guide*

---

[10] Chad Van Dixhoorn, *The Minutes and Papers of the Westminster Assembly 1643-1652*, Vol 2 (Oxford: Oxford University Press, 2012), 83.
[11] Ibid., 116.
[12] Ibid., 229.
[13] Joel R. Beeke and Randall J. Pederson, *Meet the Puritans: With a Guide to Modern Reprints* (Grand Rapids, MI: Reformation Heritage Books, 2007), 285.

to Goe to God, an expansive exposition of the Lord's Prayer.[14] It aimed at teaching Christians how to come to God in private prayer.[15] Dividing the Lord's Prayer into six[16] petitions, Gouge began with a reflection on the opening line, "Our Father which art in heaven," noting that, "Many other more magnificent titles might have been attributed to God, but none more pertinent to Prayer than this title Father."[17] In the first petition, we called upon to "hallow" God's name, which Gouge interprets as giving sufficient esteem with all our being to God's nature, attributes, triune distinction, titles, Word, and works. In the second petition, for the coming of God's kingdom, Gouge draws a distinction between God's "universal kingdom" (God's absolute rule over the entire creation) and "peculiar kingdom" (the church). It beckons Christians to pray for local churches and the church world-wide. The third petition calls for God's will to be done on earth as it is in heaven. It is a prayer for the realization of God's secret and revealed will on earth. And since we are unable to comply with God's will in our own strength, the petition is a call for God to enable us to do His will. Gouge expands on the need for Christians to read, study, and apply the teaching of Scripture as the expression of God's revealed will.

The final three petitions "aim at man's good."[18] The fourth petition is for daily bread, including such practical things as sleep, health, children, peace, and prosperity. The fifth peti-

---

[14] A facsimile edition of this work was published by Reformation Heritage Books (Grand Rapids: MI, 2011).
[15] Eric Rivera, *Christ is Yours*, 144-178.
[16] Augustine and Roman Catholics divided the Lord's Prayer into seven petitions, making "Lead us not into temptation" and "Deliver us from Evil" two separate petitions.
[17] Eric Rivera, *Christ is Yours*, 147. Rivera cites the original spelling, which I have modernized here.
[18] Ibid. 149.

tion, "forgive us our debts as we forgive our debtors," provides an "insight into Gouge's theology of assurance of salvation and practical divinity."[19] Among other matters Gouge denies the distinction between "mortal" and "venial" sins. People need to feel the weight of all sins. The issue of forgiveness leads Gouge into a lengthy, fascinating treatment on the penal nature of the atonement, the imputation of Christ's righteousness/obedience, the Reformed doctrine of justification and its relationship to biblical assurance, as well as criticism of Roman Catholic teaching, and especially that of Cardinal [Robert] Bellarmine, who died five years before the book on the Lord's Prayer was printed, on the nature of the relationship between baptism and the forgiveness of sins.

The sixth petition, "lead us not into temptation but deliver us from evil," falls into two parts: The first asks God to prevent us from falling into evil and the second asks God for help whenever we do fall. By way of application Gouge provides no less than twenty-seven prayer requests, including patience under duress, growth in sanctification, and participation in the Holy Spirit's ministry in us and through us.

In concluding his treatment of the Lord's Prayer, Gouge, sounding amazingly like Calvin in his magisterial treatment on prayer in the Institutes,[20] asks the question:

---

[19] Ibid., 150.

[20] John Calvin, *Institutes of the Christian Religion*, trans. Ford Lewis Battles, 2 vols., Library of Christian Classics, 20-21 (Philadelphia, PA: Westminster, 1960), 3.20.34-48. Earlier, in Calvin's treatment on prayer, Calvin wrote: "We have noted another point: not to ask any more than God allows. For even though he bids us pour out our hearts before him, he still does not indiscriminately slacken the reins to stupid and wicked emotions; and while he promises that he will act according to the will of the godly, his gentleness does not go so far that he yields to their willfulness. Yet in both, men commonly sin gravely; for many rashly, shamelessly, and irreverently dare importune God with their improprieties and imprudently present before his throne whatever in dreams has struck their fancy."

Q. How may we believe the obtaining of those things which we pray for?
A. By praying for such things as we know to be promised. When God has promised something we can be assured that he will provide it. Always. In every circumstance.

In republishing William Gouge's treatment of the Lord's Prayer in modern English Don Kistler has served the church well. It ranks with older treatments of the Lord's Prayer by John Calvin, Thomas Watson, Richard Baxter, and Herman Witsius, as well as more recent works by R. C. Sproul, J. I. Packer and Albert Mohler.

Tolle lege.

Derek W. H. Thomas

Senior Minister, First Presbyterian Church, Columbia SC
Chancellor's Professor, Reformed Theological Seminary
Teaching Fellow, Ligonier Ministries

Dedication

To the Truly Honored Sir James Fullerton, Knight
Groom of the Stool to the King's Most Excellent Majesty
And Gentleman of His Majesty's Bed Chamber

And

To the Right Honorable His Most Worthy Consort
The Lady Bruce, Baroness of Kinloss

Grace on Earth and Glory in Heaven

It is the nature of some soil to long retain good corn with the life and heart of it in the bowels thereof before it puts it forth. Such a soil has my soul showed herself to be. The solid seed of your Honor's goodness has been plentifully cast on me ever since you dwelt where I exercised my ministry. The proper crop expected from the seed of goodness is gratefulness. This crop has not as yet grown to the desired measure of maturity. Nor has forgetfulness or ungratefulness been any cause thereof, but want of opportunity, which being at length offered now puts forth this fruit of gratitude that in all humility is presented to your honorable acceptance.

There are (worthy Sir James) public and private respects that induce me thus openly to make reverend mention of your honorable name. Public respects, for which all the King's subjects are bound to bless God for you, your faithful service to the King's most excellent majesty from his childhood to this day. Private respects in my own and my children's behalf, whom you have forever in all duty bound to you. Besides your profound and sound judgment, your much and great experience in controversial and case divinity in matters of disputation and devotion, though they somewhat discourage me from presenting so unpolished an explanation of so perfect a pattern of prayer to such as eagle-eye as can soon discern and discover the defects and deformities thereof, yet they also encourage me to seek such a patron that through the patronage of so judicious a censor it may be embolden to lie open to the view of all sorts of readers. Wherefore not the manner of explaining this perfect prayer, but the matter explained; not any worth of the workman, but the goodness of your own disposition (that makes you ready on all occasions to do all good offices of courtesy and kindness) promise a favorable acceptance of that which is humbly commended to your patronage.

There are (good Madam) general and particular respects that move me by this means to manifest my humble bound duty to your Honor—in general your true piety and holy devotion to God, your love of His Word and of His ministers, in particular your good respect of my ministry, and of my person for my ministry's sake, your entire love of my dear deceased wife, of blessed memory, and the many evidences whereby the truth of these have been demonstrated. All these induce me to testify my humble thankfulness to your Honor in this manner, that it may be the more real and prove some help and furtherance to your pious devotion, which may at this time be somewhat more seasonable because of that long weakness of body wherewith it has pleased the wise God, your heavenly Father, to visit you. To take occasion from the weakness of the body to use means of strengthening the spirit is a blessed advantage. This makes God's fatherly chastisement to turn to our profit and, through a true apprehension and due consideration thereof, it works in us a hearty and earnest desire of going to God for direction. Behold here a help, *A Guide to Go to God*, which desires as a handmaid to attend your Ladyship and to be entertained by you that she may be the more ready at hand to guide you in your way to God.

Grant, therefore, I beseech you, graciously to accept this small testimony of gratitude here tendered to your Honor by him, that being utterly unable of himself to return any recompense for your many great kindnesses, yet exceedingly desirous that they may be abundantly recompensed, does not cease to solicit the Throne of Grace (where plenty of all blessing is to be had) for your Honor's present and future happiness in this and the other world, and in that respect is and will be, as in all duty he acknowledges himself most bound to be,

Your Honor's Daily Orator

William Gouge

To the Reader

To the Right Honorable, Right Worshipful, and My Much Respected Parishioners, Inhabitants in BlackFriars, London

All Needful Prosperity in This World, and Eternal Felicity in the World to Come

I desire, my much honored and entirely beloved parishioners, so long as the Lord of life shall preserve me in the land of the living, to go on promoting your spiritual edification in every way that I can privately, publicly, by prayer, by preaching, yea, and by printing too. Behold here an evidence thereof. What privately I first digested in my own meditation, and then publicly delivered by word of mouth, whereof in the open church you heard your children and servants examined, and for a blessing whereupon many prayers by us all jointly and severally have been poured out before God, is now through God's gracious providence so published as it may be reviewed as often as you please. Well accept it for it is *A Guide to Go to God.* God is the highest and chief Good, below which we may not remain and beyond which we cannot attain. To place our rest in anything before we come to God is dangerous. To attain to any rest beyond God is impossible. This therefore is that proper place where the well-enlightened and rectified soul aspires, as all hot light things aspire to the high hot region. The means whereby we men on earth have access to God in heaven is prayer. By prayer we enter into the court where God sits in His majesty, and we present ourselves before Him, speaking unto Him, as it were, face to face. That therefore which instructs us to pray aright directs us to God. This the Lord's Prayer does. And nothing can do it better. For this end, to teach us how to pray, it was first prescribed. It is not only a most absolute prayer in itself, but also a perfect pattern for other prayers. And in this respect it is the only way wherein we can go to God. Full of matter is this form of prayer, but few are the words thereof. Such fullness of matter in so few words make it to many as the prophesy of Christ was to Candace's eunuch, whereof he said (to him that moved this question, "Understandeth thou what thou readest?") "How can I except I had a guide?" A guide therefore is needful for many to direct them in this way to go to God.

Lo, a guide is at hand. This explanation of the Lord's Prayer is offered to you for that purpose. But as a guide that directs a traveler in his journey to the king's court does not make the way better, but shows him how to order his travel in that way, so this guide, this explanation, adds nothing to the perfection of the prayer, but only helps you in the use thereof. The many particulars that minister just matter of ardent supplication, hearty gratulation, deep humiliation, and conscionable observation of our ways, are in this explanation distinctly set out. Thereby you may see how rich a cabinet the Lord's Prayer is, how full of most precious jewels, useful for the soul of man. The excellence of this form of prayer is set forth in the first section of this explanation. Whatsoever is therein performed is the fruit of my affected retiredness and suspected idleness in the country. So many, so continual are my employments in the city, so many interruptions from my studies day after day are there caused, as I never yet could find any leisure to set down distinctly such points as by God's assistance were uttered out of the pulpit. Whatever has hitherto been published by me has in my retiring time been prepared for the press. This benefit of a few weeks' absence in the year from my charge (there being in that time a good supply made by my reverend Brethren) may gain a sufficient dispensation with those that are not too supercilious, which I hope you, my parishioners, will not be. For I have ever found such true love, such good respect, such kind usage, such favorable acceptance of all my pains in every kind as I have just cause to bless the divine providence for bringing me to this place. May the Lord God so bless all my labors unto you all as we may have all just cause to bless Him one for another, and to continue mutually and heartily to pray for one another. Do so, and so will

Your Careful Pastor
William Gouge

From the Church-Court
in BlackFriars, London,

February 17, 1625

The Lord's Prayer

Our Father, which art in heaven, hallowed be Thy name.

Thy kingdom come, Thy will be done in earth as it is in heaven.

Give us this day our daily bread. And forgive us our trespasses, as we forgive them that trespass against us.

And lead us not into temptation, but deliver us from evil.

For Thine is the kingdom, and the power, and the glory forever. Amen.

1

The Excellence of the Lord's Prayer

Those two things that are of greatest weight to commend unto our diligent consideration the reading or hearing of anything after a special manner commend the Lord's Prayer.

The Author and the Work Itself

Two things in an author make his work to be esteemed: eminence of place and excellence of parts. The work of a king is honored because it is the work of a king, even for his place's sake. The work of a great scholar is admired for his learning's sake, though in his estate he is never so mean.

Two things also in the matter or work itself commend it: The perfection of it and the profit that may be gotten by it. If an art is accurately handled, and so perfectly set out as nothing can be found defective, and yet no superfluous redundancy therein, every good student will be sure to have it and will diligently study it. Or if a work that may bring much profit to such as carefully use it is published, he will be thought careless of his own good who does not use it.

When all these meet together, an excellent author and a worthy work—an author to be respected for eminence of person and excellence of parts, a work to be regarded for the absolute perfection of it in itself, and for the necessity and utility of it to us—they are as a fourfold twisted cord to draw our minds thereto and to bind them thereon.

Such an Author is the indicter of this prayer, and such a work is the prayer itself. This title, "The Lord's Prayer," implies as much. The Lord is the Author; prayer is the work.

By the Lord is meant that one Lord Jesus Christ by whom are all things, and we by Him. The eminence of His person is such as He has a name given Him above every name. No monarch on earth, no angel in heaven is to be compared unto Him.

In regard of the excellence of His gifts, God gave Him the Spirit without measure, "for it pleased the Father that in Him all fullness should dwell." For He is the only begotten Son that is in the bosom of the Father and knows what is the will of the Father, what is most pleasing and acceptable to Him and what suits He is willing to grant unto His children. God would have many things to be spoken and heard by the prophets, His servants, but how much greater are the things that His Son utters?

As for the work, none is so heavenly, none so profitable as prayer. And among prayers none is to be compared unto this whether we consider the matter contained in it or the manner of setting it down.

The matter is in every way sound, complete, and perfect. Every word in it has its weight. There is not one superfluous word in it that could be spared. Nor is it any way defective. Whatsoever is lawful, needful, and fitting to be asked in prayer is therein contained; yea, whatever is to be believed or practiced by a Christian is therein implied. There is no particle of any good prayer commended in the Scripture, or at any time by any person well-conceived, but may be found couched in this. In this form are comprised all the distinct kinds of prayer, as requests for good things, deprecation against evil, intercession for others, and thanksgiving.

The manner of setting down the things contained in this prayer is answerable to the matter. By it we are taught how to begin prayer, in what order to set every petition that we make, and how to conclude our prayer.

The order therein is as admirable as any other point. Though the things comprised in it are innumerable, yet are they all couched under so few words as they may easily be remembered.

In a word, nothing that is in any way pertinent unto prayer is omitted in this form. And nothing is set down therein that is not pertinent unto prayer. It may therefore be fitly called a catholic and a canonical prayer—catholic in that it comprises the substance of all warrantable prayers in it, canonical in that it is the canon or rule to square and frame all prayers by.

Is not this then a fit subject for the greatest that are in dignity, in learning, in judgment, in wit, or any other excellency to exercise their meditation thereon? Can too much pain be taken to open and discover the rich treasure contained therein? Are they not ungrateful to the Author of it, and injurious to themselves, who lightly esteem it?

What may we think of Papists that do not allow the vulgar people to learn it in their own mother tongue? Indeed they suffer, yea, and enjoin them to tumble it up and down, and to mumble it again and again, as it were, by tale upon their beads in an unknown tongue, whereby they make it a matter of mere babbling.

What also may we think of Anabaptists and such like schismatics as forbid people to use it at all? Of all prayers this, without all contradiction, is the most perfect, so as if any form at all may be used then this most of all.

OBJECTION. It is so profound and deep as it is impossible for any to fathom the depth of it.

ANSWER. It will not thence follow that it is not to be used at all. Many of those petitions that Christians in their own form of prayer make imply more matter than in the time of uttering them they are able to conceive. Who can comprehend the infiniteness of Gods glory? May we not therefore pray as Christ did, "Father, glorify Thy name?" Who can understand his faults? Shall not a sinner therefore ask pardon for all his sins?

Who can in the time that "amen" may be uttered think of every particular point that in a long prayer has been mentioned by way of petition or thanksgiving? May not therefore "amen" be said at the end of our own or another's prayer if it has been long?

Assuredly, a general apprehension of more particulars than can be distinctly conceived at once is acceptable to God or else many approved prayers recorded in Scripture were not acceptable. No man can in particular express all things that are needful and fitting to be mentioned in prayer. It is therefore very requisite that after we have particularly and expressly mentioned in our prayer such things as we conceive to be most needful and profitable we should use some such general words and phrases as may include all other needful and profitable things. In this respect the common custom of concluding our own prayers with this perfect form of prayer prescribed by the Lord is very commendable.

OBJECTION. This clause, "After this manner pray ye," implies rather a platform to frame other prayers by than an express form to be used word for word.

ANSWER. That phrase may imply as well the very form prescribed as a like form. But Luke uses a phrase that puts this doubt out of doubt. It is this, "When ye pray, say." What should they say? Even the words following: "Our Father, which art in heaven."

QUESTION. What need is there for any other form of prayer to be used seeing this is so absolutely perfect?

ANSWER. To show that we take a particular and distinct notice of the things that we pray for. On this ground both Christ Himself, and the apostles also, to whom this form in special was prescribed, used other forms that are expressed in the Scripture.

By comparing these two forenamed places of the two evangelists together we may well gather that both this very form may be used, and that other forms also may be framed answerable to this.

Behold here the goodness of God, who is not only ready to hear us in His Son, but also by His Son has taught us how to call upon Him. Does He not herein show Himself to be a Father indeed? Is not this a great motive to provoke us with boldness to go to the Throne of Grace? How much more effectually may we obtain what we ask in Christ's name if we ask it in His form of prayer?

That we may be the better directed and the more encouraged to call upon God, and that by this excellent form here prescribed, we will distinctly consider the several branches thereof.

The Several Branches of the Lord's Prayer

The Lord's Prayer being (as we have heard) a most perfect pattern of prayer, it contains both the circumstances pertaining to prayer, and also the very substance of prayer.

The circumstances are two. One is precedent, which is the preparation thereto in the preface. The other is subsequent, which is the ratification thereof in the past particle "Amen."

The substance of the prayer consists of two parts, petition and thanksgiving.

The petitions are six in number, all which may be reduced unto two headings, God's glory and man's good. The three first petitions aim at God's glory, as this particle "Thy," having relation to God, shows. The last three petitions aim at man's good, as these particles "our" and "us," having relation to man, imply.

Of those petitions that aim at God's glory, the first desires the thing itself, the second the means of effecting it, and the third the manifestation of it.

Of those that aim at man's good, the first desires his temporal good, the last two his spiritual good, and that in his justification and sanctification.

In the form of praise three things are acknowledged: God's sovereignty ("Thine is the kingdom"), God's omnipotence and power, and God's excellence and glory.

All these are amplified by the perpetuity of them, "forever," which notes out God's eternity.

These are the several parts and branches of the Lord's Prayer, which with the Lord's help shall be more particularly opened, and that by way of question and answer for the better perspicuity.

Preparation to Prayer

QUESTION. What is first to be considered in the Lord's Prayer?

ANSWER. The preface prefixed before it in these words: "Our Father, which art in heaven."

QUESTION. What general instruction thence arise?

ANSWER. Preparation is needful unto prayer. For this preface is purposely prefixed to fit and prepare our hearts to prayer. To this very purpose tends this direction of the wise man, "Be not rash with thy mouth, and let not thine heart be hasty to utter anything before God." He there renders a weighty reason thereof taken from God's eminence: God is in heaven, a most high and glorious God. Men do not rashly enter into the presence of a king on earth. They will, as Joseph did, change their raiment; yea, they will think beforehand both of the matter that they intend to move and also of the manner of propounding their suit. Should we not much more come preparedly into the presence of the King of Kings?

To the eminence of His person before whom we come, I may well add the excellence of the work that is done. No other work is more excellent than prayer. If preparation is required unto any work, then most of all unto prayer.

The Means to Prepare Us to Prayer

QUESTION. How does this preface teach us to prepare ourselves to prayer?

ANSWER. By describing and setting forth God.

QUESTION. What is thence taught us?

ANSWER. A due consideration of His person to whom we pray is a special means to prepare us unto prayer. They who duly weigh the majesty of a king above other men will with better respect approach his presence. I find it usual with the saints whose prayers are recorded in the Scripture to be ample in setting forth the glorious properties of God in the beginning of their prayers, for which purpose note the prayers of Solomon, Jehoshaphat, Hezekiah, Jeremiah, Daniel, Nehemiah, Christ, and the apostles.

Meditation hereon is a special means to thrust out of the heart all bye and base thoughts, and to make the soul soar aloft and fly up even into heaven; yea, when a man's spirit is dull it will exceedingly quicken it to call to mind God's excellent attributes and great works, and to ponder them seriously.

The neglect hereof is one cause of that little devotion that is in many men's hearts while they are praying unto God. Yea, he who comes to God in prayer and does not duly weigh that surpassing excellence before which he approaches unawares dishonors the divine Majesty with unfit and unseemly suits.

Praying to God Alone

QUESTION. To whom may that description noted in the preface of the Lord's Prayer be applied?

ANSWER. To God and to God alone. None else can be called our Father in heaven.

QUESTION. What do we learn we from this?

ANSWER. God alone is to be prayed unto. This prayer is in that point defective if any saint, angel, or other creature is to be called upon. We have good warrant both from the light of God's Word, and also from the light of nature to call upon God; but there is no good warrant in any way to call upon any other.

God's Goodness and Greatness Jointly Considered Together

QUESTION. How is God described in the foresaid preface?

ANSWER. By His goodness and by His greatness.

QUESTION. What is thence inferred?

ANSWER. God's goodness and greatness are both to be thought on when we pray to God. Read the prefaces of the prayers before quoted, and of other like prayers in Scripture, and you shall find those two properties of old usually joined together. The heathen by the light of nature observed these two to be the most principal attributes of God, and thereupon called Him *Optimus Maximus*. The one of these shows how ready God is to hear, the other how able He is to help. So these are two strong pillars to support our faith.

A due consideration of them both together is a special means to preserve in us a blessed mixture of confidence and reverence, both which are necessary because the place before which we present ourselves in prayer is a throne, at the footstool whereof we must with all reverence fall. And it is a throne of grace to which with all confidence we must approach. And thus shall we be kept in the golden mean between two dangerous extremes, the gulf of despair and the rock of presumption, by either of which prayer is made altogether fruitless. For God does not turn to the doubting mind, and turns from the proud heart, so as both must return empty from God. And no marvel, for "he that believeth not maketh God a liar," and the proud thinks there is no God.

Learn therefore by the forenamed meditation on God's goodness and greatness to preserve this sovereign balance of faith and fear. On God's goodness, first let the eye of your meditation be fixed. For Christ teaches us to say, "Our Father," before He puts us in mind of God's glorious place in heaven, which order He observed when He Himself prayed, saying, "Father, Lord of heaven and earth." In this order the apostle calls Him, "The God of our Lord Jesus Christ, and Father of glory."

I do not deny but that there may be good use of setting God's greatness before us, and that it may in prayer be first expressed as it is in the prayers of Daniel, Nehemiah, and other saints; but it must be by such as have a steadfast faith in God's goodness, and at that time also God's goodness must be in their minds, as it was in Daniel's. For so soon as he had said, "O Lord God, great and fearful," he immediately added, "which keepest covenant and mercy, etc." The brightness of God's greatness would utterly dazzle the eye of man if first, immediately and only it should be fixed thereon.

This direction is of singular use to us base, sinful, wretched creatures who cannot but be astonished at the thought of Gods greatness, power, justice, jealousy, and other like attributes.

Hitherto we have dealt with such general instructions as the preface of the Lord's Prayer teaches. The particular branches shall in order be handled. The first concerns God's goodness in this clause, Our Father, wherein we are to consider, first, the relative title given to God (Father), second, the correlative particle (our) whereby a particular application of that general relation is made. In handling the title we will declare, first, the thing itself here attributed to God, which is paternity or fatherhood. Second, we will declare the manner of expressing it in the vocative case and second person, as if more fully it had been thus said, "O Thou our Father."

This Title "Father" Applied to God

QUESTION. Is this title "Father" proper to God?

ANSWER. Yea, most properly it pertains to Him. For it is the true and proper title of him who gives being to that whereof he is called a father. They therefore among men who under God are instruments of the being of others, who bring children forth into this world, are most usually called fathers. But it is God alone who truly and properly gives a being to things, whereupon Christ says of Him, "There is but one your Father, which is in heaven." And the apostle to like purpose, "There is but one God, the Father." And among other unities he reckons this, "One God and Father."

Now God is called Father both in relation to His Son, the second Person in the Trinity, and also in relation to His creatures. In the former respect it can be applied only to the first Person in the Trinity, whose only begotten Son the second Person is, and that by reason of His eternal generation and the hypostatic union of His two natures in one person. In the latter respect it may be applied to all the three Persons in the Trinity. For not only the first, but the second Person also is expressly called Father; and we are said to be born of the Spirit, which is a work of paternity. All the three persons then are included under this title Father. And prayer may be made to them all jointly as one in substance, and to any of them expressly by name, yet so as when one only is named, neither of the others is excluded. For the Father is always to be called upon in the name of the Son by the assistance of the Spirit, else we do not know what to pray as we ought.

This one God distinguished into three Persons is said to be the Father of His creatures, first generally as He has given being to them all; second, especially as He has set His image on some of them above others.

His image is set on His creatures in two ways: By that excellence wherein He created them and by renewing an excellence in some of them after their fall. By reason of that primary excellence Adam and angels are called sons of God; for in regard of those divine qualities, and that glorious estate wherewith He adorned them above other creatures at the beginning, they are said to be made after the image of God.

The image of God, which is a kind of divine excellence, is renewed only in some of the sons of men, and that in a civil and spiritual respect. It is in a civil respect as they have dignity and dominion given to them over others, such as all magistrates and governors, in whom there is a resemblance of God's sovereignty, in which respect they bear God's image and are called gods, and sons of the most High. It is in a spiritual respect as God through His grace has adopted some to be His sons and by His Spirit has begotten them anew.

Though out of the fatherhood of God here is meant that relation that the first Person in the Trinity has to the second, may not be excluded (for they who do not apprehend God to be a Father of Jesus Christ cannot in faith and with comfort call upon Him), yet it has special relation to His creatures who say, "Our Father," and among them to sons of men since their fall who say, "Forgive us our trespasses," and among the sons of men to such as are adopted of God, and born anew after His image, who only in truth say to God, "Hallowed be Thy name." Thus we who with our own voice confess God to be our Father profess ourselves to be taken from a servile condition into the adoption of sons.

Many other more magnificent titles might have been attributed to God, but none more pertinent to prayer than this title "Father." Christ therefore usually in His prayer used it.

The Instructions that the Title "Father," Applied to God Import

QUESTION. What instructions may be gathered from this title "Father" applied to God in prayer?

ANSWER 1. God is to be called upon in the mediation of Christ. Only in Christ is God a Father; and only in Christ are we adopted and born again. Out of Christ God is a terrible Judge and a consuming fire. This title therefore includes Christ and faith in Him. Thus Saint Peter first had an eye to God's fatherhood in relation to Christ, His only begotten Son, and then in relation to the saints, His adopted sons.

ANSWER 2. They only have this privilege to approach by prayer into God's presence who can in truth call Him "Father," which none can do but they who believe in Christ. "For as many as received Him, to them He gave power to become the sons of God, even to them that believe in His name." To them only will God reach out His golden scepter of grace, as Ahasuerus did to Esther. They therefore by a kind of property are said to call upon God.

ANSWER 3. Prayer must be made in confidence of God's fatherly love. How else shall they else call him "Father?" The apostle says, "Because ye are sons, God hath sent forth the Spirit of His Son into your hearts crying, 'Abba, Father.' " Now the ground of this confidence rests only in God's fatherhood. For here are no other motives, either from ourselves or from others. But paternity promises all blessings.

ANSWER 4. There is ground of returning to God after we have gone from Him. For a father is ready again and again to receive. "I will arise and go to my father," said the prodigal. And when that father saw his son yet a great way off he had compassion. After David had justly banished his son Absalom, he longed to go forth unto him. As fatherhood promises all blessings, so it promises all forbearance. It makes one ready to give and forgive. A father's love is of all others most constant and immutable. Though he is provoked to correct, yet will he not forget to love.

ANSWER 5. There is sufficient encouragement against everything that may in any way dishearten us from approaching into God's presence, whether it is excellence in God or infirmity in ourselves. A father will lay aside in his child's presence whatever may dishearten him.

ANSWER 6. They who call on God must bear a childlike affection for Him. For they who with their lips call God "Father," and in their hearts do not respect Him as a Father, apparently mock Him. On this ground God says to His people, "If I be a Father, where is mine honor?" And Saint Peter says, "If ye call Him 'Father,' pass the time of your sojourning here in fear." This childlike affection will provoke us to seek both His favor and His honor, how to be accepted of Him and how to please Him. This answerable disposition is a main end of the relation between God and us. And when He commands you in prayer to call Him "Father," this He wills you, that by a divine course of life you should be like your Father.

So much of the title "Father." The manner of expressing it follows in the vocative case and second person.

The Prerogative of God's Children to Speak to Him Face to Face

QUESTION. What does the manner of expressing this title "Father" in the vocative case and second person import?

ANSWER. A dignity, and a duty of God's children.

QUESTION. What is that dignity?

ANSWER. Such a familiarity with God as to speak to Him face to face. For this title, "Father," is so set down as directed to God Himself in His own presence. David excellently sets forth this privilege where he says, "Lord, I pour my whole desire before Thee." All do not have this liberty as an evidence whereof they have no ability thus to come into Gods presence.

They upon whom God pours the Spirit of grace, He also pours the Spirit of supplication—but upon no other. It is therefore a gift appropriated to the saints to call upon God in faith, by which term they are described. Others may use this word, and with their lips say to God, "O Father," but their supposed prayers are but mere lip-labor. At best their inward desires are but wishes. Now there is a great difference between wishing and praying. A wish may intimate some sense of that which a man wants, and some desire of having it, but small care in using the means to get it, and less faith in obtaining it. But the faithful prayers of the saints argue sense, desire, care, faith, and all. Balaam could wish and say, "Let me die the death of the righteous." Like to whom were they that said, "Who will show us any good?" But David goes directly to God, and thus expressly prays to Him, "LORD, lift Thou up the light of Thy countenance upon us."

We know that any man may in any place wish and say, "I would the king would grant me this or that suit." But at all times to have a free access to the king's presence, and to say unto him, "O my Liege, I beseech thee grant me this suit," is a great privilege, pertaining only to the king's favorites; and so much the greater when there is assurance of prevailing by this free access, as there is assurance by that free access that saints have to God's presence.

This is little considered by them who make all their prayers rather by exhortation unto prayer than by express petition in the third person thus: "Let us pray that God would do this or that," which argues too light an esteem of the forenamed privilege. And is a declaration of what ought to be done rather than an actual performance thereof.

Their Duty Who Have Free Access to God

QUESTION. What is the duty that is expected of such as have the forenamed free access to God?

ANSWER. That in prayer especially their heart be struck with a due respect of God's presence. For then they stand face to face before Him. This follows as a just consequence from the foresaid dignity. When dutiful children or loyal subjects stand in the presence of their father or sovereign, they will manifest all the due respect they can, especially when they make a suit to them. Should not we the children and subjects of God do it much more? When we come to speak of the glory and greatness of God, we shall have further occasion to press this point.

So much for the relative title "Father." The correlative is noted in this particle "our." In handling this, first, we are to consider in general the parties that are comprised under it, and then, more particularly, the person and number wherein it is expressed.

The Parties Comprised Under This Particle "Our"

QUESTION. Who does this correlative particle "our" set out?

ANSWER. Mortal men who live on earth.

QUESTION. What is hereby given to be understood?

ANSWER. The love of God and the honor of those mortal men.

QUESTION. How is the love of God set forth?

ANSWER. By condescending to be a Father to such base wretches. There is an infinite disparity between God and man. God is a Lord of incomprehensible majesty and perfect purity. Man, in regard of the mold from whence he came, and where he must return, is but dust. And in regard of the corruption of his nature is worse than the most brute beast and most unreasonable creature. May we not then on this ground with a holy admiration say, "Behold, what manner of love the Father hath bestowed upon us that we should be called the sons of God!" Who would dare call God "Father" if Christ had not warranted us to do so?

QUESTION. What is the honor that is hereby done unto the sons of men?

ANSWER. The greatest that can be, for what greater honor can there be than to be the king's son? David thought it was a great matter to be Saul's son-in-law (yet Saul was but a king on a small part of the earth and David was then anointed to be his successor). What is it then to have the King of Heaven to be our Father? This is far more than to be an angel, who is but a messenger and servant. "Are they not all ministering spirits, sent forth to minister for them who shall be heirs of salvation?"

Herewith they may all who have this honor granted to them uphold themselves against that vile esteem wherein the world holds them. Why should they care for the world's despising of them who have God to be their Father? "For this cause the world knoweth us not, because it knoweth not the Father."

This much of the parties whose Father is God. The manner of applying God's fatherhood by the first person follows.

Applying God's Fatherhood to Ourselves

QUESTION. What do we acknowledge by this correlative particle "our" as it is in the first person?

ANSWER. We acknowledge that God is not only the Father of Christ, and of other men, but our Father also; as if one praying alone and for himself should say, as Christ did, "O my Father," and as Thomas said to Christ, "My Lord and my God."

If it is objected that that which is uttered in the plural number is not particularly applied to one's self, I answer that though it is not applied to one's self only and alone, yet it may be to him jointly with others. Though I believe God to be a common Father of many (which the plural number implies), yet that does not hinder me from reckoning myself in that number and so to make the application to myself. This much is fitly expressed in this speech of Christ, "I ascend to My Father and to our Father." Here He acknowledges God to be a common Father of others in these words "your Father," and yet makes a particular application thereof in these words, "My Father."

QUESTION. What instruction arises from this application of God's fatherhood to us?

ANSWER. A particular persuasion of God's fatherly affection to us is then especially required when we pray to Him. We cannot in truth say to Him, "our Father," without such a persuasion. The benefits of that particular persuasion are great and manifold.

1. It distinguishes the sound faith of true saints from the counterfeit faith of formal professors and the trembling faith of devils. They may believe that God is a Father, but they cannot believe that God is their Father and therefore they believe and tremble.

2. It makes us to come more boldly to the throne of grace. When the prodigal child did not know to whom to go (though he could not be ignorant that there were many fathers in the world) he, remembering that he had a father of his own, said, "I will go to my father."

3. It makes us to rest upon God more confidently for provision for all needful things and protection from all harmful things. For this particular relation of God's fatherhood to us shows that God takes a special care of us to whom the promise of God's care especially belongs.

4. It much upholds us in all distresses. With this particular persuasion the Jews upheld themselves when they seemed to be forsaken. Yea, herewith Christ upheld Himself in His greatest agony.

5. It strengthens our faith in all the properties and works of God. For to believe that it is my Father who has made all things and continues to uphold and order them; that it is my Father who is the Fountain of all blessings, and gives what He

will to whom He will; that my Father is everywhere present, knowing all the necessities and extremities of everyone; that the mighty, merciful, wise, provident God is my Father; to be truly persuaded hereof must minister much comfort at all times, in all places, whatever our present condition is. But otherwise, to know that by God the whole world is ordered, that His eyes are in every place, that He is omnipotent, just, wise, and true, and not to apprehend Him to be our Father cannot but much strike our hears with much terror and make us flee from Him, as Adam did when he heard the voice of God in the garden.

6. It affords much comfort against our manifold infirmities. For it assures us that God will take no advantage against us for them, but will rather accept our poor endeavors; and when we cannot pray as we should He will put desires into our hearts and words into our mouths. A child's own father will accept any manifestation of his mind and meaning, yea, and will say to him, "Do you not mean this? Would you not rather have that?"

7. All that can be said of God's fatherhood will bring no comfort to a man unless he can apply it to himself. Children do not go to a man for the things they want because he is a father of other children, but because he is their own father.

As the manner of expressing the correlative particle "our" in the first person, whereby he who makes the prayer is included, was observed, so it is also in the plural number, whereby it is extended to others.

God's Impartial Respect to All His Children and the Sufficiency of Blessing for All

QUESTION. Why is the application of God's fatherhood set down in the plural number "our"?

ANSWER. To show that God is the common Father of all the saints, even of the whole church, and of every particular member thereof. As there is one God, so that one God is a

Father of us all. To this purpose is that emphatic interrogation of the prophet in Malachi 2:10, "Have we not all one Father?"

QUESTION. What does this teach us?

ANSWER. It teaches us God's respect to us, our duty to one another, and the privilege of saints.

QUESTION. How is God's respect manifested?

ANSWER. By His impartial favor to all alike, and by the abundance of blessing that He has that is sufficient for all.

Concerning God's impartial respect, Christ here teaches all, of whatever degree, to say to God, "Our Father." God then is the Father of all, and as a Father He carries Himself towards all. He is good and merciful and of great kindness to all who call upon Him. He upholds all who fall. In this respect especially He is said to have no respect of persons. That title therefore that notes out an only son on whom all love is cast, and by a property attributed to Christ, the only begotten Son of God, that very title is attributed to all the saints to show that though they are many, yet so impartial is God's affection to them all, and to every one of them, as if they were all but one only child of God. On this ground they are all called firstborn, heirs, kings, and other such names as set forth an equal respect of God to them all. Yea, they are all one body, and one spouse of Christ, the Son of God. If the ground of this impartial respect is well weighed, the truth of it will more clearly appear. For it wholly rests in God Himself and proceeds from His free grace and mere mercy, and not from any gifts or parts that are in the saints. If it depended on anything in the sons of men then might it be partial, as the love of earthly parents is.

Concerning the abundance of blessing our common Father has, it appears to be sufficient for all in that Christ directs all to go to Him, and that for others as well as for themselves, and not to fear to put us in mind that He is the Father of others as well as of ourselves, and that He has others to bless as well as us. So God is not like Isaac, who had but one blessing, and having therewith blessed one son could not bless the other. He is as a springing fountain that ever remains full and continues to overflow though never so much is taken out of it. Men who are very cautious in keeping standing ponds private to themselves allow springs to flow out in common for others. Thus God's fatherly bounty flows out to all who in faith come to partake thereof. Did not saints know and believe as much they would urge and press all the evidences they could of God's fatherly respect to them in special (as Esau did to Isaac, saying, "I am thy son, thy first born, bless me, my father") rather than make mention of His common fatherhood.

The Mutual Duties of Those Who Say, "Our Father."

QUESTION. What are the duties on our part to be performed by reason of God's common fatherhood?

ANSWER. 1. Great ones must make themselves equal to those of the lower sort. Though in outward privileges they are greater than other saints, yet ought they as brethren to respect the meanest because God is their Father also. Who was greater in the church than the apostles? Yet they accounted and called the meanest their brethren, which they learned of Christ their Master, who expressly told them that they were all brethren. Yea, Christ Himself (though He was Head and Lord of all) was not ashamed to call them brethren. Is it not intolerable arrogance to scorn to account him your brother whose Father God is as well as your? Such insolent persons cannot in truth say, "Our Father."

ANSWER 2. Mean ones must be content in their estate, and that because God is their Father as well as the Father of the greatest. Though in some outward respects they are meaner than others, yet in the greatest prerogative, which is to be a child of God, they are equal to the greatest. There is neither bond nor free, but all are one in Christ Jesus, and this is a ground of great contentment.

ANSWER 3. Saints must take occasion of praying together. So shall they most fitly say to God, "Our Father." This is the rather to be noted because Christ has promised His presence after a special manner where two or three agree together.

ANSWER 4. Saints must pray one for another. For Christ has so ordered this prayer as thereby, in using it, we are put in mind one of another. The Teacher of peace and Master of unity would not have prayer so singly made that when one prays he should pray only for himself. By this mutual intercession of one for another, as we acknowledge God a common Father, according to the scope of this phrase, "Our Father," so we profess Him to be the Fountain of all blessing, able to help all, even others as well as ourselves, which is a great honor done to God. And we also hereby profess that we are willing and desirous that others should partake of the same blessings that we crave for ourselves. Of this mind was that prophet who said, "Would God that all the Lord's people were prophets," and that apostle who said, "I would to God that all that hear me were such as I am." Note every one of the petitions that we are taught to make for ourselves and you shall observe every blessing craved for ourselves to be craved also for others, as these two words, "us" and "our," expressed in every one of them plainly shows.

There is a double bond to bind us hereunto, one of love, the other of justice. Christ notes it to be the duty of love to pray for others. And the apostle notes duties of love to be a due debt. Herein lies a main difference between faith and love. Faith is as a hand that is closed, grasping all for itself. Love is as a hand that is opened, ready to communicate what it has to others. Whereas therefore in our belief, in the singular number each one says, "I believe," in prayer each one says in the plural, "Our Father, give us, forgive us, deliver us."

ANSWER 5. Saints must pray in brotherly love, and with hearts and minds united. This phrase, "Our Father," puts them in mind of a brotherly affection one towards another. To this purpose may be applied that consequence, which on such a ground the prophet infers in these words, "Have we not all one Father? Why do we deal treacherously every man against his brother?"

The Saints' Participation in One Another's Prayers

QUESTION. What is that privilege of the saints that is gathered out of this phrase, "Our Father?"

ANSWER. They mutually partake of the benefits of one another's prayers. For it may well be taken for granted that this form being prescribed by Christ, they in whom the Spirit of Christ is accordingly use it, and so pray for all whose Father God is. For this is a public and common prayer, and when we pray we pray not for one, but for the whole Church because we are all one. This will appear to be a great privilege if the benefit of prayer is rightly discerned. And a great comfort it must be to such weak ones as cannot pray as they desire. The privilege of the communion of saints appears in nothing more than in the mutual participation of one another's prayers.

QUESTION. May not God be called upon in the singular number thus, "My Father?"

ANSWER. Yes, in private by one alone He may, as did Christ. St. Paul also did in such a manner give thanks unto God. Yea, thus we are directed by the prophet to call upon God, and to say, "My Father." Yet one may not so apply in particular God's fatherhood to himself as to appropriate it to himself, nor yet to be unmindful of others in his prayers, contrary to the scope of expressing this relation in the plural number, "our." This form is not set down to bind us so strictly to the words or syllables as never to swerve from them, but it is set down rather to teach us what to aim at in the manner and matter of our prayers.

QUESTION. May this form ("Our Father") be used by one alone?

ANSWER. Yes, so did Daniel when also being alone he used the singular number. "O our God," he said, "hear the prayer of Thy servant." And in the next clause, "O my God, incline Thine ear." In regard of that particular confidence that he had in God, he said, "my God." And in regard of his respect, even when he was alone, to other children of God he said, "our God." For our love to the brethren and our persuasion of their union in Christ must be manifested to God when we are alone as well as in company.

Thus much of God's goodness. It remains to speak of His greatness.

Of God's Being in Heaven

QUESTION. How is God's greatness set forth?

ANSWER. By His mansion place that is in heaven. A mansion place is a usual means of greatness or lowliness. When wee see a little thatched, ruinous cottage, we imagine that he is a poor, lowly person who dwells there. Thus Eliphaz set out the baseness of men who dwell in houses of clay, whose foundation is in the dust. But if we see a fair and stately palace we think that he is a great person who inhabits there. Great Nebuchadnezzar thus set out his own greatness: "Is not this great Babylon that I have built for the house of the kingdom, and for the honor of my majesty?" Yea, if beggars see but a fair porch before the door of a house they deduce that one who can spare them something abides there. To our capacity, therefore, the Lord (who dwells in the light that no creature can approach unto) is pleased thus to set forth His greatness, glory, and magnificence.

Many so pervert this description of God's greatness as thereby they much impeach the excellence of His majesty. For...

1. Some thence infer that God may be circumscribed and compassed in a place, which is contrary to His infinite greatness by reason whereof He is said to fill heaven and earth; to have heaven for His throne and the earth for His footstool; to be everywhere so as none can withdraw themselves from His presence; yea, to be so incomprehensible as the heaven and heaven of heavens cannot contain him.

2. Others thence infer that He is so high as He cannot see the things below, which Eliphaz notes to be the mind of the profane in his time who say, "Is not God in the height of heaven? How does God know? Can He judge through the dark cloud? Thick clouds are a covering to Him so that He does not see and He walks in the circuit of heaven." But this notion is directly contrary to that omniscience and perfect sight of God that the Holy Ghost thus sets out: "Out of heaven doth the Lord behold the earth. The eyes of the Lord are in every place, beholding the evil and the good." There is not any creature that is not manifest in His sight.

3. Others thence infer that though it is granted that God sees the earth and all things done thereon, yet He does not order them, which was the thinking of many philosophers. This is a notion directly contrary to that excellent discourse that God Himself had with Job, and to the evidences of God's providence extending itself to the smallest things, as to all kinds of creatures, even to little sparrows, to the hairs of our head and to the grass of the field.

But let pass all such false, erroneous, absurd, and blasphemous collections. Know that this placing of God in heaven is not properly, but comparatively and respectively to be taken, and that to give us occasion to conceive something of God's excellence, which is in truth inconceivable and incomprehensible.

QUESTION. Why is God thus set forth?

ANSWER 1. To make our souls ascend as high as possibly can be when we pray unto Him. Above heaven our thoughts cannot ascend. Therefore He is said to be in heaven, which is the highest place of all. "I lift up mine eyes to Thee who dwellest in heaven," says the psalmist.

2. To distinguish God from earthly parents and to show that He is far more excellent than they, even as heaven is higher than the earth and things in heaven are more excellent than things on earth. No kings or monarchs, though they should rule from one of the earth to the other, can like to our Father who is in heaven. Who is like the Lord our God who dwells on high?

3. To show that He is free from all earthly infirmities, and from that changeableness whereunto things on earth are subject. In heaven there is no corruption, diminution, or alteration. Much less can there be any such thing in Him who is the chiefs of all in heaven, and with whom is no variableness or shadow of turning.

4. To set Him forth in the most glorious manner that can be. As kings are most glorious in their thrones, so is God in heaven, which is His throne. Heaven is where the angels behold the face of God and where thousand upon thousands minister unto Him, and ten thousand of thousands stand before Him. In heaven Christ is set at the right hand of the throne of majesty. Heaven it where St. Paul heard unspeakable words, which it is not lawful (or possible) for man to utter. In a word, in heaven truly and properly are the things that eye has not seen, nor ear heard, nor have entered into the heart of man.

5. Because as His glory is most manifested in heaven, so from heaven. For from heaven especially the glory of His power, providence, justice, mercy, and other attributes is declared. The heavens declare the glory of God. From heaven God caused judgment to be heard. From heaven the wrath of God is revealed. From heaven the Lord beheld the earth to hear the

groaning of the prisoners. From above is every good giving, and every perfect gift.

The Direction That God's Being in Heaven Gives Us for the Manner of Praying.

QUESTION. Does this description of God's greatness give us any direction for prayer?

ANSWER. Yes, both for the manner and the matter of prayer.

QUESTION. What direction does it give for the manner of prayer?

ANSWER 1. In prayer we are to conceive no image of God. For whereunto can He who is in heaven be resembled? It cannot but much impair the surpassing excellence of God's glorious majesty to be likened to any creature, and that much more than if a great monarch should be said to be like a toad or a viper. Often and earnestly God forewarned His people to take heed thereof, and much contested against them for it. This one point of palpable idolatry, if there were no other, is enough to keep us from communion with papists.

2. We are to conceive of no earthly or carnal thing of God who is in heaven. To think that God deals hardly with us, misjudges our intentions, does not accept our good deeds, respects persons, or any such thing, is to conceive a carnal thing of God. Is it fit to say to a king, "You are wicked"? Or to princes, "You are ungodly"? How much less to Him who is in heaven, who does not accept the person of princes?

3. We are not to measure God, His Word, or His works by the use of our reason. He is in heaven; we are on earth. This therefore is to measure things that are heavenly with an earthly measure, which is too scanty. "As the heavens are higher than the earth, so are My ways higher than your ways," says the Lord. This is to be noted especially against such as in their distresses, when they can see no ordinary means of help, think

God Himself cannot help. This would be like the Israelites that said, "Can God prepare a table in the wilderness?" and like the prince that said, "Though the Lord would make windows in heaven, could this come to pass?" (2 Kings 7:2) This also is to be noted against such as utterly despair of mercy, as did Cain, Judas, and others.

4. We are to apply all the goodness of earthly parents to God after a transcendent and super-eminent manner. For as the heaven is higher than the earth, so great is His mercy. "If ye being evil know how to give good gifts unto your children, how much more shall your Father which is in heaven give good things to them that ask Him" (Matthew 7:11). On this ground the saints in former times have said, "Though Abraham be ignorant of us, and Israel acknowledge us not, yet thou, O Lord, art our Father" (Isaiah 63:16). "Can a woman forget her sucking child? Yea, though they may forget, yet will not I forget," the Lord says (Isaiah 49:15). "When my father and mother forsake me, then will the Lord take me up" (Psalm 27:10). According to this transcendent application of fatherly love to God we ought to have our faith strengthened therein. How much comfort may such parents as are tender over their children, or such children as have tender parents, or any others who know the tenderness of earthly parents, receive by this application if they believe as they ought that our Father who is in heaven is as much more tender than fathers on earth, as heaven is higher than earth? Yea, such as have impotent and unnatural parents on earth may uphold themselves through faith in their Father who is in heaven, being, as a Father, ready, and as in heaven, able to supply all their necessities.

5. With all reverence we are to prostrate ourselves before God our Father in heaven. For this end, first, a true fear of God must be planted in our hearts, according to this pathetic wish of God Himself, "O that there were in their hearts a fear of Me!" Then this fear must be manifested by beseeming

gesture and words, neither overly curious nor overly careless. Hereof we have an excellent pattern in the Lord's Prayer wherein there is admirable art (as we have shown before) and yet no frothy curiosity. The wise man, upon the ground here noted, gives a like direction. His direction is this, "Be not rash with thy mouth, and let not thine heart be hasty to utter any thing before God" (Ecclesiastes 5:2). His ground is this: God is in heaven. As for our gesture, on a due consideration of the greatness of God, we are exhorted to fall down and kneel before Him. The publican with all humility carried himself in prayer before God, and He who pardons the humble heard his prayer. To conclude this point, all the reverence, both inward and outward, that possibly may be is to be manifested to our Father in heaven lest His fatherhood makes us overly bold. Thus shall we in truth say unto God, "Mercy is with Thee, that Thou mayest be feared."

6. We are to make no place a pretext to keep us from prayer. For as the heaven and the sun therein is everywhere over us, so as we cannot withdraw ourselves out of the compass thereof, so much more is God in every place over us and with us; neither can we withdraw ourselves out of the compass of His presence. We may, therefore, yea, we ought (as just occasion and fit opportunity is offered) pray in any place. We read of the saints' prayers made in the temple, in their own houses, on the housetop, in the open field, on a mountain, in a ship, in the midst of the sea, in a fish's belly, on a journey, in a battle, and in sundry other places. This being so, what need is there of going on pilgrimage to this or that shrine? Is our Father who is in heaven tied to one country, or to one place in a country more than to another? This is a heathenish concept! For the heathen imagined their Apollo, from whom they received their oracles to be at Delphi, Cumae, Dodona, and such other particular places.

7. We are to lift up pure hearts in prayer. For heaven, where God is on His throne of grace, and where our souls in prayer ascend, is a pure and holy place into which no unclean thing can enter. Besides, from heaven can God spy with what minds and hearts we come before Him. His throne being in heaven, His eyes behold, His eyelids try the children of men. Now He can endure no iniquity, no hypocrisy. If we regard wickedness God will not hear our prayers. They are an abomination to Him.

8. Our prayers are to be made with a holy subjection to God's will saying, as Christ did, "Not my will be done, but Thine." God being in heaven has an absolute sovereignty. His will must and shall stand whether we will or not. But by our willing subjection we make a virtue of necessity, which is a great point of wisdom.

9. We must see that in faith we lift up eyes, hands, and hearts into heaven. Our Father on whom we call is in heaven. But locally in our bodies we cannot go there. Spiritually, therefore, with the wings of faith we must fly up there. Faith is the eye, hand, and foot of the soul.

10. Our prayers are to be so sent forth as they may pierce the heavens where God is. This is to be done with extension not of voice, but of spirit. The shrillest sound of any trumpet cannot reach unto the highest heaven, no, nor the strongest report of any cannon. But ardency of spirit can pierce to the throne of grace. Such a prayer was that which Moses poured out when God said, "Why criest thou unto Me?" The apostle called such desires as God's Spirit raises in our spirits, groans that cannot be uttered.

11. We may pray with confidence in God's almighty power, believing that God is able to grant whatever we shall ask according to His will. As the title "Father" gave us ground of confidence in God's fatherly love, so this placing of Him in heaven gives us as good ground of confidence in His power. Thus shall

we (as Abraham did) give glory to God, being fully persuaded that what He has promised He is able also to perform.

12. Let us see that we pray with courage, not fearing what any on earth can do to hinder the fruit and success of our prayers. For our Father to whom we pray, and from whom we expect the accomplishment of our desire, is in heaven, higher than all. Daniel without question well knew and considered this ground of confidence when, notwithstanding the decree made against all that should ask any petition of any God or man, he prayed three times a day his window being open.

The Direction That God's Being in Heaven Gives Us for the Matter of Prayer

QUESTION. What direction does this placing of God in heaven give us for the matter of prayer?

ANSWER. It teaches us what things especially to ask.

QUESTION. What are they?

ANSWER ONE. Things of weight and worth, fit for such a Majesty to give. When subjects prefer a petition to their sovereign sitting on his throne or chair of estate, they do not usually make suit for pins or points. This would be dishonorable to his majesty. Shall we then make suit to this highest Majesty in heaven for toys and trifles? Shall a dice-player pray that he may win his fellow's money? Shall an angry man pray to God that he may be revenged on him with whom he is angry? Shall any one desire God to satisfy his lusts? In this respect St. James says, "Ye ask and receive not because you ask amiss that you may consume it on your lusts." For this general direction about the matter of prayer we have a perfect pattern in this platform prescribed by our Lord wherein is nothing but what is of great moment mentioned.

OBJECTION. We are there taught to pray for daily bread, which seems not to be so great and weighty a matter.

ANSWER 1. Under bread all temporal blessings are comprised. Now all temporal blessings jointly considered together are a matter of much moment and fitting to be craved of that Lord who is in heaven, and to whom the earth and the fullness thereof belong.

ANSWER 2. We do not there only crave the thing itself, but a blessing with it. Now the blessing of the least creature is a weighty matter: more than all the world can give. Without the blessing the creature itself is nothing. For man does not live by bread only, but by every word that proceeds out of the mouth of the Lord man lives.

ANSWER 3. Though temporal blessings in their kind are comparatively small, yet in their end they are of great worth. Their proper end is to enable us the better to do that work which God has enjoined us to do, and to honor Him in this world, which only the living can do. In this respect we are to crave them not singly and simply in themselves, but as means to enable us to honor God and to do good unto our brethren.

ANSWER TWO. From this placing of God in heaven we are taught to crave heavenly things, which are such as tend to the glory of God who is in heaven and such as help us to heaven.

These are the things that Christ especially intends where, making a comparison between our father on earth and our Father in heaven says, "How much more shall your Father which is in heaven give good things to them that ask Him?" St. Luke, expressing the same point, in the place of good things, puts the Holy Ghost, whereby is showed what are the good things that Christ means, namely such as proceed from the sanctifying Spirit of God. These heavenly things are most meet for Him who is in heaven to give. To this purpose tends this exhortation of the apostle: "Seek those things which are above." Well had Solomon learned this lesson, for when God said to him, "Ask what I shall give thee," he answered, "Give Thy servant an understanding heart," which is one of those good gifts that come from above.

OBJECTION. If the things that we are here taught to pray for are heavenly, how is it that temporal blessings come in the rank and number of them?

ANSWER. They come as appendices and accessories to heavenly and spiritual blessings, for so they are promised. First seek the kingdom of God and His righteousness, and all these things shall be added unto you. As when a man purchases manors and lands, the wood in hedgerows for fire-boot, plow-boot, and other like purposes is given in the gross. Or, more plainly, when a man buys spice, fruit, comfits, or any such commodities, paper and packthread is given into the bargain. If you get heavenly blessings, temporal things, so far as they are needful for you, shall be cast in.

ANSWER THREE. From placing God in heaven we are taught to crave heaven itself, that we may be where our Father is and where we may most fully enjoy His glorious presence. Thus the apostle desired to depart to the end that he might be with Christ. And the holy patriarchs are said to desire a heavenly country, which also the apostle noted to be the desire of all true saints. Where God is, there must everyone lay the foundation of His abode.

There are two things that will testify the truth of our desire hereof.

1. A studying to enter into that rest, together with a cheerful walking in the way that leads thereto.

2. A cheer and joy of heart when we see any sign of our dissolution approaching. Old Simeon and Paul were exceedingly affected in this case.

Thus far of the preface; the petitions follow.

2

The Manner of Handling Every Petition

In handling every petition six points shall be distinctly observed.

1. The meaning of the words.
2. The order and dependence of one point upon another.
3. The particular good things that we are to crave.
4. The particulars for which we are to give thanks.
5. The duties that we ought to endeavor after.
6. The failings for which we are to be humbled.

The three former of these are most proper and natural. For by opening the meaning of the words the true and full intent of Christ will be better found out.

By noting out the dependence, one point will give much light to another. For the order is very accurate.

By reckoning up the particulars that are to be craved we may easily discern what abundance of matter is couched under a few words.

The other three points follow by just consequence. Whatever we pray for, when we have obtained it, we must be thankful for. We must do what we can to get what we pray for or else we mock God. The want of such things as we ought to pray for ministers just matter of humiliation.

These three latter points therefore are to be considered in every petition as well as the former.

The Name of God and the Things Comprised Under It

QUESTION. Which is the first petition?

ANSWER. "Hallowed be Thy name."

QUESTION. What is the name of God?

ANSWER. It is that whereby God is made known. For that is the end and use of a name, to make known and distinguish that whose name it is. Thus Adam gave names to every living creature to make them thereby be the better known and to distinguish them one from another. Whatever Adam called every living creature was the name thereof, namely a name proper and peculiar unto it whereby the nature of it was expressed and so the creature made known. Thus whatever it is whereby God is made known unto us may be comprised under this title "name" attributed to God.

QUESTION. How many things are there whereby God is made known?

ANSWER. Six especially.

1. His nature, which is a Spirit. Hereby we know Him to be invisible and in no way subject to corporeal grossness or weakness. Yea, hereby we know that He must be worshipped in spirit and truth.

2. The distinction of Persons in the holy Trinity. Hereby is Jehovah the true God distinguished from all false gods. For it never came into the imagination or apprehension of any heathenish idolater to conceive that his god could be one in nature and three in persons. Hereby also may we know how to approach unto the Father, namely in the mediation of His Son by the assistance of His Spirit.

3. His titles. The Jews have ten several titles that they apply to God, and whereby they distinguish Him from all creatures. Among the rest "Jehovah" is the most proper. For that is applied to none but God. These two titles, "Lord" and "God" are most usual in our tongue.

That the titles applied to God are properly His name is evident by that answer that God Himself gave to Moses, inquiring what he should say if the children of Israel should ask what the name of that God who sent him was. God's answer was this, "Say, 'I AM hath sent me to you.' " By the forenamed titles is God distinguished from all creatures.

4. His attributes. Of these some are incommunicable, so proper to God as in no respect they can be attributed to any creature, such as eternity (without beginning), simplicity (without mixture), infiniteness (filling all places), prescience (knowing all things before all times), immutability (not subject to any change), all-sufficiency in Himself, omnipotence and such like. When we hear any of these to be attributed to any we may thereupon infer surely that is God, or else they are falsely attributed. Other attributes are indeed communicable, and in some respects may be applied to creatures, such as purity, wisdom, truth, justice, mercy, and others such like. Yet in that they are originally, infinitely, unchangeably in God they declare that God to be Jehovah, the supreme Lord of all. Such as these were reckoned up when the Lord proclaimed His name to Moses.

5. His Word. This of all others most clearly, distinctly, and fully makes God known unto us. Christ, speaking of the Holy Scriptures, thus says, "These are they which testify of Me."

6. His works. "For the invisible things of God from the creation of the world are clearly seen, being understood by the things that are made, even His eternal power and Godhead." God's works evidently declare Him to be God, yea, to be the only true God, infinitely wise, just, merciful, powerful, etc. In a word, God's name is His glory.

Of God's Making Himself Known

QUESTION. What do we learn from this mention of God's name?

ANSWER. God may be known. Though He is invisible, inconceivable, incomprehensible in Himself and in His divine essence, yet it has pleased Him to set Himself forth according to our capacity, as is evident by all those places where mention is made of His name.

QUESTION. Why has God taken a name to be known by?

ANSWER 1. To work in our hearts a due respect of Him. Who will or can respect that which he does not know? But the name of God is in every respect glorious. It therefore makes those who know it to respect Him.

ANSWER 2. To show us how we may draw near unto Him, call upon Him, trust in Him, and receive from Him all needful blessings. If He had no name, or were in no way known of us, how could we seek Him and find Him? Thus He has aimed both at His own honor and our good in taking a name to Himself. Wherefore we ought to inquire after the name of God, and to take notice of all those means whereby He has made Himself known to us, that we may the better hallow His name.

Thus much of this word "name." About the other word ("hallowed be"), we will first consider the meaning of it, and then the manner of setting it down, and that impersonally and in the form of petition.

Of Hallowing

QUESTION. What does this word "hallow" signify?

ANSWER. Properly, to make holy, being all one as to sanctify. But it is diversely used in the Scriptures. It is attributed sometimes to things that are to be made holy, and sometimes to things that are already holy in themselves.

Things to be made holy are hallowed in two ways.

1. By setting them apart or employing them to a holy use. This may be done by one creature to another. For thus God commanded Moses to sanctify or hallow all the firstborn. And to show His meaning herein He says a little after, "Thou shalt

set apart unto the Lord all that openeth the matrix." Thus ministers hallow the bread and wine at the holy communion.

2. By putting holiness actually and properly into that which is hallowed. This the Creator only can do to His creatures. The apostle therefore thus prayed, "The very God of peace sanctify you wholly." And this God does by His Spirit, which is thereupon called the Holy Ghost and Spirit of sanctification.

That which is holy in itself is said to be hallowed by esteeming, acknowledging, and declaring it to be as it is. In this sense the Lord says, "They shall sanctify My name, and sanctify the holy one of Jacob." To sanctify a holy one can import no more than (as was said) to esteem, acknowledge, and declare him to be holy. This is all the hallowing or sanctifying that can be done to the Creator. This therefore must be what is here meant.

QUESTION. Why is choice made of a word that sets out God's holiness rather than any other of His attributes?

ANSWER. Because holiness is in itself a special excellence, and also the perfection of all other excellencies. If holiness could be severed from any of God's attributes (which is impossible that it should be, for as soon may God cease to be God as to be holy), it might then be said thereof, as it was said of Israel when the ark was taken away, "Where is the glory?"

The Creature's Hallowing the Creator

QUESTION. What do we learn from the desire of hallowing God's name?

ANSWER. The Creator may be hallowed by His creature, otherwise Christ would not have taught us to make this petition; neither would there have been as many exhortations recorded in Scripture to this purpose as there are.

This is not done by the creature's conferring of anything upon His Creator, but only by the Creator's gracious acceptance of our acknowledgment of Him to be as He is. "For if thou beest righteous what givest thou to Him? Or what receiveth He at thine hands?" God is so absolute and perfect in Himself as, do the creature what it will, it can in no way increase the honor of God, no, nor darken and obscure it. His name is holy in itself, whatever we say for it or against it. Neither is it needful in regard of the Creator that His name should be hallowed; but in regard of the creatures it is very needful. For the creature's hallowing of God's name adds nothing to the happiness of the Creator hallowed, but much to the happiness of the creature hallowing. Should no creature hallow his Creator's name, the Creator would not be the less honorable; but the creature that failed therein would be much more miserable.

Behold here the admirable goodness of God to man, who accepts that which is in Himself as given to him by man. Perfectly and infinitely holy is He, and yet condescends to be hallowed. Ought not this gracious acceptance by God move us to desire and to do the things wherein and whereby God is hallowed?

The Excellence of Holiness

QUESTION. What is taught us by the express mention of hallowing in this petition?

ANSWER. God's chief glory consists in His holiness. Read the Scriptures observantly and you shall find this attribute most usually applied to Him. They who best know how most to glorify God resound this one to another, "Holy, Holy, Holy, is the Lord." Yea, by a property and excellence God is called "the Holy One."

Take heed therefore that no thought that may in any way impeach God's holiness passes from you; but let your heart give assent and your tongue say, "Amen," to this divine ditty of that heavenly choir, "Holy, Holy, Holy, Lord God Almighty." So acknowledge Him to be holy in all His counsels, words, and works. And for a more evident demonstration thereof, "As He which hath called you is holy, so be ye holy in all manner of conversation, because it is written, 'Be ye holy, for I am holy.' "

The Extent of Man's Desire to Have God's Name Hallowed

QUESTION. What do we learn from the manner of setting down this duty in the third person indefinitely thus, "hallowed be?"

ANSWER. Our desire of having God's name hallowed must be beyond that which we are able to do by ourselves. The extent of our desire in this respect must reach to all creatures, in all places, and at all times. For this purpose read Psalm 113:2–4 and the entire 148th Psalm. This shows that in this desire we simply aim at God's glory and that we respect the honor of God more than the reward that may redound to us thereby. If our desire were restrained to ourselves, that we only might hallow the name of God, not caring whether it were hallowed by others or not, it might justly be thought that the chief, if not the only end of our desire were some recompense that from thence we expected to ourselves. Moses manifested a pure zeal of God's glory when he could have been content to be blotted out of God's book rather than God's name should be dishonored.

Man's Inability to Hallow God's Name

QUESTION. Why is this set down by petition thus, "hallowed be," rather than by promise thus, "hallowed shall be"?

ANSWER. Because it is not in our power to do it of ourselves. "For we are not sufficient of ourselves to think anything as of ourselves; our sufficiency is of God." God therefore works in man that ability, mind, and will that he has to hallow God's name so as in truth it is God who in and by us hallows His own name.

The Force of This Word "Thy" in the First Petition

QUESTION. To whom is this particle "Thy" to be referred?

ANSWER. To Him who is described in the preface.

QUESTION. What does it note out?

ANSWER. A reason for the petition, a restraint of the petition, and an emphasis on the petition.

QUESTION. How does it give a reason for the petition?

ANSWER. It does so as it has relation to the two properties of Him who is described. He is Our Father, and He is in heaven, a good and a great God, a gracious and a glorious Lord. Is there not then good and great reason that His name should be hallowed?

QUESTION. How is it a restraint?

ANSWER. By implying that God's name only is to be hallowed. "I am the Lord," says this God. "That is My name, and My glory will I not give to another." And as God will not, so neither must we give that which is due to Him to ourselves or others. On this ground the psalmist thus prayed, "Not unto us, O Lord, not unto us, but unto Thy name give glory." Tyrus, Nebuchadnezzar, Herod, and many others have been severely revenged for usurping that glory to themselves that was due to God.

QUESTION. How does this particle "Thy" set out an emphasis?

ANSWER. By implying that the name of God is to be advanced above all names. As if we thus said, "Thy name be hallowed as becometh so great a name, whose glory is above the heavens." Thus this particle "Thy," directing our heart to our Father in heaven, makes it to soar aloft and extends the desire thereof.

Of Man's Honoring God Because God Honors Him

QUESTION. What is to be observed about the order of the first petition?

ANSWER. The fit inference of it upon the preface and the due precedence it has before all other petitions.

QUESTION. What do we learn from the inference of it upon the preface?

ANSWER. The honor that God grants to man should move man to seek the honor of God. And sons of God ought especially to seek the honor of God.

The first of these is a general doctrine, arising from that prerogative which God in heaven grants to men on earth, namely to be their Father. Whence is inferred as a duty their desire of hallowing God's name. To this end is a like preface prefixed before the Decalogue. In that preface are laid down the favors of God to His people; and thereupon obedience to all God's commandments (whereby God is much honored) is required. This duty of honoring God, upon the forenamed ground of God's honoring man, is much inculcated by Moses and the Prophets.

Both justice and gratitude require as much, justice because it is a due debt, and gratitude because it is a real acknowledgment of kindness received.

We ought therefore to take notice of those special favors and honors that God does to us that our hearts may be the more stirred up thereby to seek His honor.

Of Saints Honoring God Because They Are Sons

The other doctrine arises from the particular kind of honor noted in the preface, which is to be sons of Him who is in heaven. Because He is our Father, and we His sons, therefore we especially ought to seek His honor. "If I be a Father, where is Mine honor?" God most expects it at His sons' hands, as of right He may. For these sons are honored with the greatest honor that can be. Can there be a greater honor conferred on sons of men than to be sons of God? Consider this, all you who call God Father, especially you into whose hearts God has sent forth the Spirit of His Son crying, "Abba, Father." We who are in the rank of God's children ought wholly to apply ourselves for the glory of our Father, saying, "Hallowed be Thy name."

Preferring God's Honor Before All Other Things

QUESTION. What ought we to learn from the precedence of this petition?

ANSWER. God's honor ought to be preferred before all things. And God's honor is the main end whereat all our desires ought to aim.

The order of the Decalogue and the placing of the first commandment before all the rest confirm the former of these instructions. So does this exhortation: "First seek the kingdom of God." All priorities are comprised under that particle "first." Both before and above all things is that to be sought. Christ preferred His Fathers glory before His own life, yea, and before freedom from that bitter agony whereunto He was brought being our Surety. For thus in His prayer He reasoned about that point: "What shall I say? Father, save Me from this hour. But for this cause came I unto this hour. Father, glorify Thy name." And then He rested in that above all He desired. This mind by the same Spirit was wrought in St. Paul, who did not count his life dear, but was ready to die for the name of the Lord.

QUESTION. Is God's honor to be preferred before our eternal salvation?

ANSWER. These two cannot stand in opposition. The more we seek God's honor, the more we help forward our salvation; and the more we seek our salvation aright, the more we advance God's honor.

If they could stand in opposition, then without contradiction God's honor should be sought rather than our own salvation. On this ground Moses made this transcendent prayer, "If not, blot me I pray Thee, out of Thy book which Thou hast written."

God's glory is of all things the most excellent and precious. If a man's name is better than precious ointment and great riches, what is God's? Now the more excellent a thing is the more it is to be esteemed and preferred. Besides, by seeking and setting forth God's honor we seek and set forth our own. For as it is in itself an honorable thing to honor God, so God, who can and will perform it, has said, "Them that honor Me will I honor." Is there not then good reason to desire above all other things that God's name be hallowed?

Aiming at God's Honor in All Things

That God's honor is also the main end whereat all our desires ought to aim is evident by that pertinent exhortation of the apostle, "Whatsoever you do, do all to the glory of God." This was his rejoicing, that the Lord should be magnified in him whether by life or by death. God Himself makes His glory the end of all His counsels and actions. But that end which He aims at we also must set before us. As for this end it is the highest, chief, and best end whereunto anything can be referred. It is the end of this first petition, and of all the rest; for the perfection of God's kingdom and subjection to His will tend directly to His glory. As for the other three petitions, though in the matter of them they concern our good, yet in the manner of seeking our good, namely of God, they make to God's glory. For in the fourth petition God's providence in the things of this life is acknowledged, in the fifth His mercy in pardoning sin, and in the sixth his power in keeping safe from all assaults.

This may serve as a touchstone to try the soundness of a religion. In opposition between diverse religions, mark which come nearest to this mark and most tend to this end. If the religions of Protestants and of Papists are well touched with this touchstone, and equally poised in these balances, it will easily be found that the reformed religion is much more sound than the other. For one main difference between us and them in all our controversies is this, that we take away from man all manner of glorying in himself and give the glory of all to God. But they rob God to give to man matter of trusting unto himself, and unto others like himself, and of boasting in himself and others. Instance the controversies we have with them about the authority of the Church above the Scriptures, the power of popes and priests, the adoration and invocation of angels and saints, their intercession, the inherent virtue of sacraments, man's free will to good, works of satisfaction and supererogation, the merit of works, indulgences, pilgrimages, and many others like these.

This also may serve as a touchstone to try particular actions. The more they aim at this end the better they are. Though a work seems otherwise never so good, yet if God's glory is not the end of it, it only seems to be good, as that which seems to be what it is not. To give alms, to pray, to fast, are works that in the general matter and substance of them are good; yet in these Christ censored the Pharisees and warned His disciples not to be like them, and that because they missed this end. Let us therefore in all things aim especially at God's glory.

The Particulars to Be Prayed for Under the First Petition

QUESTION. Unto how many headings may those particulars that in the first petition we are taught to pray for be referred?

ANSWER. Unto three especially, for we are taught there to desire:

1. Such graces in ourselves as may enable us to hallow the name of God.
2. Such graces in others as may enable them thereto.
3. Such an over-ruling providence in God as may direct everything thereto.

QUESTION. What are the graces that we desire for ourselves to the aforesaid end?

ANSWER. Such as are requisite for every power of our soul and part of our body to make them fit instruments for hallowing God's name.

1. For our understanding, we desire knowledge of God, that (as the apostle prayed) God would give to us the Spirit of wisdom and revelation in the knowledge of Him. This we may the more confidently pray for because it is absolutely promised; and we ought the more earnestly to desire it because it is the groundwork of all other graces. Before the understanding is well enlightened, neither can the will be made subject to God, nor the heart set upon God, nor any other power of soul or part of body be serviceable to Him. The light of the body is the eye, that is, the understanding in man, the little world, is as that great light the sun in the great world. "If therefore thine eye be single thy whole body shall be full of light." If the understanding is well illuminated and clearly discerns the truth the whole man throughout will be well ordered. But if your eye is evil your whole body shall be full of darkness. If the understanding is blind the whole man must be out of order. The knowledge here desired ought to be a particular and distinct understanding of all the things whereby God is made known unto us, as of His nature, persons, titles, and attributes, yea, also of His Word whereby all these, together with His whole will, are plainly revealed; and of His ordinances wherein and whereby He is worshipped; and finally of His works whereby His wisdom, power, justice, and mercy are evidently made known. Yea, further, we ought to desire that, knowing God to be the only true Jehovah,

we may acknowledge Him to be worthy of all honor, as the celestial spirits do.

2. For our will, we desire a thorough and full submission of it to God as to our sovereign Lord. Hereof we have a worthy pattern in Eli, David, and Christ Himself. Hence will follow patience under all crosses as laid upon us by God, contentment in our estate as appointed to us by God, thankfulness for every blessing as bestowed upon us by God, and other like virtues, which as they have respect to God make much to the hallowing of His name.

3. For our mind and will jointly together, we desire faith whereby we give all due credence to the truth of God's Word and believe in Him. This is a great honor done to God, for he who receives His testimony has set to his seal that God is true. Under this heading is comprised confidence in God's mercy wherein the glory of God most brightly shines forth (for His mercy is great above the heavens), confidence in God's power whereby Abraham gave great glory to God, trust in God's providence (a point much pressed by Christ), persuasion of God's divine wisdom whereby all things are turned to the glory of God's name, and other virtues of the like kind, whereby God's name is also much hallowed.

4. For our heart, we desire that it may be wholly set upon God, and that He may be made the object of all our liking affections, to love Him with all our heart, with all our soul, with all our mind, to joy in the Holy Ghost, to delight in His Word, to care how to please Him, and to be eaten up with a zeal for His glory. And on the other side we desire that our disliking affections be set on that which dislikes Him, such as to hate sin and obstinate sinners who are hateful to Him, to fear His displeasure, to grieve at His offence, and to tremble at His judgments.

5. For our speech, we desire to mention the name of God as we have occasion with all reverence, yea, and to take all oc-

casions of speaking of the glory of His name; for in this respect especially is our tongue, by an excellence, called glory. We desire therefore (when in truth, righteousness, and judgment it may be done) to swear by His name, to call upon His name, to praise His name, to declare His name to others, and to instruct them therein so that the name of God may be the more hallowed. Yea, above all, we desire to use our glory, our tongue, in maintaining the truth of God and in making a just apology when question is made thereof.

6. For our life and outward actions, we desire that they be holy, just, and blameless that men may see our good works and glorify our Father who is in heaven. "Herein, Christ said, "is My Father glorified, that ye bear much fruit." And St. Paul notes that works of mercy tend to the glory of the Lord.

QUESTION. What graces do we desire for others to the hallowing of God's name?

ANSWER. All those that we are to desire for ourselves, that God's name may be hallowed by others as well as ourselves, which we are to desire not only for our children, families, kindred, neighbors, and country-men, or such as we are by outward bands bound unto, but indefinitely for all of all sorts. We have a worthy pattern in Psalm 67. Thus shall we show that in our desire we aim more at God's glory (which is the main scope of this petition than at the good of such as are in any way dear unto us.

QUESTION. What things do we desire that God by His over-ruling providence would turn to the hallowing of His name?

ANSWER. Everything whatsoever, such as:

1. The virtues of His saints whereby else they may be puffed up.

2. The peace and prosperity of His saints whereby else they may be drawn away from God.

3. The failings and folly of His saints, as He turned the envy of Joseph's brethren to the accomplishment of His Word.

4. The troubles and crosses of His saints, that they do not sink under the burden of them.

5. The wicked plots and practices of his enemies, and of the enemies of His Church.

6. All that all creatures do so that thus, in all places, at all times, in and by all things, the name of God may be hallowed.

The Particulars for Which Thanks Is to Be Given Under the First Petition

QUESTION. To what headings may those particulars, for which by reason of the first petition we ought to give thanks, be referred?

ANSWER. To the same headings that the particulars for which we ought to pray were referred, which are:

1. All things whereby we ourselves are enabled to hallow God's name, whether in our soul, as the gifts and graces thereof, or in our body, such as health, strength, agility, and dexterity to anything that makes to that end, or in our calling, whether it pertains to church, commonwealth, or family, or in our outward estate.

2. All things whereby others are enabled to hallow God's name, and that in their soul, body, calling, or estate.

3. All events that in any way make by the overruling providence of God to the hallowing of His name, such as:

a. All manner of blessings bestowed on His churches and children.

b. Judgments executed on His or their enemies.

c. Providence manifested in and upon any creatures.

The Duties Required by Reason of the First Petition

QUESTION. To what headings may the duties that by reason of the first petition we are bound unto be referred?

ANSWER. Unto two especially, one that respects ourselves, the other that respects others.

QUESTION. What are we bound unto in regard of ourselves?

ANSWER. To make the best use that we can of all the means that God affords to enable us to hallow His name, by giving us knowledge of God, bringing our wills in subjection to Him, drawing our hearts unto Him, and breeding and increasing any of the forenamed graces in us.

1. For this end we ought so to behold the creatures, and meditate on them, as we may discern the stamp of God in them, and the evidences that they give of His wisdom, power, justice, mercy, providence, and so forth. By this means God brought Job to a more full knowledge and a more reverend respect of His divine majesty than he had before. David also by this means had his heart even ravished with a holy admiration of God.

2. We ought to take more distinct notice of God in and by His Word. The Scriptures are they that testify of God. And because for our help the Lord has ordained and sanctified the preaching of His Word as a powerful means to breed and increase in us all those graces whereby we may be the better enabled to hallow God's name, we ought diligently to attend to it.

3. We ought to take all occasions of stirring up our glory (as David called our tongue) to speak of and to spread abroad the glory of God's name; yea, and to be willing to open our ears to those who are ready to speak of the same subject, and by our mutual conference to minister more and more matter thereabouts.

4. We ought to order the whole course of our life so as it may be worthy of the Lord, and a means to bring honor to His name.

QUESTION. What are we bound unto in regard of others?

ANSWER. We are bound to do our uttermost to endeavor to draw others to hallow God's name. For this end we ought:

1. To instruct such as are ignorant of God in the knowledge of God.

2. To draw them to set their whole heart on God by commending to them the greatness and goodness of God so as they may be enamored therewith.

3. To encourage them to all good works whereby God is glorified.

The Things to Be Bewailed in Regard of the First Petition

QUESTION. What are we to bewail in regard of the first petition?

ANSWER 1. Whatever is in any way defective and wanting to the honor of God, so as, if it were more complete, God might be more honored thereby. The older Jews who had seen the first temple built by Solomon, when they saw the foundation of the second temple laid, wept with a loud voice because that latter temple was not so fair as the former. Thus if the brightness of the gospel does not shine forth so brightly as it has done formerly, or if in any other way the glory of God is obscured, it ministers just matter of much humiliation.

ANSWER 2. Whatever brings dishonor to God's glorious name, as all manner of sins committed against any of the four commandments of the first table, under which heading may be comprised:

1. Atheism, which is an utter denying of God.

2. Ignorance of the true God. This makes men transfer the honor of God upon others. Against such therefore will Christ come in flaming fire.

3. Errors of God. As when the unity of His nature, trinity of persons, perfection of power, mercy, justice, wisdom, truth,

or any other attributes are denied; or when God is in any mean respect made like man, or any other creature.

4. Light esteem of God, as when He is not trusted, feared, loved, and obeyed with all the mind and might.

5. Neglect of due worship, or yielding false or careless service to Him.

6. Undue use of His Name, such as abusing the same by rash swearing, forswearing, blasphemy, and the like.

7. Profaneness and all manner of impiety.

8. Contempt of His image in such as He has set over us. These and such like tend directly to His dishonor.

To this heading may be referred all such sins as make men attribute to others, or arrogate to themselves, that which is due to God. Base flattery and foolish admiration make some to deify others, as the Tyreans did Herod. Self-conceit, pride, and arrogance make others to deify themselves as Tyrus did.

ANSWER 3. The sins of others, especially of such as profess themselves members of the Church, which cause the name of God to be blasphemed.

ANSWER 4. The evil events that follow from any of the troubles that befall the Church, such as fear of man more than of God, denying the truth of God, and apostasy.

ANSWER 5. All the advantages that enemies of God and of His saints in any way get, their insults and cursed reproaches, and those against God Himself.

3
The Second Petition

God's Kingdom, What it Is and What Are the Kinds of it

QUESTION. What is the second petition?

ANSWER. "Thy kingdom come."

QUESTION. What is the kingdom of God?

ANSWER. It is that estate where as a King He rules. For that is a kingdom where a king reigns and rules. Where God therefore reigns, there is His kingdom.

QUESTION. How does God reign as a King?

ANSWER 1. By His absolute power He reigns over the whole world.

ANSWER 2. By His special grace He reigns over His church.

According to this different manner of God's reigning is His kingdom distinguished. For:

1. He has a universal kingdom called His kingdom of power because by His absolute and supreme power He rules over all creatures whatever or wherever they are. In regard of this universal sovereignty of God the Scripture says, "His kingdom ruleth over all. For who hath resisted His will?" And thereupon the psalmist says unto God, "How terrible art Thou in Thy works? Through the greatness of Thy power shall Thine enemies submit themselves to Thee."

2. He has a peculiar kingdom, called His kingdom of grace, whereby He reigns over a select people culled out of the world who voluntarily yield obedience unto Him. The company of this people is, in one word, the church; and it is a society chosen of God, redeemed by Christ, called and sanctified by the Holy Ghost, that has been in all ages of the world, some in

heaven, others on earth, spread over the face thereof far and near, in which respects it is called the holy catholic church. This is properly the kingdom of Christ in and by whom the Father reigns. For it is said that a kingdom was given to the Son of man, of whom the Father says, "I have set My King upon My holy hill of Zion," whose people shall be willing in the day of His power.

Herein lies a main difference between God's manner of government in His universal and in His peculiar kingdom: The world's subjection is forced, but the church's subjection is free.

God's Reigning Over Rebels

OBJECTION. Touching that universal kingdom of God over all creatures in all places, seeing there are many who rebel against God and say, "Let us break His bonds asunder and cast His cords from us. We will not have Him to reign over us." Thus they "walk according to the prince of the air, the spirit that works in the children of disobedience." And seeing the devil is the god of this world, a doubt may be made how God can be said to be their King, and God's kingdom thus universally extended over the whole world.

ANSWER 1. Rebellion of subjects does not take away the right of a sovereign. Christ, therefore, notwithstanding the tumult of people, is said to be a King.

ANSWER 2. None can do anything at all without His permission. Instance the arch-rebel of all, Satan, in the case of Job. Instance also the many plots and practices of the wicked, who in all ages by an over-ruling hand of God have ben disappointed and made void.

ANSWER 3. God can, when and as it pleases Him, restrain them, as He restrained Sennacherib. Yea, and He can beat them down and utterly destroy them, as he destroyed Pharaoh and his whole host.

ANSWER 4. Satan, to whom the forenamed rebels are subject, is but God's executioner. He is one of the number of God's servants, though of his guilty and reprobate servants. So even in that power that Satan has over them God shows Himself to be their King.

QUESTION. Is this universal kingdom of God here meant?

ANSWER. No further than that God would order it to the good of His peculiar kingdom, which is here principally intended.

The Kingdom of Grace and Glory

QUESTION. How may the peculiar kingdom of God be considered?

ANSWER. In the beginning and progress of it and in the consummation and perfection of it.

In the former respect it consists of a mixture of evil persons with good ones, and of evil qualities in those good persons with good ones. In regard of these mixtures it is resembled to a field wherein tares grow with wheat, and to a net that gathers all sorts, and to corn that arises with straw and chaff as well as with sound and solid grain.

In the latter respect it consists only of such as are in every way perfectly good, and therefore are said to shine as the sun, that has no darkness, nor any speck or spot in it. In the former respect, especially, it is called a kingdom of grace, and that in opposition to those who never were, nor ever shall be, of it. And therefore they are objects of God's severe justice and revenging power.

But in it grace reigns for distinction from those who are translated out of it into heaven. For by reason of the many temptations and imperfections whereunto the saints on earth are subject, they stand in need of much more grace than the saints in heaven, who are just and perfect.

In the latter respect it is called a kingdom of glory, and that by reason of the place where it is, and of the persons who are of it.

The place where it is is the most glorious place of all the world, even the highest heavens.

The persons, both King and subjects thereof, are decked with unspeakable glory. The King there manifests His glory more than anywhere else, as brightly as can possibly by the creature be discerned. The subjects there partake of as much glory as they are capable of, and that in soul and body. So they are all glorious within and without.

The Difference Between the Kingdom of Grace and Glory

This kingdom of Grace and of Glory is but one and the same kingdom, distinguished into two parts that differ in six circumstances. They differ:

1. In time. The kingdom of grace is now present while here we live. The kingdom of glory is to come.

2. In place. This kingdom of grace is on earth; that of glory is in heaven.

3. In condition. This kingdom is continually warring against many enemies, in which respect it is called the church militant. That kingdom triumphs over all the enemies, in which respect it is called the church triumphant.

4. In order of entering into them. This one is to be entered into and passed through before we can enter into that one. The priest was to enter through the sanctuary into the Sanctum Sanctorum.

5. In the manner of government. This one is governed and ordered by many subordinate means, such as magistrates, ministers, and sundry ordinances. That one is governed immediately by God Himself.

6. In continuance. This kingdom has a date and is to come to an end. That one is everlasting without end.

The Church's Government

QUESTION. What can we learn we from this title "kingdom," here applied to the church?

ANSWER. God's church is a well-governed estate. There is governed by a King, a just, wise, and potent King. No king is or can be like Him. He not only can restrain and subdue His enemies, but can also change their hearts and link them to His subjects. He can make the wolf dwell with the lamb. Therein are righteous laws, excellent privileges, and all things requisite for a well-ordered polity, all tending to the good of the subjects. For it is the estate whereof God takes most care.

They therefore who seek to take away order, and to bring confusion into the church, much dishonor this kingdom and the King thereof, who is not the Author of confusion, but peace. So do they also who profess themselves to be members of the church, and yet live as if they were without law, in no kingdom and under no government.

This condition of the church, to be a kingdom (if the King, scepter, laws, and privileges thereof were well known) would be a strong motive to draw such as are out of the church into it, and to retain such as are of it, in it, and to make them say, "It is good to be here." There is nothing worthy to be desired in a kingdom but is after a most excellent manner in this kingdom, as sufficient supply of all things needful and safe protection against all things hurtful.

Thus much of this title "kingdom." The next word to be considered is, "come."

The Increase of the Church

QUESTION. What does this word "come" import?

ANSWER. A want of perfection and progress thereto.

The word "come" is metaphoric. That which is coming is not where it would be; it may yet go further, and in that it is coming. Step by step it draws nearer and nearer to that whereunto it would come; otherwise it did not come but stood still. Hereby then we are given to understand that the kingdom here spoken of has not yet attained to the highest pitch and fullest perfection thereof. Therefore we desire that by degrees it may so proceed on thereto as it may at length attain that whereunto it proceeds, so that that which is in part may depart and that which is perfect may be accomplished.

QUESTION. To which of God's kingdoms is this metaphor to be applied?

ANSWER. To His peculiar kingdom, the church, in both the parts thereof, militant and triumphant. In the militant church it is to be extended to all who in God's decree are deputed thereto, whether called or not called. To such as are not called, that they may be called and so come into the kingdom of grace. To such as are called, that they may be more and more fitted to come into the kingdom of glory so as it may be full and perfect in all the parts thereof.

The Church's Imperfection

QUESTION. What doctrine does this desire of the coming of God's kingdom imply?

ANSWER. God's church is not yet perfect. This is true of both the parts of the church, militant and triumphant.

The militant church, whether it is considered in the several assemblies and congregations thereof (which consist of such as are but hypocrites as well as such as are upright), or in the best of those particular persons (who make up those congregations, and have in them flesh as well as spirit), cannot be denied to be imperfect. Whereupon, as in regard of the mixture of good and evil persons, Christ says of His church, "As a lily among thorns, so is My love among the daughters" Thorns are called so for their wicked disposition, but daughters for their communion in holy things). So in regard of the mixture of spirit and flesh in such as are upright she says of herself, "I am black, but comely," black by reason of her infirmities and imperfections, as well as of her afflictions and persecutions. For with some comeliness there may be blackness.

The triumphant church also, though in regard of that part thereof which is in heaven it is glorious, not having spot, or wrinkle, or any such thing; yet because the combat of all that blessed communion is not yet full, and the bodies of them whose souls are in glory are yet in the power of death, may be truly said to be imperfect. For the times of restitution, or perfection of all things is come. God will have His creatures wait for it. The vision is yet for an appointed time; though it tarries, wait for it because it will surely come.

Shall now particular churches, which by the true notes of a church may be proved to be true churches, be denied to be churches and forsaken because of some imperfections therein? They who will abide in no church but in that which is perfect may wander from church to church and fine none on earth to abide in. Were it not for the church's imperfection there would not be so great need of this petition. This is thus noted not to justify any corruption or imperfection. For this petition, that implies imperfection, enjoins us to pray against it. And that which is prayed against must not be patronized, but rather the best means that can be must be used to redress the same.

As not particular churches, so neither particular persons must be misjudged by reason of the imperfection of grace or the corruption of flesh remaining in them. All here on earth is in part; all is imperfect. Spirits of just men made perfect are to be found in heaven, not on earth. They who think themselves perfect are for the most part furthest from perfection. Let us for our parts be of the same mind whereof the blessed apostle was, not to think ourselves already perfect, but to follow hard after perfection, and to press toward the mark for the price of the high calling of God in Jesus Christ.

Man's Inability to Come Unto God

QUESTION. What do we learn from the application of this word "come" to the kingdom of God?

ANSWER. Man of himself cannot come to God's kingdom. It must come to him before he can come to it. "I was found," says the King of this kingdom, "of them that sought Me not." For no man can come unto Him unless the Father draws him, which made the church thus to pray and promise, "Draw me and we will run after Thee."

Man by nature is dead in sin. Can he who is dead come till he is come unto and has life put into him?

Hereby both the free preventing grace of God is commended unto us, and also all self-conceit in man is removed, and much matter of humiliation ministered unto him.

The Force of This Word "Thy" in the Second Petition

QUESTION. To whom does this particle "Thy" have relation?

ANSWER. Even to Him to whom the same particle had relation in the former petition. And it here imports the same things that it did there: A reason, a restraint, and an extent of this petition.

A reason, as it refers both to the preface and also to the first petition. The kingdom here meant is the kingdom of Him who is our Father who is in heaven, and whose name is to be hallowed. There is great reason therefore that we should pray for this kingdom to come.

A restraint, as it implies that this kingdom only should be desired to come. So not any kingdom that is contrary to this, and hinders the coming of this, but every kingdom that is any help to the coming of this, in that only respect as it is such a help, ought to be desired to come.

An extent, in that it implies a coming fit for such a kingdom as God's is, yea, and answerable to the excellence of Him who is the King thereof.

God's Power to Make His Kingdom Come

QUESTION. What should we learn from directing this petition unto God?

ANSWER. It is in the power of God to perfect His church. He can gather all the parts thereof together and bring them all to that measure of perfection that is best for them. Otherwise it would be in vain to make this petition to Him. It is God who gives the increase. It is He who is able to make grace to abound.

Let us therefore ever call upon Him to be favorable unto Zion, and to build up the walls of Jerusalem. And let us in faith depend on Him for the good of His church, and as long as He remains King thereof let us not fear what any creature can do against it.

This much for the meaning of the words, and the instructions arising out of them. The order and fit inference of this petition upon the former follows.

The Best Means and Fittest Persons to Hallow God's Name

QUESTION. Why is this second petition inferred on the first?

ANSWER. To point out the best means of hallowing God's name and to show what persons are most fit thereto.

QUESTION. What is the best means?

ANSWER. The church, wherein praise waits for God. For God is known in Judah. His name is great in Israel. Nowhere is God so well known as in His church.

QUESTION. Who are the fittest persons to hallow God's name?

ANSWER. Such as are members of the church. Them therefore David calls upon to praise the Lord. No other persons can hallow God's name aright for this is a work of God's sanctifying Spirit. No man can say that Jesus is the Lord but by the Holy Ghost.

Upon the two forenamed grounds we ought the more earnestly to pray for the church so that the name of God may be the more hallowed. This moved Daniel to be exceedingly fervent in prayer to God for His church.

The Spiritual Blessings to Be Craved for the Whole Militant Church

QUESTION. What are the particular good things that by virtue of the second petition we ought to pray for?

ANSWER. All such things as concern the good of the church militant or triumphant.

In our prayer for the church militant we ought to have respect to the things that concern the whole body, or the several parts thereof, whether they are more remote, or nearer to us, and so we are more special members thereof.

QUESTION. What are we to pray for in regard of the whole body of the church militant?

ANSWER. That God would bless it with all needful blessings, both spiritual and temporal.

Pray that He would protect it from all manner of evil.

Under the blessings craved for the church, pray for the means that God has sanctified for the better effecting of them are comprised.

QUESTION. What are the spiritual blessings that we ought to desire for the church on earth?

ANSWER 1. In general, that as God has chosen it to be as His vineyard and orchard so He would take a special care of it, having His eye continually upon it, to plant it, to water it, to fence it, to do for it whatever He sees requisite for it. Because we know that God knows better than we do what is good for His church, therefore ought our desire of the good thereof to be referred to Him and extended to that knowledge that He has of it. To this purpose David thus prayed, "Do good in Thy good pleasure unto Zion."

ANSWER 2. In particular we ought to desire both the daily increase of God's church on earth, and also the establishment of it.

For the increase of it two special things are to be desired, and that indefinitely without any limitation to any particular place.

1. That where no church is God would be pleased to plant one. Such ought the extent of our desire to be herein as to pray that God's saving health may be known among all nations, especially among such as have a particular promise made to them, as the Jews. On this ground when they were a people and we were none, they prayed for us.

2. That where any foundation of a church is laid God would cause the building answerably to be reared up. To this purpose David in his forenamed prayer added this clause, "Build Thou the walls of Jerusalem." This was the main thing that the apostles aimed at in that powerful prayer that with one accord they made unto God. On this ground we have just cause to pray for Virginia, and other like plantations.

For the establishment of the church, two things also are to be desired.

1. That such churches as are built up may be kept from ruin and the people thereof from revolt. On this ground we ought to pray for the churches now in Europe.

2. That if any breaches have ben made they may be repaired and such people as have revolted be restored. On this ground we ought to pray as for those churches of Greece that

were planted by the apostles, so for all those churches that having received the light of the gospel have returned to Popery.

QUESTION. Which are the means that we ought to pray for, as sanctified of God for obtaining the forenamed blessings?

ANSWER. They are of two sorts: Outward, which are the sacred ordinances of God, and inward, which is the sanctifying operation of God's Holy Spirit.

Of outward means there are three special kinds.

The chief and most absolutely necessary is the ministry of God's Word.

The next to that is the administration of the sacraments.

The last, which is also of very good use, is ecclesiastical government.

By the ministry of the Word both such as are out of the church are gathered into it, and they also that are in it are further built up in all needful graces. That is Christ's scepter whereby He governs His church and wherein His statutes, ordinances, and all the privileges of the church are contained.

By the administration of the sacraments that grace which is wrought by the Word is confirmed and established. These are Christ's seals to ratify His covenant, and all His promises made unto His church.

By ecclesiastical government that is well ordered many scandals and stumbling blocks are removed or avoided. Such as are free-hearted and forward are encouraged; such as are backward and slothful are pricked on; such as are unruly and refractory are bridled and kept in compass.

QUESTION. What are we to pray for in regard of the ordinances of God?

ANSWER. Pray that they may be freely and purely exercised. "Pray," says the apostle, "that the Word of the Lord may run [that is, have a free and a speedy passage] and be glorified," that is, be purely and powerfully preached. That which he applies to the Word may also be extended to other holy ordinances of God. That they may be freely and purely exercised we are to pray both for ministers, and also for magistrates. Pray for ministers especially, that the Lord would send forth laborers into His harvest: and give them utterance that they may open their mouths boldly to make known the mystery of the gospel. So ability, liberty, and integrity are to be prayed for in the behalf of ministers. Of all other functions none is more needful, none is more useful for the church, none can less be spared than ministers. Wherefore more instant prayer is to be made for them. Magistrates also, who are promised to be given as nourishers and nurses of the church, may by their good government procure much good to the church, as Mordecai did. We ought therefore to pray for them that God would raise up men of worth who may feed His people according to the integrity of their heart and guide them by the skillfulness of their hands, as David did. Where there are none to bear rule, every man does that which is good in his own eyes—whence must follow much confusion. And where there are evil magistrates, people are often drawn to follow their evil courses. Witness this title given to the first King of Israel, "Jeroboam, which made Israel to sin." If they will not follow their evil courses they shall be sure to be oppressed. For when the wicked bear rule, the people mourn.

QUESTION. What ought we to pray for in regard of the sanctifying operation of God's Spirit?

ANSWER. That it may always accompany all the outward means ordained of God for the good of His church. "For neither is he that planteth anything: nor he that watereth: but God that giveth the increase," which He gives by the work of His Spirit. The Spirit gives life. The apostle therefore prays for them who had heard the Word of truth, that God would give them the Spirit of wisdom and revelation. By the operation of God's Spirit are all God's ordinances made powerful and effectual.

Praying for the Outward Temporal Estate of the Church

QUESTION. What are we to pray for in regard of the temporal estate of the church?

ANSWER. All needful peace and prosperity. Though all temporal blessings are comprised in the fourth petition, yet so far as they tend to the good of the church, being a means that the gospel may be preached and the sacraments administered more freely, that people may be more encouraged to come into the church, and to abide in the church, that ecclesiastical government may be the better exercised, they belong to this petition. Yet because the church like a palm tree often grows better, at least in purity, when it is pressed with adversity, we are in our desire of the outward peace and prosperity of the church to submit our desire to the wisdom of God, and no further to desire it than God sees it to be needful and useful for the church.

The Extent of Our Prayer for the Good of the Church After Our Time

QUESTION. How far ought our desire for the good of the church to extend?

ANSWER. To present, and to succeeding times, that the church of God may prosper, flourish, and increase both in our days, and also in the days of our posterity from time to time until the day of perfect consummation, which is the day of the glorious appearing of Jesus Christ. For this end we are to pray for seminaries, ministers, magistrates and Christian people. Pray for schools of learning, colleges, universities, Inns of Court, and other such like places where youth are trained up and fitted to be useful members of the church. Yea, also we ought to pray for Christian families that in them children may from their infancy be trained up in piety. In Scripture there is frequent mention made of children of the prophets who were trained up under prophets to succeed them in their functions. And there were colleges and other like places for training up these.

Concerning seminaries, we are to desire two things especially for a continuance of them and for God's blessings on them, that they may flourish in good learning, and that their learning may be seasoned with grace. For otherwise it may prove more dangerous than commodious to the church of God.

This extent of our desire for the good of God's church after our time shows that therein we aim more at God's glory and His church's good than at any private benefit to ourselves.

Praying Against Evils That Annoy the Church

QUESTION. What are the evils from which we ought to pray that the church may be protected?

ANSWER. Pray for protection from the dominion of sin, of Satan, and of all evil men who are Satan's ministers and instruments.

These have kingdoms, for sin reigns, and that unto death, where it finds entertainment; and it makes men servants unto itself. Satan also is the god and prince of this world, and as a prince he rules and works in the children of disobedience. All tyrants, persecutors, and such like enemies of the church, being in authority, are the deputies and viceroys of sin and Satan, using the uttermost of their power to bring men into subjection under sin and Satan. The chief of these is antichrist. The kingdom of all these is contrary to Christ's kingdom, and the standing of them hinders the coming of Christ's kingdom; and in that respect we are to pray that they may be weakened and demolished. Yea, we are to pray that everything that causes offence in the church may be removed, for which we have an express promise.

These are the suits that we ought to put up for the church indefinitely, and for such parts thereof as we never knew, saw, or heard of.

The Things to Be Craved for Particular Churches of Which We Know

QUESTION. How ought we to pray for particular churches whose estate we know?

ANSWER. We ought to frame our prayers according to what we hear, see, or otherwise know of any of them.

1. If any special blessing is bestowed on any, to pray that it may be continued and increased.
2. If any mischievous plots are practiced against any, pray that they may be prevented.
3. If ministers or other members of any churches are oppressed, pray that they may be delivered.
4. If persecution is raised against any church, pray that either that fire may be quenched or else that sufficient courage and strength may be given to such as are persecuted to hold out and endure the uttermost trial.
5. If any noisome weeds of idolatry, heresy, schism, or the like sprout up in any church, pray that they may be rooted out. To sharpen our prayer herein we ought often to call to mind that which in this case is promised by Christ: "Every plant that My heavenly Father has not planted shall be rooted up."

This is that true use that we are to make of the knowledge that we have of the estate of any of God's churches.

Praying for the Churches Whereof in Particular We Are Members

QUESTION. How ought we to be affected towards those particular churches whereof we are more immediate members?

ANSWER 1. Our prayers ought to be more particularly applied to them.

ANSWER 2. They ought to be more earnestly extended for their good.

To give some instances of the particular application of our prayers in this kind:

1. We ought by name to pray for the churches in the land wherein we live, as the Jews in a special manner prayed for Zion and for Jerusalem. Thus we of England ought in particular and by name to pray for the churches therein. Yea, because Scotland and Ireland are under the same government that we are we ought by name to pray for those churches also.

2. We ought by name to pray for the magistrates that are set over us; as for the king's majesty, so also for inferior magistrates, and for the ministers of God's Word in the said dominions.

3. We ought more especially to pray for the city, town, or parish where we live. Jeremiah exhorted the Jews, when they were in captivity, to pray unto the Lord for the city where they abode. Ought we not much more to pray for the city or parish where we are in our own country, and where we freely enjoy the holy ordinances of God? Here we ought by name to remember the minister that is set over us. "Pray," says the apostle, "and for me."

4. Yet more frequently and earnestly ought we to pray for the family where we are, whether we are the head or other members thereof. Christ bid His disciples into whatever house they entered to pray that peace might be to it; much more ought we to desire the good of the family where we have our continual abode. We ought by virtue of this petition to pray that our family in particular may be a seminary and nursery of the church; yea, that it may be a church (as the houses of Philemon, Aquila, and Priscilla were), which they are when morning and evening sacrifices of the calves of our lips are constantly offered up therein, and that other duties of piety meet to be performed in a family are there conscionably observed. Such

ought everyone's desire to be for his own family, that if piety should be banished out of the land or parish where he lives, yet it should find harbor in his house. This was the holy resolution of Joshua.

5. Finally, because everyone's person is most near to himself, everyone ought most of all to pray for himself, that his person may be a fit temple for the Holy Ghost, and though the house where we live is an impure and impious place, no member of any true church, yet that he himself may be as Joseph was in the house of Potiphar, a faithful member of the true church, a free-hearted subject of the kingdom of God. And for this end everyone ought to pray that in his person he may be sanctified throughout, and his whole spirit, soul, and body be kept blameless unto the coming of our Lord Jesus Christ.

This is that true and proper use that we are to make of those bonds whereby we are outwardly linked one to another, that as we are more nearly knit one to another, so more specially and instantly to pray that they to whom we are in outward bonds linked may with us be fast knit to the body of Christ, and as true members thereof may beautify and honor it and that all the body by joints and bands having nourishment ministered and knit together may increase with the increase of God.

Thus we see how our desire ought to be ordered for the militant church. It ought in general to be extended to the whole body wherever, and more particularly applied to the several parts of it as we have any notice thereof, and more earnestly extended for such parts as we ourselves are more nearly knit unto.

The Things to Be Desired for the Church Triumphant

QUESTION. What are we to pray for in regard of the triumphant church, the kingdom of glory?

ANSWER. Pray for the full perfection and consummation thereof, whereunto tend these following particulars:

1. That we who live in this kingdom of grace may be fitted and prepared for that kingdom of glory, that we may be presented as a chaste and pure virgin to our husband Christ. Such a prayer the apostle used to make for the members of the militant church.

2. That we may be loosed and be with Christ in that glorious place. For the gathering of such into the kingdom of glory as belong there helps forward the consummation of it.

OBJECTION. How can this desire of being dissolved stand with the unchangeable decree of God concerning the appointed time of man's death?

ANSWER. This kind of prayer rather shows what we could desire, if the will of God were so, than what we would whether it was God's will or not. Neither is it made to alter God's determined purpose, but to manifest our longing desire after that which God in His eternal counsel has purposed for us. Thus many of the faithful Israelites, who lived long before the Messiah was exhibited, desired to see Him. An absolute desire of present death (as was the desire of Elijah and Jonah) is not warrantable, but a longing after death to be in the kingdom of glory (as was the desire of Paul) is very commendable.

3. That the number of those whom God has ordained to make full the body of Christ may be accomplished. For there is a certain number ordained unto eternal life, and until that number is full the kingdom of glory cannot in all the parts thereof be consummate.

4. That the signs that in God's Word are foretold to go before the coming of Christ may accordingly fall out; that by the sight of them we may be more erected to look for the glorious appearing of Christ. There are signs foretold; these therefore must be prayed for.

5. That all the obstinate enemies of the church who in any way hinder the full and perfect consummation thereof may be destroyed, and not only those wicked men, cruel tyrants, and persecutors, but also death, and him who has the power of death, the devil. The destruction of these is promised, so there is good ground to pray for it.

6. That the bodies of all the saints who from the beginning have slept may be raised from death to be united to their souls and brought unto the kingdom of glory. For this is absolutely promised.

OBJECTION. This is to pray for the dead.

ANSWER. Not for this or that particular friend departed whose estate we certainly do not know but in general for all the true members of Christ's celestial body; nor to obtain that for them that was to be obtained in the times of their life, remission of sins; nor yet to alter their final estate, the doom whereof passed upon them at the moment of their dissolution, but only as their resurrection is a degree to the perfecting of the kingdom of glory. We are taught to pray for the full perfection of that kingdom, so pray indefinitely for the resurrection of the saints, which is a degree thereto.

7. That Christ would come in His glory to judgment and make a perfect separation between the elect and reprobate, for so much is foretold and promised.

8. That all the members of Christ's mystical body being glorified with Him, He may deliver up the kingdom to God the Father, that God may be all in all. For so much is also foretold.

The Things for Which Thanks Is to Be Given by Reason of the Second Petition

QUESTION. For what are we to give thanks by virtue of the second petition?

A. Everything that makes to the good of God's church, whether directly, by blessings bestowed on it, or consequently, by restraining or overthrowing the enemies of it, ministers just matter of thanksgiving. We are therefore to be thankful in the behalf of the church in these cases that follow, and others like them.

1. When churches are planted where none were before. Thus the Jews glorified God when they heard that the gospel was embraced by the Gentiles.

2. When such churches as are planted thrive and prosper. For this St. Paul gave thanks in the behalf of the Thessalonians.

3. When good magistrates are raised up. In which case the Queen of Sheba blessed God for setting Solomon on the throne of Israel. Much more are we to bless God for good ministers of His Word, and that not only when they are first raised up, but also when, being restrained by sickness or any other means, they are again restored.

4. When the gospel has a free passage and sounds forth from one place to another.

5. When the ministry of the Word is in power and is fruitful among the saints.

6. When the church has rest, peace, and prosperity.

7. When such as are persecuted stand steadfast in the faith and are not terrified with any oppositions against the truth, or drawn to deny the same.

8. When the church is delivered from any plots of the enemies against it.

9. When vengeance is executed on the enemies of the church.

10. When seminaries of the church, just as schools of learning, colleges, and universities do prosper.

11. When piety is planted in families, especially in our own.

12. When private Christians grow in grace, especially if withal they edify one another.

13. When saints who have given undoubted evidence of their perseverance in the true faith depart out of this life. Though that loss which the church on earth may have of them ministers matter of mourning, yet in that the triumphant church is increased by their departure is matter of thanksgiving.

14. When we see the time of our own departure to be at hand.

15. When we observe any of those signs to fall out that Christ has foretold of the end of the world, and of His glorious coming unto judgment.

The Duties Required Under the Second Petition

QUESTION. What duties are we to endeavor after by virtue of the second petition?

ANSWER. Everyone ought, according to the estate and condition wherein he is, to do what lies in his power to help on the coming of the kingdom of God, and that both in himself and in others also. For which end these particulars following are carefully to be observed.

1. They who are out of the church must come into it. If they are in the kingdom of darkness they must not abide therein. This is especially to be observed of them to whom the light of the gospel appears and reveals their darkness. To such it is said, "Awake thou that sleepest, and arise from the dead, and Christ shall give thee light."

2. They who are in the church must walk worthy of their calling. To such it is said, "Ye were once darkness but are now light; walk as children of light."

3. They who being of the church are among such as are out of it must labor to win them. St. Paul went so far herein as he became as without law that he might gain them who were without law. To show that this is a common duty belonging to every member of the church, St. Peter exhorted women so to

carry themselves towards their husbands, as if any do not obey the Word they may without the Word be won by the conversation of their wives.

4. Fellow members of the church must edify one another and hearten, encourage, and provoke one another unto good works, and to stand steadfast in the faith.

5. They who are strong must bear with the weak; and everyone must take heed that they lay no stumbling block before any to make them fall or give any offence.

6. If any are parents of children, they must be careful to bring them to be incorporated into the church by the sacrament of baptism, and that while they are infants; and as they come to any years of discretion to bring them up in the nurture and admonition of the Lord so that when they are translated into the triumphant church they may leave their children behind them true members of the militant church, and that successively generation after generation.

7. If any are householders, their care must be to make their houses (as the houses of Philemon, Aquila, and Priscilla were) churches of God, and in this respect take upon them the faithful endeavor of Abraham and the settled resolution of Joshua.

8. They who are ministers must take heed to all the flocks whereof the Holy Ghost has made them overseers to feed the church of God and do all things unto edifying.

9. They who are magistrates must maintain true religion in their dominions, and cause all who are under their jurisdiction to stand to the covenant of God. Yea they ought to be so watchful over the Lord's vineyard as to suffer neither wild boar to root it up, nor foxes to make any havoc therein. They must suffer neither professed enemies nor running seducers to harbor therein.

The Things to Be Bewailed Under the Second Petition

QUESTION. What are the things that we ought to bewail by virtue of the second petition?

ANSWER. Bewail all such things as in any way make to the disadvantage or disparagement of the kingdom of Christ.

1. Bewail that great sway that Satan has in the world whereof he is the god and works in the children of disobedience and that all the world worships him. For all infidels, idolaters, heretics, schismatics, hypocrites, and profane persons are his vassals—and these are they with whom the world is filled.

2. Bewail the small circuit of Christ's kingdom. The prophet thus brings in the church herself bewailing her small number: "Woe is me, for I am as when they have gathered the summer fruits, as the grape gleanings of the vintage."

3. Bewail the mixture of Satan's subjects with Christ's in that small circuit. For where the Lord of the field sows good seed, the envious man sows tares, which makes the servants of the Lord to complain.

4. Bewail the many clouds that obscure the light of the gospel. I mean the clouds of error, superstition, human traditions, and such like, whereby the clear light of the gospel is hindered from shining forth in its full brightness. Christ Himself complained that the Word of God was made of none effect through the many traditions of the Jews.

5. Bewail the spoils of the church made by open enemies, whereof David much complained, as did also other prophets.

6. Bewail treacheries of false-hearted brethren. The church complained that all her friends dealt treacherously with her, and Christ complained that His own familiar friend in whom He trusted, who ate of His bread, lifted up his heel against Him.

7. Bewail unfaithfulness in magistrates suffering such as bear no good will to the church to creep into it, lodge in it, and work mischief against it. This good Nehemiah greatly com-

plained of. Much more cause of complaint there is when princes in the church are roaring lions and her judges are ravenous wolves.

8. Bewail unfaithfulness in ministers when they are insufficient, idle, or corrupt in doctrine or life, whereby the edification of the church is much hindered. The prophets often complained of such.

9. Bewail desolation of seminaries, of schools, colleges, universities, and such like. David lamented the destruction of the city of priests, which was a seminary. The coming of the kingdom of God is much hindered by the desolation of seminaries. So also is it as much, if not more, hindered by corruption in seminaries. If fountains are poisoned, can wholesome streams be expected to flow from thence? In corrupted seminaries more vassals of Satan than true subjects of Christ are bred and brought up.

10. Bewail the disorder of families. When piety finds in private families little or no entertainment, if it is not clean thrust out of doors, and such licentiousness used, when houses are rather made sties for Satan than churches of God, great cause of mourning is given. Jeremiah complained that husbands and wives, parents and children, were all given to wickedness.

11. Bewail the unworthy walking of professing believers. It is a means to keep such as are not of the church from entering into it when they see such as profess themselves to be of the church to walk as children of darkness and to turn the grace of God into wantonness. St. Paul bitterly complained of such.

12. Bewail the reproaches cast upon the saints. Sarah, when she beheld Ismael scoffing at Isaac, was exceedingly moved. So was David at Michael's scorning of him for the manifestation of his zeal. Some weak members of the church may be discouraged thereby; and in that respect it is a matter to be lamented.

13. Bewail the persecution raised against the church. This Elijah much bewailed; yea, it made him weary of his life. A free passage of the Word, and a free use of other holy ordinances of God, is much hindered thereby; and many are thereby brought to deny the faith. Therefore it is to be bewailed.

14. Bewail the timorous backsliding of professing believers. This St. Paul complained of in his time. This tends greatly to the discouragement and disadvantage of the church, and is much to be lamented.

15. Bewail the schisms, sects, and dissentions in the church. These greatly hinder the growth of the church; yea, they often cause greater desolation than open oppositions of professed enemies.

16. Bewail too much love of life in this world and fear of death. If men might live as long as they desired, how slowly would God's kingdom come! That we who desire the kingdom of God to come speedily should seek to live long in this world implies a contradiction.

4
The Third Petition

The Will of God That Is Here Meant and Doing It

QUESTION. Which is the third petition?

ANSWER. "Thy will be done in earth as it is in heaven."

QUESTION. What is here to be considered?

ANSWER. The thing desired and the manner of performing it.

The substance then of the petition is in these words, "Thy will be done in earth." In the words following is a direction for the better performing of that which is desired. Of these two points therefore we are to speak in order. And first of the petition that sets out the rule that in all things we ought to set before us, namely the will of God.

QUESTION. How does God will a thing?

ANSWER. He does it by ordaining and determining it and by liking and approving it.

By this differing manner of willing things God's will may be distinguished into His secret counsel and His revealed Word.

The former of these is that sovereign, absolute will of God by which all things are, and without which nothing can be. For "He worketh all things after the counsel of His own will," and has done whatsoever He pleased. For who was His counselor?

The latter is called God's good and acceptable will whereby He manifests what is pleasing unto Him.

QUESTION. Which of these is here especially meant?

ANSWER His revealed Word, as is evident by these reasons.

1. "The revealed things of God belong to us and our children forever" (Deuteronomy 29:29).

2. God's revealed Word is that rule that we must lay before us, and the mark whereat we ought to have an eye in all things (Psalm 119:9).

3. This will of God may be resisted, and is much resisted, by the sons of men. For as Christ says, "How oft would I . . . and ye would not?" (Matthew 23:37) God's good and acceptable and perfect will is not everywhere, as His power is.

There is therefore great need that we should pray to have this done. Not that God would do what He will, but that we may be able to do what He wills. As for God's secret counsel (as it is kept secret), it cannot be here meant as appears by these reasons.

Secret things belong unto the Lord our God.

The counsel of God shall stand; it cannot but be done so we need not pray that it may be done.

A desire may be made contrary to God's secret will without sin. Instance the desire of David to build a temple for the Lord, which desire both Nathan the prophet of the Lord, and God also Himself approved; and yet it was the determined purpose of God that David should not do that which he desired.

Yet if the foresaid counsel of God is made known, either extraordinarily by special revelation or ordinarily by events (for events declare the determined counsel of God), then there ought to be yielded thereto a willing submission, which submission is commended in the examples of Job, Eli, David, Hezekiah, Paul, and other saints. And thus this phrase ("be done") imports both obedience to God's Word and also subjection to His work, or a willing yielding to whatever God says or does. It is a phrase both of action and passion, of action in relation to God's Word and of passion in relation to His guiding providence. And it imports patience and contentment even in such things as cross our own minds. In this sense Paul's companions, when they heard his resolution to go to Jerusalem where the prophet had foretold that he should be bound, said, "The will of the Lord be done."

In regard of God's secret will, we pray that nothing that God does displeases us, and in regard of His revealed will that nothing we do displeases Him. Obedience therefore to God is here principally prayed for.

The Extent of Our Desire to Have God's Will Done

QUESTION. Why is this desire set down impersonally thus, "be done"?

ANSWER. To show the extent of our desire. If it had been expressed in the first person ("Let us do"), our desire might seem to be appropriated to ourselves. If in the third person ("Let men do"), it might seem to be posted over to others from ourselves. But this indefinite phrase, "be done," may indifferently be referred to ourselves and all others whoever they are.

The Rule of Our Obedience, God's Will

QUESTION. What do we learn from the express mention of God's will in this petition?

ANSWER God's will is the rule of our obedience so as if such a question as the people, publicans, and soldiers propounded to John, or the ruler to Christ, or the Jews to the apostles, be moved, and it is demanded what is to be done, in a word out of this petition this answer may be given, "God's will." This is that which often we are enjoined to understand, to prove, to practice, and that is so much pressed in Psalm 119, and that not without just cause. For God's will is the very ground of goodness. Whatever is willed of God is good, and therefore good because it is willed by God. Where the apostle prayed for the Hebrews that God would make them perfect in every good work, by way of exposition he added this clause, "to do His will."

They who make decrees of councils, traditions of elders, statutes or canons of men, or any other thing besides God's Word their rule, have but a leaden rule, which may be bowed this way or that way. What may we then think a man's own reason, will, lust, appetite, or humor to be? And yet many make these the rules of their obedience.

For our part let us thoroughly acquaint ourselves with God's Word, and therein exercise ourselves day and night. Let us make it our counselor to be resolved thereby in all doubts, our guide to be directed thereby in all our ways, our light to be enlightened thereby through the darkness of this world, our touchstone to prove and try all things thereby. And let us have it in as high account as ever David had it.

Practicing God's Will

QUESTION. What does this phrase ("be done") teach us?

ANSWER. Nothing is sufficient without practice. It says nothing because neither knowledge of God's will, nor a good disposition thereto, nor profession thereof without doing it is anything. All these are in their kind needful, for practice without knowledge cannot but be very preposterous; without a good disposition merely hypocritical; and without a free profession too timorous. So knowledge of God's will is as light to give direction unto practice; a good disposition thereto is as salt to season it; a free profession is as wine to make it quick and cheerful. Yet all those without practice are as nothing. He who knows his master's will and does not act according to it shall be beaten with many stripes. He who has a good mind and disposition to God's will, and yet does not do it, condemns himself in that which he allows. And he who makes a fair profession of it, but yet does not do it is like that fig tree that Christ cursed, and he has this doom denounced against him by the Judge of all, "Depart from Me, thou worker of iniquity." I may therefore well say to them that know, like, and profess God's will,

"Blessed are you if you do it." But without doing all is in vain. For…

1. There is no truth of grace where there is no practice of grace.

2. Doing God's will is the main end of revealing God's will.

3. The benefit of all consists in practice for by it God is most glorified, our fellow saints stirred up to a holy emulation, they who are without are either won or made ashamed, and we ourselves are assured of our election before the world and salvation after the world, gaining also thereby a good name while we live and a blessed memorial after we are dead.

If these motives are not sufficient to move such as know the will of God to add practice thereunto, and to do it, I do not know what can be sufficient.

Man's Inability to Do God's Will

QUESTION. What are we taught by desiring of God that His will be done?

ANSWER Man is unable of himself to do God's will. "Without Me," said the Lord, "ye can do nothing." It is God who works in us both to will and to do. As for man, take him as he is of himself, and it will appear that every imagination of the thought of his heart is only evil continually. And by the weakness of this corruptible body we are held back from bringing our wills to yield unto and agree with God's will. Is it then possible that of himself he should do that which is so pure and perfect as the will of God is?

On this ground we see that there is just cause…

1. To deny ourselves, and not to lean unto our own wisdom, will, conceit, or any natural ability.

2. To call upon God to draw us so that we may run after Him, and wholly to depend on Him for His preventing, assisting, and perfecting grace.

3. To use such means as God has sanctified to enable us to do His will.

4. To give the praise of all that ability we have to do God's will unto God who works in us both the will and the deed.

5. To use and employ the said ability to the glory of God.

The Force of This Word "Thy" in the Third Petition

QUESTION. To whom does this particle "Thy" in the third petition have relation?

ANSWER To the same person to whom it had relation in the two former petitions; and it imports the same things in this petition that it did in the other two, namely a reason, a restraint, and an emphasis.

A reason, because it shows that the will here mentioned is the will of our Father who is in heaven, whose name is above all to be hallowed, and whose kingdom is before all to be preferred.

A restraint, because it implies that His will only is to be done.

An emphasis, because it intimates an advancing of God's will above all others.

Preferring God's Will Before All Others

QUESTION. What then does this particle "Thy" teach us?

ANSWER God's will is to be preferred before all others. This Joseph, Daniel and his three companions, the apostles and many others well observed when they refused to yield to man's will against God's. And David, Paul, and Christ, when they submitted their own wills to God's in such things as if it had been the will of God, could have desired to have been otherwise. Among others the example of Christ is to be observed because He was a Son and we are but servants. If the Son yielded to do the will of His Father, how much more ought the servant to yield to do the will of his Master.

Both the supreme sovereignty of God, and also the absolute perfection of His will, require as much. As for our own and other men's will, they are subject to much error and often prove very pernicious.

This is especially to be noted of such as can be content to do God's will so far as it is agreeable to their own humor or does not cross the will of those men whom they are loath to offend. But if in these cases they refuse to do God's will, they do not have it in that high account that here they are taught to have it, and they come very short of the extent of this petition whereby we are taught always to have one eye on God's will and not on our own. For in our will there are many contrarieties, but in the Lord's will there is always life and goodness.

Praying Only for Men in Earth

QUESTION. Who are comprised under this phrase "in earth"?

ANSWER. Sons of men inhabiting the earth. In this phrase there is a double figure of speech. First, the place is put for them who are therein. Second, a general is put for a particular. For there are sundry sorts of creatures that live on earth, yet only the chief and principal of them are meant, even they who have the dominion over all the rest. Now men are here thus set forth because while they live on earth they are most backward to do God's will.

QUESTION. What instruction may be raised from this phrase "in earth"?

ANSWER. Men, while they live in this world, need our prayers. All the directions given in Scripture to pray for any, all the promises made to prayer, all the warrant that is given for performing this duty, is restrained to prayer made for them who live on earth. And they are to be prayed for:

1. Because they are subject to manifold infirmities.

2. Because they may reap benefit by our prayers, which they that are taken from earth cannot do. For they who are translated from earth to heaven are made perfect so as they do not need our prayers. And they who are cast down from earth to hell are thrown into such irrecoverable misery as they can reap no benefit by our prayers.

Let us not therefore offer up so precious incense as prayer is in vain for such as can reap no benefit thereby. But in faith let us pray for them that are on earth.

The Meaning of This Phrase "In Heaven"

QUESTION. Who are comprised under this phrase in heaven?

ANSWER. The glorious angels and glorified saints with Christ their Head.

Some think the middle heaven is here meant, where the sun, moon, and other stars are placed, and that partly because the creatures in that heaven constantly keep that course wherein by the will of their Creator they were at first placed, and partly because they are visible so that constant course of theirs, according to the will of God, may be seen by men on earth. But however that constancy of theirs may be a witness against our manifold aberrations and swervings from that course wherein our Creator has set us, yet in that they have no understanding to take notice of the will of God or do what they do by any free, willing choice, but by a natural motion from which they cannot swerve we must ascend higher than that heaven, even to the highest heaven of all, where the forenamed angels and saints are, who in all things by a most free and willing choice perfectly fulfill the will of God.

QUESTION. How can they whom we do not see be a pattern for us?

ANSWER. By the Word we may know what is done by them. For God has thereby manifested how they do His will.

The Manner of Following a Perfect Pattern

QUESTION How can we do God's will as they do it, seeing they in all points do it most perfectly and it is impossible for us to attain to such a perfection?

ANSWER 1. In such a manner as they do we may also do God's will, though not in so complete a measure. A candle gives light in a house even as the sun does in the world, in such a manner, not in so great a measure. There may be in quality and likeness a comparison between things that are in quantity and measure very unequal. In this respect they who have hope in Christ are said to purify themselves even as He is pure.

ANSWER 2. All the saints even on earth have the beginning of that heavenly perfection wrought in them, which beginning the apostle calls "the first fruits of the Spirit." Now we may be confident of this very thing, that He who has begun a good work in us will perform it until the day of Jesus Christ that we may be blameless in that day.

ANSWER 3. Our desire and endeavor may and must be beyond our ability, as shall be proved by and by.

The Matter of Patience that the Inhabitants of Heaven Have

QUESTION. How can there be a sufficient pattern where there is no trial of patience, as in heaven there is none? For the angels and saints in heaven are not subject to any crosses that would try their patience.

ANSWER. This pattern is especially for active obedience. Those heavenly spirits do many things that they would not but for the will of God. When it is the will of God the angels willingly descend from heaven to earth, sometimes to bring glad tidings to the church and sometimes to execute vengeance on sinners. Yea, the souls of the saints that have been taken out of their bodies and carried into Abraham's bosom, that place of joy and bliss, have been content at the will of God to leave their glory and to return again into their bodies, even as Christ came down from heaven not to do his own will, but the will of Him who sent Him and as His soul, after it had been in Paradise returned into His body in earth. Now heaven, Paradise, and Abraham's bosom is a place of such glory, and so conspicuously does the brightness of God's glory there shine forth, as the celestial spirits would never be willing to depart out of it, but to do the will of their Lord.

There is a compassion in them for the afflictions of the church in earth. For the saints in earth and in heaven are fellow members of one and the same body, in which respect there cannot but be some sympathy and fellow-feeling of their fellow-members afflictions even as there is in the head of that body, Jesus Christ. The main reason why the souls of the departed martyrs desire vengeance on the enemies of the church is for those saints' sake who were living, and so subject to their tyranny and cruelty. It is said that there is joy in the presence of the angels of God over one sinner that repents. Why not then compassion also over the church that is afflicted?

The saints in heaven through patience inherit the promises (for through many afflictions men enter into the kingdom of God), and therein we are exhorted to be followers of them.

With patience they expect the resurrection of their bodies, and perfect consummation of that glory that is ordained for the whole body of Christ and all the members thereof. When it was told the souls of the forenamed deceased martyrs that they should rest until their brethren should be fulfilled, they were silent and patient; they did not reply again.

Thus, then, we see that in heaven there is a pattern of patience.

Of Rightly Doing Good

QUESTION. What do we learn from this direction ("as it is in heaven") added to the petition?

ANSWER. Good things are to be done after a right manner. So much is noted in the sum of the moral law, as Christ has set it down. The good things enjoined are to love God and our neighbor. The manner of loving God is to do it with all the heart. The manner of loving our neighbor is to love him as our self. If the Scriptures are observantly read we shall find them as copious in prescribing the right manner as in pressing the main matter of any duty, and in declaring God's approbation of the one more than of the other. Take for example the first work of piety recorded to be done after man's fall. In the sacrifices that Abel and Caine first offered God did not behold the offering, but the heart that he might please God in his offering who pleases Him in his heart. The offering declared the work, the heart the manner of doing it.

God's will is manifested in the manner as well as in the matter. Yea, if a good thing is evilly done God will say, "Who required this at your hands?" A good thing is clean perverted and made evil by an evil manner of doing it.

It is therefore very requisite that we examine good things even by the manner of doing them, and not think it sufficient that the thing we do is for the matter and substance of it lawful and warrantable. As many (if not many more) transgressions are committed by failing in the manner of doing good things as by doing things that are simply evil.

Propounding a Perfect Pattern Before Us

QUESTION. What are we taught by the kind of pattern set before us?

ANSWER. The pattern that we follow must be perfect; such a pattern is the example of those who are in heaven. They are the spirits of just men made perfect. Like patterns cannot be found on earth except the pattern of Christ in the days of His flesh, which is also set before us.

QUESTION. How are examples of saints on earth to be followed if our pattern must be perfect?

ANSWER. No saints example that ever lived on earth for the time of his abode on earth is made a pattern in all things without exception to be followed. But their examples are set before us to be imitated.

1. Imitate them in such particular good things as they did well as Abraham in believing God's promises, Moses in being faithful in God's house, the prophets in long-suffering, Job in patience, and other saints in other particular graces are made patterns.

2. So far forth as they followed a perfect pattern we must follow them.

We are very prone to follow imperfections. As a stream where a breach is made will leave the channel to run in that breach and by striving to run therein will make the breach greater and greater, so we, where we see any defect in the pattern, are ready not only to fail by that defect, but to be far worse. A proselyte made by a Pharisee proved two-fold more a child of hell than the Pharisee. We are, by that corruption of nature that is in us, prone to swerve from the pattern that is set before us, even where the pattern itself is good and right. How much more shall we swerve when the pattern is defective? Yet by a perfect pattern we shall be kept the nearer and held closer to perfection.

It is therefore a point that greatly concerns us to make choice of our pattern, and not to be beguiled with glorious titles of antiquity, universality, multitude, and consent of men on earth. Perfection was never found in these, much less in some few or single men that are blinded and puffed up with honor, wealth, power, or any such earthly pre-eminence. Yet how does the whole world almost follow such and make them their only pattern?

Aiming at More Than We Can Attain To

QUESTION. What do we learn from setting those who are in heaven as a pattern before those who are in earth?

ANSWER. Such perfection as in this life cannot be attained to may be aimed at. For it is not possible for any on earth to be so perfect as they who are in heaven, yet must we aim at their perfection and endeavor after it. For Christ exhorts us to be perfect as our heavenly Father is perfect.

1. Thus shall we better discern how far short we come of perfection, and of that integrity that is requisite for all those who stand in God's glorious presence. On this ground Job said, "How should man compared unto God be justified?"

2. Thus we shall be the more humbled and brought to say to God as Job did, "Behold, I am vile. What shall I answer Thee? I will lay my hands upon my mouth. I abhor myself and repent in dust and ashes."

3. Thus shall we be brought to a thorough and utter denial of ourselves and from all self-conceit and confidence in our own righteousness, and to pray unto God not to enter into judgment with us.

4. Thus shall we be the more stirred up to put forth our uttermost ability, as it is in the old proverb, "He who will shoot high must aim at the sun," a mark far beyond his reach. A man who shoots at a mark within his reach may shoot short for want of putting out his full strength.

Little do they regard these helps who set the examples of mortal, weak, sinful men before them and think all is well if they are any better than the worst sort of people, as that Pharisee who said, "O God, I thank Thee that I am not as other men are, extortioners, unjust, adulterers, or even as this publican." Hence is it that they are so far from judging themselves for many of their sins that they are ready rather to justify themselves when they are reproved and say, "Do not such and such men do the like?" What sin almost might not be justified if the pattern of men on earth, yea, of the best, were a sufficient plea and pretext? Have you not heard of Noah's drunkenness, David's adultery and murder, Lot's incest, Solomon's idolatry, Peter's denial of Christ, and other like sins committed by other like men? By such patterns men are many times made to stumble in the way wherein they should walk, if they are not clean turned out of it.

The pattern here propounded by our Lord stirs us up to covet earnestly the best gifts and to seek to excel.

By this pattern in heaven set before us, the common scoffs of profane libertines (upbraiding such as endeavor to follow this direction with the nicknames of "angels on earth," and "young saints") are wiped away. How can those taunts be imagined to be otherwise made than in derision of this direction, which assuredly He who gave this direction will not suffer to pass unavenged.

The Order of the Third Petition

QUESTION. To which of the former petitions does this third petition have reference?

ANSWER To both of them.

To the first, as a manifestation of the truth of our desire to hallow God's name. For no such evidence can be given thereof as a true and thorough subjection of ourselves in all things to the will of God. Then is God's name most hallowed when His will is best done. Of all places, in heaven is God's name most hallowed because there His will is best done. For this end Christ here sets them in heaven before us for a pattern therein.

To the second petition this references as a reason of our desire thereof. For the subjects of God's kingdom are they who most readily and faithfully do the will of God. We therefore desire that God's kingdom may come that there may be the more to do the will of God.

The Honor Done to God by Doing His Will

QUESTION. What doctrine arises out of that relation that this petition has to the first?

ANSWER. God's honor is most advanced by a faithful subjection to His will. Thus Christ proves that He glorified His Father on earth, namely by finishing the works that He gave Him to do.

For by our forwardness to do God's will we acknowledge both the greatness and also the goodness of God. We acknowledge that He is the supreme Sovereign who has power to require this and that to be done; and withal we acknowledge that what He declares to be His will is most good. For these are the motives that are of force to draw us on to do anyone's will—the sovereignty that He has over us who wills this or that and the equity of that which He wills.

We ought therefore hereby to be the more stirred up to do God's will because thereby His name is hallowed.

Showing Ourselves to Be God's Subjects by Doing His Will

QUESTION. What doctrine arises out of the relation that this petition has to the second?

ANSWER. They are the truest subjects of God's kingdom who are most ready to do His will.

Hence was it that the psalmist, where he showed that God had set up His Son as a King, infers these exhortations: "Serve the Lord," "Kiss the Son," and so on. And again upon a like ground he says, "Thy people shall be willing in the day of Thy power."

The Word of God (which is that will of God that is here especially meant) is the scepter of His kingdom and the law thereof. All the statutes and ordinances of His kingdom are comprised in His Word; therefore they who do it must be His best subjects.

This then is a true trial of our spiritual estate, whether we are indeed of His kingdom or not. If we delight to do His will, and His law is in our hearts, then have we good assurance in our own souls, and give good evidence to others, that we are true members of His church, true subjects of His kingdom. But if there is nothing but a bare profession we are like the fig tree that encumbered the ground, or like those who said they were God's people, but indeed were the synagogue of Satan. God's kingdom does not come by professing and saying, but by performing and doing God's will.

The Particulars That We Are Taught to Pray For in the Third Petition

QUESTION. What are the particulars for which, by virtue of the third petition, we ought to pray?

ANSWER. Such as concern the petition itself and such as concern the direction added thereto.

QUESTION. To how many headings may the things that concern the petition itself be referred?

ANSWER. To four especially, which are these:

1. The rule itself, in this word "will."
2. The restraint of it, in this particle "Thy."
3. The extent of it, in this phrase "be done."
4. The place where it is to be done, "on earth."

QUESTION. What do we desire in regard of the rule?

ANSWER 1. Knowledge of God's Word. For in and by God's Word is His will revealed and knowledge thereof is the ground of true obedience. "Give me understanding," says the psalmist, "and I shall keep Thy law; yea, I shall keep it with my whole heart." Desire of obedience without knowledge is very preposterous. An ignorant man's practice is like a blind man's wandering in byways. How can it otherwise be but that such should fall into many dangers?

ANSWER 2. A conformity of our wills to God's, or a readiness in our will and heart to yield to whatever we shall know to be God's will. When God said to David, "Seek My face," his heart answered, "O Lord, I will seek Thy face." For this was his prayer, "Incline mine heart unto Thy testimonies." It is a proper fruit of sanctifying knowledge to draw the will to embrace as good that which the understanding discerns to be true.

ANSWER 3. Strength of memory to hold fast God's Word, and that in the good directions and sweet consolations, in the precepts and promises thereof. Where the psalmist says that the mercy of the Lord is upon those who remember His commandments to do them, does he not imply that to remember God's Word is a special help to doing it? Things not remembered are as things not known. The apostle notes this to be the cause of the Hebrews fainting in their troubles, that they forgot the direction and consolation of the Word.

ANSWER 4. Life of conscience, both to cheer us up in doing the will of God and also to check us when we swerve from the same, and not to suffer us to be quiet until we turn to it again. For these are the proper functions of a conscience that is quickened and sanctified. The apostle notes that they who give themselves over to transgress have their conscience seared with a hot iron; the life of it is taken away.

ANSWER 5. Love of God's Word, that our hearts are so set upon it as we make it our joy and delight. This made David as forward as he was to do the will of God, for God's Word was his love, longing, joy, delight, more sweet than honey, more precious than thousands of gold or silver. This reason for doing God's will he himself renders in these words: "My soul hath kept Thy testimonies, for I love them exceedingly." Love sets all the power of a man's soul and parts of his body on work to accomplish that which is loved. But unless our heart and affections are set upon God's Word, very hardly shall we be brought to do it because it is contrary to our natural and corrupt will.

ANSWER 6. Renovation of our outward parts, that they may be made instruments in their several functions to execute God's will; that as there is a readiness to will, so there may be a performance also. And for this end we ought to pray that we may be sanctified as in our whole spirit, so in body, and that He would work in us both to will and to do. All the former without this are nothing. This is the main and principal thing here intended. The others are but preparations and helps thereunto.

Here I might take occasion to reckon up all those virtues that in God's Word are enjoined to us. For God's will comprises under it all those virtues; yea, whatever may truly be thought to be good is comprehended in the will of God. But it is sufficient thus in general to have pointed at this heading.

QUESTION. What should we desire in regard of the restraint of the forenamed rule in this word "Thy"?

ANSWER 1. A distinct understanding of the excellence and perfection of God's will so that we may addict ourselves wholly to it, not taking from it nor adding to it. Had we indeed as good an opinion and as high an esteem of God's will as David had, we would cleave as closely to it as he did.

ANSWER 2. A right discerning of the vanity and corruption of the creatures will, especially when it is not agreeable to God's, but swerves from it. In this respect it is said, "The Lord knoweth the thoughts of man that they are but vanity," and, "He taketh the wise in their craftiness." If we could truly and thoroughly discern as much would we be so blockish as to prefer the will of any man before God's?

ANSWER 3. A denial of our own will, a point that the wise man much presses in these and such like prohibitions: "Lean not to thine own understanding. Be not wise in thine own eyes." Seldom or never are self-conceited men brought to yield simple obedience to God's will. They will be so inquisitive into the ground and reason thereof that if they are not satisfied therein their own will, and not God's, shall be done. There is more hope of a fool than of such a one.

ANSWER 4. Mortification of the flesh. For the flesh lusts against the Spirit so that we cannot do the things that we would. When we would do the will of God, yea, and delight in the law of God after the inner man, we shall find the flesh warring against that law of the mind and bringing us into captivity to the law of sin. This made St Paul with so bitter an exclamation to say, "O wretched man that I am. Who shall deliver me from the body of this death!"

QUESTION. What do we desire in regard of the extent of the forenamed rule ("be done")?

ANSWER 1. An accomplishment of whatever God has determined, that what God wills to be done may accordingly be done, whether the creature wills it or nills it. For we ought to believe that God wisely wills all things for the best, and thereupon to desire that His counsel and purpose may stand, and even from our hearts to say, "The will of the Lord be done. Let Him do as seemeth good to Him."

ANSWER 2. A contented submission to everything that God brings to pass. Hereof we have worthy patterns in the examples of Job, Eli, David, Hezekiah, and other saints. We cannot be ignorant that events declare the determined purpose of God. When such and such a thing is fallen out, we may then conclude that God had so and so purposed it. For as God's Word declares His approving will, what He would have, so events declare His peremptory will, what He will have. Our submission therefore to God's will is tried in both. This is to be applied to all manner of crosses and losses, whether of God's children, or other friends, to death itself, or to any other thing that may seem bitter to us.

QUESTION. What do we desire in regard of the place here specified for doing the will of God, "on earth"?

ANSWER 1. Grace to well use the time of this mortal life. For the time while we abide on earth is the day wherein we may work, and the time of doing good. Christ took the advantage of the day; and we ought to be of the mind of Christ. Thus shall we show that we have as great a respect to God's honor as to our own happiness, and as great a desire to do the work appointed as to receive the reward promised.

ANSWER 2. Universal subjection to God's will throughout this world. For this indefinite phrase, "on earth," shows that our desire ought to be extended to all that are on the face of the earth. We do not pray that God's will be done only in our own house, or in our own country, or in the countries near adjoining to us, but on earth. All the graces therefore before mentioned to be craved for ourselves must also be craved for every member of the militant Church.

The Things to Be Prayed For in the Direction of the Third Petition

QUESTION. What are we taught to pray for in regard of this direction, "as it is in heaven"?

ANSWER In general a conformity of the church militant to the church triumphant. That, though these two parts of God's church are in one place distant one from another, yet they may be of like mind and disposition towards God and His will. In this respect we are said to be partakers of the heavenly calling and our conversation to be in heaven.

ANSWER 2. In particular such a manner of obedience as is performed by the saints and angels in heaven.

The Distinct Headings of the Manner of Doing God's Will in Heaven

QUESTION. To how many headings may their manner of obedience be reduced?

ANSWER To six especially, which are these that follow:

1. Sincerity. Whatever those heavenly spirits make show of they do it from the heart. In their mouth is found no guile for they are without fault before the throne of God. None who makes a lie can enter into that pure place. They are outside, whoever love lies. All in heaven shine as the sun. They are transparent; there is no cover for hypocrisy. This sincerity David desired where he prayed that God would take from him the way of lying and incline his heart to His testimonies, and let it be upright in His statutes.

2. Integrity, which is a universal subjection to every part of God's will. The heavenly spirits follow the Lamb wherever He goes. In all places they attend upon their Lord and always behold His face, to know what His will is that they may do it. They are therefore by a kind of excellence said to do His commandments, hearkening to the voice of His Word. Never was there any stop or stay in any who entered into heaven at anything that God willed to be done. This integrity also David desired where he said, "Oh, that my ways were directed to keep Thy statutes! Then shall I not be ashamed when I have respect to all Thy commandments." Yea, this God Himself earnestly desired for His people.

3. Alacrity. There is nothing wherein the heavenly spirits show more cheerfulness than in doing God's will. It is music and melody to them. In which respect they are said to have harps as a sign of their cheerful mind and disposition. While Christ lived on earth, it was His meat to do the will of Him who sent Him. Did He not then do it with cheerfulness? For this alacrity David prayed where he desired God to quicken him.

4. Sedulity. The heavenly spirits are both diligent, and also quick and speedy in executing the will of the Lord. They are thereupon said to have wings and to fly. Was not he of that mind who said, "I made haste and delayed not to keep Thy commandments?" For this end the church desired Christ to draw her that she might run after Him.

5. Ardency and zeal. The heavenly spirits in regard of their zeal are said to be a flaming fire. In which respect the title "seraphim" is given unto them; for it is a Hebrew name taken from heat and burning. There is nothing that more heats and enflames their love and delight than God's will. When they know that God wills this or that, they are all on fire till it is done. This zeal was in him who said, "My soul breaketh for the longing that it hath to Thy judgments always." And his expectation to have his heart enlarged shows that he prayed for this holy zeal. Be zealous therefore.

6. Constancy. The heavenly spirits serve God day and night. They do not wax weary of doing God's will. As the good angels still keep their first estate, so the glorified saints ever abide in their estate. None of them have yet, nor ever will fall away. This he prayed for who often called upon God to establish him. This constancy is the grace of all graces. It sets the crown on all their heads and brings men to the fruition of the fruit of all. "Be thou faithful unto the death and I will give thee the crown of life," says He who can make good what He says.

The Things for Which Thanks Is to Be Given in the Third Petition, and the Direction Annexed to It

QUESTION. What are the particulars for which we are to give thanks by virtue of the third petition?

ANSWER 1. All those graces whereby we are enabled to do the will of God.

1. Illumination of our minds, whereby we may understand what is the will of God.

2. Subjection of our will unto God's.

3. Happiness of memory to keep in mind the will of God, that we do not forget it after we have once known it.

4. Faithfulness of conscience to cheer us when we do God's will, and to check us when we transgress it.

5. Settledness of heart and affections upon God's will.

6. External obedience in the several parts of our body thereto.

7. Power over the flesh that draws us from the will of God.

ANSWER 2. All events of what kind so ever, be they losses or other crosses, minister matter of thanksgiving; for they are comprised in the number of those "all things" for which we must give thanks. "For this," says the apostle, "is the will of God," a reason very proper and pertinent to our purpose. Thus Job blessed God for taking away as well as for giving.

QUESTION. What matter of thanks does the direction added to the third petition afford?

ANSWER. We ought to be so much the more thankful by how much the more heavenly our obedience is, as when it is sweetened with sincerity, seasoned with integrity, quickened with alacrity, enlarged with sedulity, enflamed with ardency, and followed and crowned with constancy. The more excellent the graces are wherewith we are enabled to do God's will, the more matter of praise they afford. This was what moved David to bless and praise God again and again, that he and his people offered according to the will of God willingly in uprightness of heart and with joy.

The Duties to Be Observed by Reason of the Third Petition

QUESTION. What duties ought we to endeavor after by virtue of the third petition?

ANSWER 1. We ought to search the Scripture that we may know the will of God. For in them is the will of God contained. This is that searching to which knowledge and understanding is promised. And for our better help herein we ought diligently to frequent the ministry of God's Word. It is noted of the converted Jews that they continued steadfastly in the apostles' doctrine, whereby is declared that they were diligent and constant hearers of the apostles, and also faithful professors and practicers of their doctrine. The former was the cause of the latter. The preaching of the Word is a great help to bring us to do the will of God, and that in a double respect. First, because the will of God is thereby the more clearly, distinctly, and fully opened unto us; second, because it is a means sanctified of God to breed credence to the truth of that which is revealed and confidence therein; yea, and to bow our will, heart, and affections to yield thereto, and to be settled thereupon. In this respect, the wisdom of God, which is especially set forth in the preaching of His Word, says, "Blessed is the man that heareth Me, watching daily at My gates, waiting at the posts of My doors."

ANSWER 2. We ought to hide God's Word in our heart so that we may not carelessly let it slip. So will all the fruit and benefit of our reading and hearing be lost, as meat or medicine that is vomited up as soon as it is taken. But by retaining God's Word in mind and memory we shall be provoked the more to do God's will, and kept from transgressing it. To which purpose the psalmist says, "Thy Word have I hid in mine heart, that I might not sin against Thee." Wherefore let the Word of Christ dwell in you richly.

ANSWER 3. We ought often and seriously to meditate on the excellence of God's will, to draw our hearts the more to it. Whose heart was ever more set upon God's will to do it than David's? And who did more meditate on the excellence thereof than he? It was his meditation day and night. The many excellent properties and effects that he attributes thereto and the many sweet and precious things to which he prefers it show how excellent he accounted it to be.

ANSWER 4. We ought by solemn vow and oath to bind ourselves to do God's will. This is a special means to keep our words, thoughts, and actions within the compass thereof. For sacred vows and oaths are as tutors and schoolmasters that will often put us in mind of that which we have vowed. And when we are about to start from them they will restrain us and hold us in.

ANSWER 5. We must keep our own will from rebelling against God's. There is naturally in our will an antipathy and contrary inclination to God's. It is very prone to oppose and resist the will of God. As therefore as we hold in headstrong horses with bit and bridle, so must we hold in our own will, no way yielding unto it, but rather crossing it when it rises against God's. This is a special branch of denying ourselves.

ANSWER 6. We ought to endeavor that our will may be one with God's, as Christ's was, who sought the will of His Father in all things (John 5:30), and that whatever pleases God may please us. So shall the will of God be done by us indeed.

ANSWER 7. We must lay it down as a rule not to be altered, and as an inviolable law to obey God rather than man. For there is no comparison between them. Yet is our foolish and corrupt heart ready to yield to such things as they who are over us, or from whom we may expect any advantage, will have to be done, yea, though it be expressly against God's will. But the forenamed settled resolution will be a special means to keep us, as it kept the apostles, from preferring man's will to God's. Thus this block being removed out of the way, we shall much more readily do the will of God.

ANSWER 8. We ought steadfastly to believe that all things are ordered by God, and that most wisely. This is the best means that can be prescribed to bring us to a contented submission to God's determined counsel and will manifested by events. He who believes that as God is a Lord of absolute sovereignty—doing what He will (will or nil the creature), so He is a God of unsearchable wisdom and infinite goodness, ordering all things for the best—will not grudge against that which God does. For he will know that as there is a necessity of yielding to His will, because it cannot be resisted, so there is also great equity therein because it cannot be bettered.

ANSWER 9. We must ever be striving to do the will of God more and more, better and better. This duty arises from the pattern here set before us. While we are on earth we cannot attain to the perfection of them who are in heaven. We must therefore, forgetting those things that are behind, and reaching forth to those things that are ahead, press toward the mark for the price of the high calling of God in Christ Jesus. And as we were taught before to desire the best gifts, and therein to seek to excel, so for this end we must stir up the gifts of God in us, and to the uttermost put forth that spiritual strength that the Lord is pleased to bestow upon us, wisely observing both what is to be done and after what manner it is to be done.

ANSWER 10. We ought, as much as in us lies, to provoke others to do the will of God. For we pray not only for ourselves, that we may do it, but for others also, that it may be done everywhere through the earth. Our endeavor must be answerable to our desire. Therefore ministers, magistrates, parents, tutors, schoolmasters, governors of families, and all who have authority and charge over others, must most especially look to this because they have the best means to cause others to do the will of God. Thus shall they better discharge that charge which is committed to them, and also much better accomplish the extent of that which is here desired. In this respect even private Christians must also provoke one another hereunto.

Sins Against God's Will Revealed by His Word

QUESTION. What are the things that we ought to bewail by virtue of the third petition?

ANSWER. Both transgressions against the petition itself and also against the direction added thereto. Against the petition are all manner of sins both against the revealed Word of God, and also against the manifested works of God.

Sins against the revealed Word of God to be bewailed by virtue of this petition are such as these:

1. Ignorance of God's will revealed by His Word. Is it not a lamentable case that the Creator should be careful to reveal His whole counsel so far forth as is requisite for the happiness of His creatures, and yet the creature be careless in taking notice thereof? This was a thing whereof the prophets much complained. And it is a matter for which we who live under the bright light of the gospel have great cause to complain. Never was there more means of knowledge, yet very small is the measure of knowledge whereunto many have attained. How can it be thought that such as do not know the will of God should do it? Can he who does not know follow it as a guide?

2. Obstinacy of our will against God's. This may be in such as know the will of God. Christ complained of the Jews' obstinacy against the good will of God made known to them. Not doing God's will is hereby much aggravated, and in that respect is the more to be bewailed.

3. Slipperiness of memory whereby the will of God made known is forgotten. By this the benefit of knowledge is lost. God much complained hereof and threatened for this to forget their children.

4. Deadness of conscience, which is the cause that men go on in sin greedily and securely. The apostle complained that men have their conscience seared with a hot iron, "who being past feeling give themselves over to lasciviousness, to work all uncleanness with greediness."

5. Hatred of God's Word, which is that light that shows the good will of God. Wisdom complains of these. There is no hope that such should do the will of God, for every man who does evil hates the light. Whereupon God thus expostulates with such a one, "What hast thou to do to declare My statutes, seeing thou hatest instruction?"

6. Actual transgressions. These David greatly bewailed. They are directly contrary to that which is desired in this petition. Yet these are everywhere, by of all all sorts committed. Oh, what cause have we to be humbled for our own sins, for the sins of others who are under our charge, for the sins of our families, for the sins of the parish, town, city, or nation where we live, and for the sins of the times where we live! In this respect we have as great cause as ever Jeremiah had to wish and say, "Oh, that mine head were waters, and mine eyes a fountain of tears," that I might weep day and night for the transgressions that are daily committed against the will of God.

Sins Against God's Will Manifested by Events

QUESTION. What are the sins against God's manifested works that we ought to bewail?

ANSWER 1. Inward discontentedness.

ANSWER 2. Outward impatience.

The former is the cause of the latter. It is noted of the Israelites that first they tempted God in their hearts (namely by their discontentedness at that provision which He had made for them), and then it is added that they spoke against God, of both which the psalmist there complained. When that which God causes to fall out in any way crosses our desire, as when children or others whom we love are taken from us, when sickness, pain, poverty, or any other cross is laid upon us, then we grow discontented in our minds. We mutter with our mouths and betray much impatience in our actions, and many times do not spare to blaspheme the sacred name of God and say, as that profane king did, "Behold, this evil is of the Lord. Why should I wait for the Lord any longer?" Who does not have cause in this respect to be much humbled for the bitterness of his own and other men's spirit, out of which much gall is oftentimes spit into the very face of God Himself?

Sins Against the Manner of Doing Good

QUESTION. What are failings against the direction that we ought to bewail?

ANSWER. An evil manner of performing good things when they are performed:

1. Hypocritically, in show and appearance only, and not in truth.

2. Partially, or by halves, so far as seem good to ourselves, but no further.

3. Grudgingly, as if it were done more by compulsion than by any free disposition of will.

4. Negligently and carelessly, without taking heed, or without such respect as is becoming so weighty a matter.

5. Lukewarmly, as without any fervor of affections.

6. Inconstantly, as if we repented of that good we had done, and thereupon refuse to hold on therein.

Hitherto we have addressed the three first petitions that concern the glory of God. The three others that concern our good are to be handled next.

5
The Fourth Petition

The Meaning of This Word "Bread"

QUESTION. What is the fourth petition?

ANSWER. "Give us this day our daily bread."

QUESTION. What points are here distinctly to be considered?

ANSWER. The thing desired, bread.

The property that we have therein, our.

The kind of it, daily.

The Giver of it, our Father in heaven.

The ground of asking it, give.

The parties for whom it is asked, us.

The time limited for it, today.

QUESTION. What is meant by bread?

ANSWER. All manner of temporal blessings. For bread in its most usual and proper acceptance signifies a special kind of food whereby our bodies are nourished. Yet so as by a synecdoche: 1. One kind of food is put for all other kinds. 2. One means of refreshing our bodies for all other means. 3. One temporal blessing for all sorts of temporal blessings. For there are so many temporal blessings whereof in this world we stand in need as it would have ben too tedious to have reckoned up every particular by name. Wherefore Christ contents Himself to mention only one kind (bread), which is of all the most usual. Everyone, poor and rich, in all places, uses bread, and so have they done in all ages. Whether they live on flesh, fish, butter, cheese, roots, herbs, or anything else, they must withal have bread. Nothing can be less spared. For as food of all other temporal things is the most necessary, so bread, of all other kinds of food. Where other things refresh a man, this strengthens him and has therefore very fitly the title of "staff" attributed to it. The want of no temporal thing brings a man to such distress as the want of bread, which especially causes famine, whereupon by a kind of property it is called a famine of bread. Under this term "bread" are comprised meat and drink, yea, food, raiment, sleep, medicine, and other things needful for our bodies, even for preserving or recovering the health and strength of them; and such a competent estate also as is meet for the place wherein God has set us, for the charge of children and others that He has committed to us, and for that function and work that He has appointed for us together with peace and all manner of prosperity. In a word, whatever is needful and useful for man's temporal estate in this world is here comprised under this one word "bread." Most usually in Scripture is it put for temporal blessings. If at any time it is put for spiritual food there is some circumstance or other that necessarily implies as much, and plainly demonstrates that there it cannot be meant of corporal food. But there being no such circumstance in this petition it is safest to take it in the literal, usual, and proper sense. If it is not here so taken, this form of prayer is defective and does not comprise in it all things requisite to be prayed for. For it is most requisite to pray for temporal blessings, as shall afterwards be proved.

The Arguments Alleged for Spiritual Food to Be Meant by "Bread" Answered

They certainly mistake the meaning of this petition who in this place apply this title "bread" to Christ Jesus, the spiritual manna, which is that bread of God that comes down from heaven and gives life unto the world. Though in John 6 bread is taken in that mystical sense, yet is it not in that place singly and simply used, but with such a description as plainly points out the mystical meaning of it, as bread of God, bread from heaven, bread of life, living bread, bread that gives life to the world, which Christ expressly applies to Himself when He says, "I am the bread of life." In that place therefore it cannot but be mystically meant. But here in this petition there is no such circumstance to point out any such mystery.

The chief arguments alleged for that mystical interpretation are these:

ARGUMENT 1. If bread is not here put for Christ, then the chief good thing that possibly we can desire is left out of this prayer.

ANSWER. Christ, as the very foundation and root of every good thing, is included in the first clause of this prayer. For in Christ is God our Father. Christ being the Head of the Church is expressly prayed for in the second petition.

ARGUMENT 2. Temporal blessings are promised as additions to the kingdom of God. They need not therefore by name be prayed for.

ANSWER. That does not follow. So they are not preferred before the kingdom of God and His righteousness they may expressly by name be prayed for. Beside the warrantable practice of Jacob, Agur, and other saints, the apostle commands us to pray for such as are sick that they may be healed.

Others observing that temporal blessings may not be excluded apply this title "bread" both to spiritual and also to corporal food. But this is to confound things of far different kinds in a form where Christ very accurately distinguishes things that differ one from another.

As for Papists who apply this to the sacrament of the body and blood of Christ, they infer thereby that the Lord should teach His disciples to pray for that which was not then instituted, and whereof they were utterly ignorant.

Praying for Temporal Blessings

QUESTION. What are we taught by the mention of bread in this prayer?

ANSWER. Temporal things are to be prayed for. Beside the warrant of this petition, and of other prayers of saints guided therein by God's Spirit, we have express precepts and promises whereupon to ground our faith in this case. On these grounds the saints who have called upon God for temporal blessings have also given thanks to God the Giver of them because…

1. These are good things in themselves.

2. They are very needful and useful. They are needful (as means sanctified of God) for preserving our being in the world, which like a lamp would soon be extinguished if a continual supply of new oil were not added thereto. In which respect they who bestow the things of this world on such as want them are said to contribute to their necessities. They are useful for enabling us the better to do the work that God appoints to us.

3. The want of them is a great hindrance to the work of our calling, to works of charity and piety, and a temptation to injustice.

Herein then the goodness of God in affording to us everything needful for body as well as for soul, and for this present life as well as for the life to come, is evidently set forth; and hereby we may and ought to take the more notice thereof.

Men's Right to the Things of This World

QUESTION. How is bread said to be ours?

ANSWER. It is ours in regard of a just and true right that we have thereunto, which right is two-fold, spiritual and civil. The spiritual right is proper to the saints who believe in Christ. For that right which God gave to Adam unto all things under heaven was forfeited by sin. But Christ, the Lord and Heir of all, uniting them who believe in Him as members of His mystical body, thereby gives them a new right to all that Adam lost. On this ground the apostle says to the faithful, "The world, things present and things to come, are yours." Of which right he gives this reason, "Ye are Christ's."

The civil right is that which is agreeable to justice and equity, and that in the courts of men. Thus children have a right to the inheritance and portion that their parents leave them, which right Naboth had to the vineyard that Ahab unjustly coveted. Thus they who bona fide purchase a thing have right to it, as Abram to the field of Ephron, and the cave in it. Thus have men a right to that which they, by God's blessing on their honest diligence, in their lawful calling get, as Jacob had to the party-colored sheep that his uncle as wages allowed to him. Thus that which is given to a man by the owners thereof he has a right unto, as Job had to the gifts that his friends bestowed upon him. And there are sundry other ways agreeable to justice and equity whereby we have a right to the goods of this world before men.

Now both the forenamed kinds of right must concur to make a thing truly and properly a man's own. They who are not Christ's have no right to anything at all before God, but are usurpers of whatever they possess and use. Unto the unbelieving is nothing pure. They who are Christ's, though they have a right to all things, yet they may possess and use no more than what they can justify to be theirs before men, and that in justice and equity. Their general right in Christ is to give them liberty to hold and occupy so much as God, by the hand of His providence, shall reach out unto them. Justice is this hand of God's providence. That which unjustly is gotten cannot properly be said to be given by God. It is with saints as with an only child and heir while his father lives. Though he has a right to all that his father has, yet he may not possess and use any more than his father allots to him.

Sundry Lessons Arising From this Particle "Ours"

QUESTION. What are we given to understand by calling bread ours?

ANSWER. Two things especially.

1. The saints have in Christ a true right to the things of this world. They who are taught to say, "Our Father" in Christ (which all the saints, and none but saints can do) are also taught to say, "our bread" (for to the pure are all things pure), which is a good motive to draw us unto Christ, so that we may with good conscience use whatsoever the Lord by His providence shall bestow upon us.

2. We may not desire that which is another's. For we are here taught to pray for that which we may call ours. Now we may justly call anything but that whereunto we have a civil as well as a spiritual right. The moral law expressly forbids coveting that which is another's.

By this word of property, "our," the Anabaptist conceit of a community of all things is evidently refuted. And we are taught to rest contented with that portion which the Lord is pleased to allot us as our own.

The Meaning of This Word "Daily"

QUESTION. What is meant by this word "daily"?

ANSWER. Ordinary and usual bread whereof we every day stand in need, being most fit for our substance to preserve soul and body together, and nourish and cherish us here in this life. Thus it imports the very same thing that the wise man sets out under this phrase, "bread of my allowance," or "convenient for me." This word is thus used to distinguish the food here meant from that which coming down from heaven endures to everlasting life, whereof whosoever eats shall never be hungry or thirst again, and to prescribe a means to our desire.

Desiring No More Than Is Needful

QUESTION. What instruction are we taught by this word "daily"?

ANSWER. Our desire must be for no more than is needful for us. On this ground the apostle advises to be content having food and raiment. Thus was the desire of Jacob, Agur, and other saints moderated. Superfluity is very dangerous. It is Satan's bait whereby he allures and beguiles many, his snare whereby he catches and holds them fast, his hook whereby he pulls them down and drowns them in perdition.

QUESTION. What may be accounted needful?

ANSWER 1. That which very nature requires, such as meat and drink to feed the body, and clothing to keep it warm. Without these the body cannot but pine away and perish.

ANSWER 2. That which is meet for the estate wherein God has set us, such as fit tools for craftsmen, books for scholars, ammunition for captains and other soldiers, yea, also for public persons, and for men of great birth, place, and dignity, such sufficiency as is fit for the same. Thus much the wise man intended under this phrase, "Give me not poverty." A man may have to sustain nature and yet be poor.

ANSWER 3. That which is requisite for the charge committed to us. As if a man has a wife and children, that which is meet for them as well as for himself may justly be accounted needful, so for others of his household and kindred lying on his charge. The apostle pronounces him worse than an infidel who does not provide for his own, and especially for them of his own house. It behooves us therefore to pray for so much as may be sufficient for them for whom we ought to provide.

ANSWER 4. That which is apparently needful for the time to come. Fathers ought to lay up for their children. When Joseph foresaw seven years famine to come, he laid up great plenty of corn beforehand.

Covetousness, Ambition, and Voluptuousness

Contrary to the forenamed moderation of our desire is covetousness, which like hell can never be satisfied. For by abundance this desire is increased; so that the more it is filled, the less it is satisfied. Hereof our Lord advised us to take heed and beware. For as it is an insatiable sin, so also a devouring sin. As Pharaoh's lean cattle devoured the fat ones, so covetousness devours all God's blessings and graces; it chokes the Word and makes hearers thereof unfruitful. It so entangles men with the things of this world as it makes it easier for a camel to go through the eye of a needle than for a rich man to enter into the kingdom of God. No sin more bewitches a man, drawing his heart from God, the only true ground of confidence, and making him trust in vanity, that is plain idolatry. Yea, it is truly called the root of all evil. For it so blinds man's mind and hardens his heart as he makes conscience of no sin; no, not of denying God and renouncing true religion, nor of perjury and blasphemy, nor of profaning and breaking the Sabbath, nor of rebellion against superiors and neglect of inferiors, nor of murder or any other unmercifulness, nor of oppression, deceit, falsehood, or any other evil.

Contrary also to the forenamed moderation of desire are ambition or affectation of worldly honors and promotions, which like a wind make a man swell above that which is meet, but yet do not fill him; and voluptuousness, or an eager hunting after earthly pleasures and delights, wherewith he used to be sooner wearied than contented.

God's Giving Temporal Blessings—That He Gives Them and How He Give Them

QUESTION. Of whom are we taught to ask bread?

ANSWER. Of our Father who is in heaven. For all the petitions of this prayer are directed to Him.

QUESTION. What is thence to be gathered?

ANSWER. The Lord in heaven is the Disposer of all things on earth. For He is the Possessor of heaven and earth. The earth is the Lord's and the fullness thereof. He therefore gives the earth and the things thereof to whom He will. We neither have them of ourselves nor can any have them of any other but of God. Whatever the means of getting them are, they are but the hands of God's providence whereby He gives us what we have.

QUESTION. How does God give bread and the things here comprised under it?

ANSWER 1. By causing them to be brought forth. For God at first made everything that is fit for man's use; and He continues still to cause the earth, sea, and other like means to bring forth all things needful for man. "I will hear," says the Lord, "I will hear the heavens, and they shall hear the earth, and the earth shall hear the corn and the wine and the oil, and they shall hear Jezreel." God is there set forth as the first Mover, and the highest Orderer and Disposer of all secondary means,whereby things meet for man are brought forth.

ANSWER 2. By bringing them to us so as we may partake of the use of them. "Thus saith God to Israel, 'I gave her corn, and wine, and oil.' " It is the same God to whom the psalmist says, "The eyes of all things wait upon Thee, O Lord, and Thou givest them their meat in due season."

ANSWER 3. By giving them a blessing. Such a blessing God gives to the things that are brought forth, and brought to us, as by virtue thereof they nourish and cherish us. This blessing is in Scripture called the staff and stay of bread. This is that Word of God by which man lives. By this man thrives. For the blessing of God makes rich. Whence this proverb has ben raised, Give me God's blessing, and cast me into the sea. In regard of this blessing they who have abundance have need to make this petition. For "a man's life consisteth not in the abundance of the things which he possesseth." Without God's blessing nothing can do him any good.

ANSWER 4. By sanctifying them to us. This is done (1) by accepting our persons in Christ and accounting us pure. To the pure all things are pure. (2) By giving us in Christ a right to what we have. All things are theirs who are in Christ. (3) By giving us a warrant out of the Word for enjoying and using the same. It is sanctified by the Word of God and prayer. (4) By giving us grace to use well what we have. By virtue of this grace St. Paul was instructed both to be full and to be hungry, both to abound and to suffer need.

In the three first respects, namely by causing things fit for creatures to be brought forth, by bringing them to his creatures, and by giving a nourishing virtue to them, God may truly be said to give bread to all sorts of men, good and evil; yea, to all sorts of creatures, reasonable and unreasonable. Yet in the last respect, namely by sanctifying it, He gives bread to the saints alone.

The Instructions Taught Us by Asking Bread of God

In that we are directed to ask bread of our Father in heaven, we are taught thereby…

1. To acknowledge Him as the Giver thereof.
2. In all want to fly to Him.
3. To give the praise of all we have to Him.
4. To honor Him with our substance.
5. To ascribe nothing that we have to any false gods, as the idolatrous Israelites did.
6. Nor to our own power, as proud Nebuchadnezzar.
7. Nor to other men, as flattering Tertullus.

God's Freely Giving the Things of This World

QUESTION. On what ground do we ask bread of God?

ANSWER. Merely on the free grace of God. This word "give" imports as much. For what is more free than a gift?

QUESTION. What does Christ hereby teach us?

ANSWER. All that we have comes from the free gift of God. For who has given to Him first? We neither can deserve anything of God nor repay anything to Him. Well did Jacob understand this lesson, which made him acknowledge himself less than all God's mercies, and unworthy of the least of them.

We ought hereby to be stirred up to more thankfulness, as David was. For the freer a gift is the better it is, the more acceptable to him who receives it and the more worthy of praise to be rendered to him who gives it.

Praying Both for Ourselves and for Others

QUESTION. What persons are comprised under this particle "us"?

ANSWER. All they whose Father God is. For "our" in the preface and "us" in the three last petitions import the very same persons.

QUESTION. What do we learn we from this manner of expressing the parties prayed for in the first person and plural number "us"?

ANSWER. In prayer we must be mindful both of ourselves and of others also. It is usual with the saints so to express their desires as they show thereby they have respect to themselves and to others too. Sometimes, therefore, having in the singular number prayed distinctly for themselves, they add thereto petitions for others, as where David thus in particular prayed for himself, "Keep my soul and deliver me, and then added, "Deliver Israel, O God."

As for ourselves, we must especially pray on these grounds.

1. Everyone is nearest to himself. And this is the tenor of the law, "Thou shalt love thy neighbor as thyself." If then you pray for any, ought you not much more to pray for yourself?

2. Everyone (if at least he is not blinded in his mind) best knows his own needs and is most sensible of his own wants, according to the proverb, "The foot best knows where the shoe most pinches." Not unfitly to this purpose may this principle be applied, "What man knows the things of a man save the spirit of a man that is in him? Who can better know when a man is hungry or thirsty, or what he best relishes than himself?

3. Everyone's prayer is most effectual for himself. No faithful prayer made for one's self will God reject. But Moses and Samuel, or Noah, Daniel, and Job may pray for others and yet deliver but their own souls.

Of praying for others see what was written before in the fourth duty.

This much of the general doctrine gathered out of this particle "us," being common to the three last petitions made for man's good. The persons here intended are further to be considered in a more particular relation to this fourth petition.

Praying for Others' Outward Welfare

QUESTION. What does the mention of others beside ourselves in this petition for temporal blessings teach us?

ANSWER. We must as truly desire the outward welfare of others as our own. This precept of the prophet, "Seek the peace of the city, and pray unto the Lord for it," is very pertinent to this purpose. For by peace he means especially outward prosperity. So does the psalmist, where he says, "Pray for the peace of Jerusalem," for he adds, "Peace be within thy walls, and prosperity within thy palaces." This might easily be exemplified by a particular enumeration of all those temporal blessings that we may pray for in our own behalf, applied to prayers for others.

Others are of the same mold as we are, and subject to the same infirmities. They are supported and sustained by the same means that we are, and they stand in need of temporal blessings as well as we. These therefore must be prayed for in their behalf.

This is the rather to be noted because many who can be well content to pray for others spiritual welfare fail exceedingly in praying for their temporal welfare, which arises from too much love of themselves and of this world. Men ordinarily are so addicted to this world as, if it were possible, they would wholly have it for themselves. They do not desire therefore to have it much communicated to others. As for grace they observe it to be as communicable as light. No man has the loss by the abundance of another. It rather increases by communication and participation. They do not care therefore how much others have thereof. But the things of this world are of another nature. The more of them is given to some, the less remains for others. This makes many the less forward to pray for the temporal estate of others. Let these two pernicious roots, love of ourselves and love of this world, be rooted out of our hearts and the forenamed duty of praying for the temporal welfare of others will be much more readily and heartily performed.

From hence, by necessary and just consequence, it follows that we ought to succor one another with the goods of this world according to the rule of love, which is our brother's necessity and our own ability. For what we pray for in the behalf of others we must to our power endeavor to do for them. This is also the rather to be noted because many who are ready to minister spiritual comfort to others—as to instruct them, to encourage them, to strengthen them in grace and godliness, and by Christian reproof to pull them out of the way of perdition, yea, and to exhort others to be merciful and bountiful in distributing to the poor—are very backwards themselves to give of the goods of this world that they have to such as are in need. Surely such men's religion is vain and their pretence of faith and love a mere pretence. The love of God does not dwell in such a person.

Resting Content with Our Present State

QUESTION. Why is our desire here limited to "this day"?

ANSWER. 1. Every day we stand in need of the bread that we are here taught to pray for. For it nourishes but for a day. He who on one day eats as much as he can will be hungry the next day.

ANSWER 2. Our life is but as a day. He who this day is alive does not know whether he shall see the morrow or not. So we are to account every day as if it were our last day, and accordingly every day renew our prayers. This is to pray continually

QUESTION. What special instruction does this limitation of our desire for the things of this world teach us?

ANSWER. We must be content with the things that are present. For God Himself has said, "I will never fail the nor forsake thee." If the promise of Him who is able to supply all our necessities is not sufficient to work contentment, I do not know what can be.

Cast off therefore all burdensome distrustfulness and take no thought for the morrow. Pray in faith for bread this day, and let the morrow take thought for the things of itself. He who boasted of his abundance laid up for many years, when he had not many hours to live, is branded for a fool. For when his life was even wasted and gone, his care was for plenty of provision.

Seeking the Things That Concern Our Own Good as Well as the Glory of God

QUESTION. What is to be observed about the order of the fourth petition?

ANSWER. 1. That which is common with the petitions that follow.

ANSWER 2. That which is proper to itself.

QUESTION. What is it that is common with the petitions that follow?

ANSWER. The fit inference of such petitions as concern our good upon such as concern the glory of God. For as in the three petitions before this we are taught to seek the things of God, so in this and the two following we are taught to seek the things that tend to our own good.

QUESTION. What do we learn from that inference?

ANSWER. It is lawful to seek such things as tend to our own good as well as such as tend to the glory of God. Can a better warrant than this platform of prayer be expected? To add other proofs, whereof the Scripture affords many, would be to light candles in sunshine.

Behold here the good respect that God bears to man. Though He might use us as galley slaves, and other slaves are used, wholly and only for His own turn, yet He does not deny us liberty to seek our own good. Yea, if the services that we perform to Him hinder our good indeed, He wills that they give place to this; and on that ground He says, "I will have mercy and not sacrifice." And again, "The Sabbath was made for man, and not man for the Sabbath."

Should not this enflame our hearts with zeal for the glory of God? Should we not hereupon be even eaten up as Christ was? It is most meet that God's goodness to us work gratefulness in us to Him.

As in respect of God this requires gratefulness, so in respect of ourselves it requires providence that we are not careless in seeking that for ourselves that God in His care over us gives us liberty to seek. Ordinarily men are given to seek their own good. Yea, nature inclines everything to seek that which is good for itself, so as I need not use many words to press this point. Most fail in seeking their own too much. Yet there are also failings in the defect, and that both of such as neglect their best and truest good concerning their eternal salvation, and also of such as neglect even their temporal estate.

The Principal End of This Life

QUESTION. What are the things proper to this petition to be observed about the order of it?

ANSWER 1. The inference of such things as concern this present life, upon such as concern God's glory.

ANSWER 2. The placing of temporal things before spiritual ones.

QUESTION. What are we taught by that inference?

ANSWER. The end of this life is to glorify God. For being taught to pray for such things as tend to the glory of God we are thereupon taught to pray for bread that our life may be preserved to that end. Directly to this purpose the psalmist thus prays, "Let my soul live and it shall praise Thee." This moved Hezekiah to pray for life when he had received the sentence of death, as may be gathered out of this reason, "The grave cannot praise Thee, death cannot celebrate Thee. The living, the living he shall praise Thee."

In God we live, move, and have our being. There is great reason therefore that our life should be ordered to His glory.

Let us on this ground set this end before us in sustaining this present life, and so order it as when we are to depart we may say to God, as Christ did, "I have glorified Thee on earth." Whenever we pray for the things of this world we ought to have this end in our minds, that whether we eat, or drink, or whatever we do, we may do all to the glory of God.

On this ground also we must be the more watchful over ourselves that we do not misspend our life, health, strength, or goods on anything contrary to that end, as in pursuing carnal pleasures, worldly honors, earthly trash, and such like things. Note for this purpose that item that the wise man gives to the young man persisting in misspending his precious time, to whom ironically he says, "Rejoice O young man in thy youth, and let thy heart cheer thee in the days of thy youth, and walk in the ways of thine heart, and in the sight of thine own eyes. But know thou, that for all these things God will bring thee to judgment."

Placing the Petition for Temporal Blessings Before Those for Spiritual Ones

QUESTION. Why is this petition for temporal blessings set before the petitions for spiritual blessings?

ANSWER. Many good and weighty reasons may be given of this order that will plainly show that placing this petition before the two following is no sufficient argument to prove that by "bread" Christ is here meant. Some of them are these:

1. This is an express petition for good, as the three former are; but the last two are deprecations from evil. It was therefore requisite that all the good things to be craved should be mentioned before the evils against which we pray.

2. The Lord, by placing temporal blessings whereof we are more sensible before spiritual, endeavors by degrees to raise up in us a desire of spiritual blessings that, though they are more needful, are less sensible. The ruler whose son Christ healed was thereby brought to believe in Christ.

3. This petition, being of least consequence, is most fitly put in the middle place. For as matters of greatest weight are first mentioned to stir up ardency, even in the beginning of prayer, so other things of much moment are reserved to the latter places to quicken the spirit and to revive ardency even in the ending of prayer. This method the best orators use in their orations. Thus Christ, beginning this prayer with the chief good thing of all, the glory of God's name, ends it with the best good things concerning man, his spiritual good.

4. Though temporal blessings are not in their kind better than spiritual ones, yet man is more hardly brought to depend

on God for temporal than for spiritual things. Witness this proverbial speech, "God, take care for my soul and I will take care for my body. Witness also that distrust for outward estate that is in many saints who steadfastly trust in God for pardon of sin and sufficient grace to bring them to eternal life. In this respect our faith in God for things of this life has a preeminence and precedence before faith in God for the things of a better life.

5. The things craved in the two last petitions are to be obtained in this life. In this life if pardon of sin and freedom from Satan's power are not had, they can never be had. He who dies with the burden of sin lying on his soul shall never be eased of it in the world to come. This life then being presupposed for obtaining pardon of sin and deliverance from evil, it is meet that it is first prayed for.

Rising from Temporal to Spiritual Blessings

QUESTION. What may we learn from placing temporal blessings before spiritual ones?

ANSWER. By our seeking such things as concern the good of our bodies, we must be led on to seek such good things as concern our souls. To this end Christ preached that excellent sermon of the bread of life to such as followed Him from place to place to have their bodies fed.

Thus shall we make a double use of the temporal good things that God bestows on us—one to refresh our bodies and another to stir up our minds to seek the things that may refresh our souls.

Blessed are they who thus use any temporal blessings, and by the sweetness of them are brought to hunger after the bread and water of life, even for that meat that endures to everlasting life.

Sundry Particulars Comprised Under the General Words of the Fourth Petition

QUESTION. What are the particular good things for which under the general words of the fourth petition we pray?

ANSWER 1. Life itself, that, so long as it pleases God, our temporal life in this world may be preserved. This good kings, prophets, apostles, and other saints prayed for, being therein guided by the Spirit of God. For the time of this life is the day to do the work of God; the time of death is the night wherein no man can work.

OBJECTION. Elijah, Jonah, and other saints desired death.

ANSWER. Therein they did not act as becomes saints. Their desire was a fruit of the flesh and not of the Spirit, and therefore it is not to be imitated.

OBJECTION. Paul, with a better spirit, desired to be dissolved.

ANSWER. That was no simple absolute desire of death, but a thing that he could in regard of his fruition of Christ's presence have desired if that work that God appointed by him to be done had ben finished.

ANSWER 2. Health and strength of body. What does the psalmist's complaint of weakness imply but desire of health and strength? Yea, he expressly prays for as much. It is noted as a special blessing bestowed on the Israelites when they came out of Egypt that none were feeble.

ANSWER 3. Means that God has sanctified to preserve life, health, and strength, such as meat, drink, apparel, sleep, and so on.

ANSWER 4. Means to recover health and strength, as doctors and all kinds of medicines, surgery and all kinds of salves, with the like. This phrase, "the sick need a physician," and the direction that Isaiah gives to Hezekiah about laying a lump of figs upon his boil, give warrant for the use of medicine and surgery. It requires learning, skill, observation and experience both to know the nature of diseases, wounds, sores, and other maladies, and also to know the different virtue that by the divine providence is given to herbs, roots, drugs, and other creatures, and wisely to apply fit and proper remedies to sundry and different maladies. These things therefore may be prayed for.

ANSWER 5. Good success in our callings, labors, and pains to get such means as are fit to preserve or recover health and strength and to maintain our estate. For all that we can do is altogether in vain unless the Lord prospers our endeavors.

ANSWER 6. God's blessing on the things that we possess and use. Without this blessing a man would be as well off to eat gravel as bread. Therefore, for obtaining this blessing, grace (as we speak) used to be said before meat, and thereby food is said to be blessed.

ANSWER 7. A divine sanctification of all we have, for every creature is sanctified by prayer.

ANSWER 8. Freedom and deliverance from all kind of external miseries, such as oppression, imprisonment, bondage, captivity, and other like distresses.

The Extent of Our Prayers for the Temporal Good of Others

QUESTION. Are we to pray for no more than is needful for ourselves?

ANSWER. Yes. What we crave for ourselves we ought to crave for others also for the petition is made in the plural number.

QUESTION. Who are those others for whom we must crave temporal blessings?

ANSWER 1. They who are of our family. It belongs to us to provide for them. We must therefore pray that we may have sufficient for ourselves and them, and that God would further bestow on them whatever is requisite for them in their places.

ANSWER 2. They who are of our kindred or alliance, though they are out of our family. The distinction that the apostle makes between these two phrases, "his own" and "them of his house," where he requires a provident care for both, shows that respect must be had to our own, that is, our kindred, though they are not of our family.

ANSWER 3. They who are of our town, parish, or city. That which the prophet advises concerning the city where the Jews in their captivity dwelt (which was to pray to the Lord for it, and to seek for the prosperity of it) may be applied to the parish, town, village, street, or any other such common place. And this reason that the prophet renders ("in the peace thereof shall you have peace") may be extended to all such places.

4. They who are of our nation. The psalmist meant his whole nation when he said, "Pray for the peace of Jerusalem." And again, "If I forget thee, O Jerusalem."

ANSWER 5. They who anywhere live in this world. That all of all sorts may in their places be maintained we ought to pray for a continuance of those things that at the beginning God ordained for the preservation of the world so that, as God has promised, there may be, while the earth remains, seedtime and harvest, cold and heat, summer and winter, day and night, and all other things meet for man in this world. Yea, also according to public extremities and necessities must our prayers be ordered, as in time of drought for rain; when fair weather is seasonable, for fair weather; in time of plague, famine, war, or any other like distress, for succor against those messengers of death—that thus so long as God has appointed us to live in this world we may comfortably pass over that time of life.

The Things for Which by Virtue of the Fourth Petition We Ought to Give Thanks

QUESTION. What are the particular good things for which, by reason of the fourth petition, thanksgiving is required?

ANSWER 1. Life itself, for every day that is renewed unto us affords matter of thanks for that life which is lent us. Thus much the psalmist intends in these words: "While I live will I praise the Lord. I will sing praises unto my God while I have any being."

ANSWER 2. Health and strength in that life. This is what Caleb, that faithful servant of the Lord, acknowledged, and that to the glory of God, for he ascribes it to God.

ANSWER 3. Sufficient means to preserve these. Moses gives this in an expressed charge to Israel, saying, "When thou hast eaten and filled thyself, thou shalt bless the Lord thy God." The Scripture under one blessing comprises all blessings of the same kind so as by virtue of that charge we ought to bless God for apparel, sleep, and other means of maintaining health and strength.

ANSWER 4. Recovery of health and strength. For this Hezekiah (as a perpetual testimony of his thankfulness) indicted a psalm of praise and caused it to be registered for all ages.

ANSWER 5. Good success in our pains. For this Abraham's servant give express thanks unto God. And Jacob ascribes that increase that he had to God, which acknowledgement is a thanksgiving.

ANSWER 6. The extent of God's providence to our family, and to such as we ought to provide for. Jacob acknowledges this much, saying, "God hath dealt graciously with me, and I have enough," meaning enough for himself and all who belonged to him; and thereupon he erected an altar in testimony of his thankfulness.

ANSWER 7. God's bounty extended to the places where we dwell. Zion was the city of David, and in Jerusalem was his habitation. He therefore praised the Lord for that peace, plenty, safety, and other like blessings that God had bestowed thereupon. On this ground we are to bless God for such good governors as He has set over us, in regard of the temporal benefits that we receive thereby.

ANSWER 8. God's providence in keeping away or removing any evils, as famine, plague, sword, plots and practices of enemies, with the like.

ANSWER 9. The common blessings that God bestows on the whole world. The consideration of this greatly enlarged David's heart to praise the Lord. Here therefore we are to take notice how all the creatures in heaven, earth, and sea still continue, as from the beginning, to be useful unto man. The heavens remain to cover him, the sun, moon, and whole host of heaven to give him light, and to send him down a sweet influence; the clouds continue to water the earth, the earth to feed divers sorts of creatures that are for man's use, yea, and to nourish sundry trees, plants, and herbs, and they in their kind to bring forth several fruits; the sea to bring forth sundry creatures that are fit to live therein; and the waters that spring out of the earth to refresh the creatures thereon. All these, and others like these, minister much matter of thanksgiving.

The Duties Required by Virtue of the Fourth Petition

QUESTION. What are the duties after which we ought to endeavor by reason of the fourth petition?

ANSWER 1. Diligence in our calling. This is that means that God has sanctified to get bread, that is, such things as are needful for our temporal estate. This was at first enjoined by God to man in his innocent estate, and afterwards again in his corrupt estate; yea, it is practiced by unreasonable creatures that in this respect are set as a pattern before us.

ANSWER 2. Good conscience in getting the things that are needful for us. Thus will that which we have be ours according to that direction of the apostle to Christians, that they eat their own bread. Thus also will that which we have be the more sweet unto us. For a good conscience is a continual feast. This is the main thing that the apostle intended where he forbade Christians to steal and enjoined them to work the thing that is good.

ANSWER 3. Confidence in God for His blessing, namely both on our pains and also on the things that we have gotten by our pains, being persuaded that He who gives the day will give things that are needful for the day. Christ's giving of thanks for the creatures that were provided gives evidence of His confidence in God's blessing.

ANSWER 4. Faith in the Lord Jesus, for a right to what we have. Thus shall we have a right before God to that which we have lawfully gotten before men. And we may reap much comfort thereby.

ANSWER 5. Faithfulness in nourishing and cherishing our bodies with that which we have. This is the main end of this petition. The wise man pronounces them blessed who eat in time for strength. Yea, nature itself draws man hereto. For "no man hateth his flesh, but nourisheth and cherisheth it."

ANSWER 6. Temperance in using such things as are most usual and useful for us. Those are the things that are here called daily bread. To this purpose tends this direction of the wise man: "Put the knife to thy throat if thou beest a man given to thine appetite." Thus shall we not be oppressed with surfeiting and drunkenness.

ANSWER 7. Contentment in that which God bestows on us. This clause "this day" imports this duty. Much quietness will this bring unto the mind. Till this is attained to, nothing will satisfy a man; but the more he has, the more he will covet.

ANSWER 8. Providence for such as belong to our charge. On this ground we pray in the plural number, Give us.” The apostle notes this to be a bound duty, saying fathers ought to lay up for their children. And he lays it so straightly to the charge of Christians that if they fail therein he accounts them worse than infidels.

ANSWER 9. Liberality to such as are in need. The extent of this particle “us” reaches to all of all sorts. Now God gives to some abundance so that out of their store they should minister to such as want. We therefore who pray that others may have bread ought, when we have sufficient for ourselves and others, give unto them.

ANSWER 10. Joy in the occasions of rejoicing that others have for God’s blessing on their temporal estate. To that general direction of the apostle, “Rejoice with them that rejoice,” may this particular be referred. We are taught to pray for others as for ourselves. We must therefore be answerably affected to their good.

The Sins Whereof the Fourth Petition Shows Men to Be Guilty

QUESTION. What are the sins contrary to the fourth petition that we ought to bewail?

ANSWER 1. A careless neglect of our own or other’s welfare.

ANSWER 2. A distrustful burden for the same.

QUESTION. Who may be accounted guilty of neglecting their own welfare?

ANSWER 1. They who do not care what harm they do to their bodies. Many bereaved of their wits, or possessed with a devil, do not care about thrusting pins, knives, daggers, and such like sharp instruments into their flesh, and to strike themselves with stones. If any in their right wits do so they are worse than mad men.

ANSWER 2. They who over-rigorously punish their bodies. Many blinded with superstition, and besotted with idolatry, do not spare their flesh. The worshipers of Baal cut themselves with knives and lances. Papists tear their flesh with whips, and in sundry other ways lacerate their bodies, whereof it may be said, "Who required this?" They who, being better instructed do, in performing such duties as are in their substance warrantable, impair their health and strength by fasting, watching, or any other kind of not sparing their bodies for duties of piety, are not free from all blame, but come too near to superstition. Their devotion carries them beyond the bounds of this petition.

ANSWER 3. They who through too eager a pursuit of what they like waste their natural vigor, as Esau, who followed his hunting till he was faint. Fearful was the issue that thereupon followed, for it cost him his birthright. All immoderate pains of mind or body are aberrations swerving from this petition, whether they are of porters, laborers, husbandmen, tradesmen, seafaring men, students, or any others.

4. They who by immoderate passion shorten their days. It is taxed as a fault in Rachel that she refused to be comforted, from which fault Jacob was not altogether free. If by intemperance in eating, drinking, or any other way men bring diseases upon their bodies, or hasten their death, their sin is much more heinous.

ANSWER 5. They who through being miserly do not afford themselves things that are needful. This is one of the great vanities that the wise man taxes, that a man to whom God has given riches, wealth, and honor, so as he lacks nothing for his soul of all that he desires, yet God does not give him power to eat thereof. Such a one is a servant, not a master; a keeper, not an owner of his wealth.

ANSWER 6. They who cast themselves into needless dangers. After David had been a means of moving three of his worthies to hazard their lives to satisfy his longing, his heart smote him for it. How fearful was the issue of those twelve couples of young men whom Abner and Joab sent to play a dangerous sport? On this ground quarrelers, challengers, undertakers of single combats, especially on private occasions, but most of all where the combats are desperate, as with pistols, or double rapiers, their bodies being naked are condemned.

ANSWER 7. Self-murderers. It is the main scope of this petition to desire preservation of life. How contrary thereunto is it to take away a man's own life? They were desperate reprobates that in Scripture are noted to have done so, as Saul, Ahitophel, and Judas. As for Samson, the thing that he aimed at was to destroy the enemies of the Church, not himself. And what he did, he did by an extraordinary spirit. And therein he was a type of Christ, who by His own death destroyed the enemies of the Church.

Neglecting the Welfare of Others

QUESTION. Who may be accounted guilty of neglecting the welfare of others?

ANSWER 1. They who are short-sighted for such as are under their charge, such as short-sighted husbands, parents, masters, and other governors. Such as are evil can give good things to their children. What may then be thought of those who do not do it?

ANSWER 2. They who are unmerciful to others in need. St. James denounces judgment that is merciless against such. A fearful doom, for mercy is the only ground of the hope that sinners can have.

ANSWER 3. They who envy the prosperity and abundance of others, as the Philistines envied Isaac and Rachel envied her sister. Well did the wise man say hereof, that it is the rottenness of the bones (Proverbs 14:30).

Sundry Branches of Short-sightedness

QUESTION. How is the forenamed short-sightedness manifested?

ANSWER 1. By idleness and negligence in a man's calling, whereby he deprives himself of the means wherewith he should provide for himself and his charge. The field and vineyard of the slothful brings forth thorns and nettles instead of wheat and grapes.

ANSWER 2. By meddling too much with other men's matters. Such a one is as he who takes a dog by the ears: he may get snapped at thereby. Therefore St. Peter wisely exhorts Christians not to suffer as busybodies. A man can have no more comfort in such sufferings than in suffering for theft, murder, and other such crimes.

ANSWER 3. By following amusements too much. For he who loves amusements shall be a poor man. Much time and money are usually spent by such. Fair inheritances have been cast away at dice.

ANSWER 4. By frequenting lewd company. For by means of a whorish woman a man is brought to a piece of bread. The drunkard and the glutton shall come to poverty.

ANSWER 5. By prodigality. The prodigal child wasted his substance with riotous living.

Caring Too Much for this World

QUESTION. Who cares too much for their temporal estate?

ANSWER 1. Profane worldlings who prefer the things of this world before the glory of God. They would have the fourth petition to be first. Such were the Jews who made sealed houses for themselves while the house of God lay waste, and the Gadarenes who preferred their swine before Christ.

ANSWER 2. Covetous men whose desire is never satisfied. They are like the things that can never say, "It is enough."

They are covetously minded and do not regard the limitation of this petition, "this day." Their mind is more on years than days, as his was who said to his soul, "Thou hast much goods laid up for many years."

ANSWER 3. Unconscionable persons, who do not care how they get what they have. They have no respect to this particle of right, "our." Under this heading all the violent oppressions and fraudulent circumventions that any use may be comprised.

ANSWER 4. Unbelievers, who before God can call nothing their own.

ANSWER 5. Ungrateful wretches who have neither mind nor time to give God thanks for the good things they have. They are like the nine lepers who, being cleansed, never returned to give thanks to Christ. Do these account their Father in heaven to be the Giver of the things on earth?

6
The Fifth Petition

Sins Are Called Debts, and the Kinds of Those Debts

QUESTION. Which is the fifth petition?

ANSWER. "And forgive us our trespasses, as we forgive them that trespass against us."

QUESTION. What is the sum of this petition?

ANSWER. Justification.

QUESTION. What are the parts thereof?

ANSWER. The petition itself and a condition annexed thereto. The petition contains the thing that is prayed for. The condition gives assurance of obtaining it.

QUESTION. How many distinct points are noted in the petition?

ANSWER. Four:

1. Debts acknowledged, debts or trespasses.
2. An appropriation of them, our.
3. The kind of discharge, forgive.
4. The parties to be discharged, us.

QUESTION. What is meant by debts?

ANSWER. Sins. Christ Himself declares His own meaning. For immediately after this prayer He returned to the condition of this petition, to urge and press the same somewhat more forcibly; and in the repetition thereof, for debts He put trespasses, and that three different times. Yea, St. Luke setting down this form of prayer thus expressed this petition, "Forgive us our sins," for we also forgive everyone that is indebted to us. That which by Matthew is called debts, by Luke is called sins. And whereas Luke in the petition expresses sins, in the condition he mentions debtors. Again, the Lord had occasion twice at one time to inculcate this question, "Think ye that these were sinners above others?" First He uses this word "sinners," then this, "debtors." It was usual with Christ to resemble sinners to debtors.

QUESTION. In what respect are we sinners counted debtors?

ANSWER 1. As we are servants of God, so we owe obedience.

ANSWER 2. As we are sinners against God, so we owe death.

Thus there is a double bond whereby we stand bound as debtors to God.

One is the bond of the law, whereunto we are tied in a double respect.

1. In regard of the supreme sovereignty and absolute authority that God has over us. This is expressed in the preface before the Decalogue thus, "I am the Lord thy God."

2. In regard of the many benefits that we have received all our days, and still continue to receive from Him. By God we are what we are and have what we have. He created us, He preserves us, He provides for us all needful things, and He protects us from all hurtful things. This also is intimated in the foresaid preface by mention of one great benefit, freedom from Egypt, the house of bondage.

The other bond is the curse of the law, whereunto we are tied by forfeiture of the former. For he who does not perform the condition of a bond stands liable to the penalty of the bond. In regard of this the law is called a handwriting against us.

Adam, even in his innocence, and all we who come from him, are in the former respect debtors by virtue of our creation. Adam since his fall, and all his wicked offspring, are in the latter respect debtors by reason of our transgressions.

QUESTION. Which of those debts do we here desire to be forgiven?

ANSWER. The latter most especially, whereby we are bound to the curse of the law, which is the penalty of it. This penalty, if it were exacted, would make us most miserable. There is good cause therefore of praying to have that remitted. As for the other debt of obedience, we ought to desire rather ability to perform it than liberty to be freed from it. Yet, notwithstanding, because it is impossible for us, so long as flesh is in us, to pay that debt as it ought to be paid, by consequence we desire a remission of that debt, namely that God would not exact of us to be performed by us in our own persons such exact and complete obedience as the law requires.

Christ's Active Righteousness Imputed to Us

QUESTION. In regard of our disability to discharge our debt of obedience to God, what may be inferred?

ANSWER. Imputation of Christ's righteousness is necessary for our justification. Christ teaches us to desire a discharge of all debts. The law requires a debt of perfect righteousness. This we are not able to pay of ourselves. But our Surety, being able, paid it. He fulfilled all righteousness. By the imputation thereof to us are we discharged. For as by one man's disobedience many were made sinners, so by the obedience of one shall many be made righteous. His righteousness is upon us to justification of life. In this respect Christ is said to be made unto us righteousness, and we are said to be made the righteousness of God in Him. This kind of debt is not duly considered of them who exclude the active obedience of Christ from our justification. They press those places that make mention only of the blood of Christ, forgetting the figure of speech that is frequent in the Scripture whereby one member or part is put for all of that kind. In particular they press this petition that places our justification in remission of sins, not conceiving that under debts here mentioned all manner of debts are comprised and under this word "forgive" all manner of needful debts are discharged. Where further they say that Christ's active righteousness was necessary for Himself, they do not duly consider the dignity of His person by virtue of the hypostatic union of His two natures, which dignity exempts Him from all necessity of obedience to the law in regard of Himself.

This doctrine of imputation, even of the active obedience of Christ, brings much comfort to poor sinners who, knowing that all their righteousness is as filthy rags, thereupon tremble at the thought of the presence of the righteous Lord. But their faith in Christ's righteousness imputed to them (instead of that debt of righteousness that they owed to God) whereby they are accounted righteous before God makes them with much comfort and great confidence present themselves before Him.

Man's Subjection to Sin

QUESTION. What observation does the acknowledgement of debt afford?

ANSWER. No man is free from sin. As this prayer, so this petition therein is prescribed for everyone on earth, which by just consequence implies that everyone is guilty of sin. Otherwise he has no need to pray for forgiveness. But besides this necessary consequence the point is in expressed terms often set down in Scripture. And everyone, whose eyes the god of this world has not blinded, and whose heart and conscience he has not hardened and seared, finds it by woeful experience to be too true. Neither can it be otherwise because original corruption, the mother and nurse of sin, abides in him so long as any breath and life remain.

OBJECTION. They who have their sins forgiven are free from sin. But in this world many have their sins forgiven.

ANSWER. Remission takes away the guilt of sin, but not the root of sin. The law of sin is remitted in spiritual regeneration, and yet it remains in mortal flesh; otherwise sin could not be propagated in the regenerate who have their sins forgiven.

Therefore this petition was prescribed even to the disciples who were justified.

We have just cause on this ground to detest the contrary positions of our adversaries, who are these that follow and such like.

1. Whatever is truly and properly sin is taken away by baptism. And to explain their meaning to the fullest, lest it should be thought that by taking away sin they understand no more than forgiving or not imputing sin, their great champion Robert Bellarmine adds that by baptism all sins are in very deed taken away so as not only it is not imputed, but there is not that which may be imputed for fault or blame. Do they not hereby show that the truth is not in them? For if we say that we have no sin we deceive ourselves and the truth is not in us.

2. The concupiscence that is in the regenerate is not truly and properly sin.

What is this but to hold that the spring of sin is clean dried up in the regenerate? If the spring is dry, whence shall any streams of sin proceed?

3. They who are justified are able to keep the whole law.

If then they do what they are able, what need is there for them to ask remission of sin, which is a transgression of the law.

4. The works of just men are perfect.

Perfection needs no remission. For such works, then, by their doctrine they need ask no pardon. Oh, presumptuous and arrogant conceits!

Let the undeniable certainty of the forenamed doctrine, that no man is free from sin, humble us for that woeful condition wherein we live while here we live. Sight of sin was what humbled the publican, whom it is better to imitate than to swell as the pharisee did who bragged of his merits and covered his wounds. Assuredly this ministers just cause of great humiliation; and it cannot but force such as have any spiritual sight and sense thereof to say, as the leper under the law was wont to say, "I am unclean, I am unclean," and in horror and detestation of ourselves, when we think of the presence of the Lord, to say as Peter did, "Depart from me, for I am a sinful man, O Lord." Yea, it will make us cry out with St. Paul, "O wretched man that I am, who shall deliver me from the body of this death!"

And that those outcries may appear to be effects of true humiliation rather than of desperation, we ought earnestly and instantly to seek remission of sin, which is the main matter intended in this petition, well weighing for the point in hand that "this is a faithful saying, worthy of all acceptation, that Christ Jesus came into the world to save sinners."

Falling Into Sin Daily

QUESTION. What observation does our daily praying for forgiveness of sin afford? For the word, "this day," expressed in the fourth petition, is to be understood in every petition.

ANSWER. Every day men fall into sin. The metaphor of drinking iniquity like water imports as much, for it shows that it is as ordinary and familiar for a man to sin as to drink, which he does often every day. Dare any man deny the truth of this doctrine upon his experience? If he dares, surely his conscience is seared with a hot iron or else he lies against his conscience. For the forenamed original corruption, as it remains in us so it remains as a spring in us, continually sending forth some salt and bitter water of sin, more or less.

Many excellent directions may fitly be inferred from this observation.

1. Set apart some time every day for examination of ourselves so that we may the better observe those several sins that every day pass from us. If they are not observed, they may lie so long festering the soul as to thereby prove incurable.

2. Let us humble our souls daily before God. Every day the fire of God's jealousy is kindled by our daily sins, whereby He

is provoked to come out in wrath and take revenge. Every day therefore we must fall down before Him with broken spirits and humbled souls. This is a means to turn His fury to pity.

3. Let us renew our covenant with God every day. For every sin gives cause for forfeiture of the covenant. The covenant being forfeited, with what comfort can we apply it to ourselves? With what confidence can we plead it before God?

4. Repent daily. Repentance is a proviso annexed to a man's forgiving his brother. Much more does God expect it of such as expect forgiveness of Him. He who sins seven times in a day must repent seven times in a day. As sin incenses wrath, so repentance for sin makes God to repent of His wrath. Because therefore there is no day wherein a man is without sin, he ought not to be one day without repentance.

5. Meditate every day on the satisfaction that the Lord Jesus once made upon the cross for our sins, and also on the intercession that He continues daily to make at the throne of grace. This gives good ground of assured hope of continual pardon for our continual sins. For the main end of Christ's continual intercession is to make continual application of His all-sufficient sacrifice for our continual sin.

6. Pray every day for pardon. This we are here expressly taught to do. All the forenamed points are but preparations unto this. This, if it is performed in faith, is what obtains pardon so often as we sin. The daily offerings that every morning and evening were appointed under the law prefigured this much.

7. Watch continually. The more subject and prone we are to fall into sin, the more needful it is that with all heedfulness we watch against sin. Satan's sedulity, the deceitfulness of sin, and our own foolishness require diligent and constant watchfulness.

The Difference Between God's Absolution and Man's Apprehension Thereof

OBJECTION. God's forgiveness is full, complete, and absolute. Whom He once acquits He never calls to account again. His discharge is of sins past, present, and to come. What need is there then of those daily duties?

ANSWER. I grant it to be so in the eternal decree and secret counsel, yea, and in that covenant that is made between Him and His Son, our Surety. But in the application thereof to us, and in our apprehension of it by faith (whereby only can our soul rest quieted and assured of it), a proceeding by degrees must be acknowledged. Though a believer for the present apprehends a full discharge of all the sins whereof he then stand guilty, yet through the violence of temptation and the weakness of flesh he may again and again make question and doubt of that discharge, especially when he has fallen into other sins, or returned to the same sins for which he before craved pardon. Frequent sinning greatly shakes and weakens faith. Christ saw it needful to give to the woman whom He Himself absolved this caveat, "Sin no more." Wherefore for strengthening our weak faith in a full pardon of all our sins, for new settling it when it is shaken, for healing the wounds that are daily made in our conscience by daily sins, for preventing the advantage that might be taken from our many forfeitures of covenant, the forenamed directions are daily to be observed.

Popish Indulgences for Sins to Come and Going to Confession in Lent

Contrary to this branch of this petition are the blasphemous indulgences that by popes and popish priests are given for sins to come, and that not only for some particular sins, whereby they egg on and embolden men to commit those sins, but also for all manner of sins, not for a day, a week, a month, or a year, but for many years, yea, all their life. And lest they should fear vengeance and punishment for their sins after this life in purgatory (with which fiction they much frighten their people), they extend their indulgences far beyond the times that they themselves set for purgatory, even unto fifteen and twenty thousand years. Are not floodgates hereby wide opened to all manner of licentiousness? Are not men hereby made not only secure, but also impudent in committing sin? By those indulgences men are taught to say, "Grant us pardon, even while we commit sin." Was ever the like heard?

To the like licentious liberty their superstitious custom of auricular confession, and of absolution thereunto given by a priest once a year in Lent, bring men. Yet this is not only by ordinary custom practiced, but warranted by their great Council of Trent.

Neglecting to Seek Discharge of Sin Until Easter or Until a Day of Visitation or Death

What now shall we say of such among us as put off all serious and thorough examination of themselves, confession of their sins, and renewing of repentance to Easter, when they intend to receive the holy communion? Though they forbear the superstitious practice of auricular confession, yet they make as wide a gap for licentiousness and wickedness as papists do. For such commonly make little or no conscience of any sin until about Easter time. And is there not just cause to think that that show of conscience that they then make is but a mere show and that it savors more of fond superstition than of sound religion? Can it be imagined that such as all the year long let loose the reigns to impiety and iniquity can once in the year make a thorough examination of their souls and confession of their sins? Neither will they have any mind to dive to the depth of such a sea; neither if they had a will thereto could they possibly do it. Such men's souls must fester for want of timely and due search thereinto.

Much more desperate must their case be who are so far from a daily, yea, and yearly searching of themselves and seeking to be discharged of their sins as all their life long they never think of any such matter unless God by some extraordinary judgment brings them, as He brought Pharaoh generally and confusedly to acknowledge that they have sinned; or unless they observe death to have seized upon them, at which time if their sins are laid before them either their heart is like, as Nabal's, to die in them, and to become senseless as a stone or else their conscience is to be, as Judas' conscience was, a rack, or rather a hell unto them, incapable of comfort. For at the time of death the body is weak, the heart faint, and the spirits dull. Yea, to him who has not before made his peace with God the thought of death cannot be but very terrible, a means even to astonish him who is otherwise feeble, dull and heavy. Satan, who is not ignorant hereof, takes great advantage thereat, and is then busiest to tempt, and most fierce and forward to assault, when man is least able to resist. And whereas all our hope of standing against Satan is in God's help, such as have all their life long provoked God's wrath and used no means to be reconciled to Him can have little hope in the last act to receive help from Him.

The Woefulness of the Debt of Sin

QUESTION. What doctrine does the resemblance of sin to debt imply?

ANSWER. Sin makes man bound to the revenging justice of God. He who thus prayed to God, "Enter not into judgment with Thy servant," well knew as much.

Every sin is a breach of covenant between God and man. It makes for forfeiture thereof. As a debtor therefore who has made forfeiture of his bond stands liable to the revenge of the creditor, or rather as a malefactor who has transgressed the law of his sovereign is liable to the penalty of the law, so a sinner is liable to the just revenge of God's law.

Take notice hereby of the horrible nature of sin. It kindles the wrath and provokes the revenge of the Creator. Who knows the power of His anger? As His greatness is, so is His anger, infinite and unsupportable. Hence is it that the creature on whom it lies lies under it eternally. For he is in no way able to ease himself of that burden. If this were duly weighed and seriously thought of when we are tempted to any sin, would we be so foolish as for a little momentary delight to run into such a debt as will cast us into that prison out of which there is no release, and in which there is torture and torment, endless and easeless? We count them miserable who fall so far into man's debt as they are never able to discharge it. What may we then think of such as fall into this debt of sin?

Take also hereby further notice of the necessity of such a Surety as Jesus Christ is, God-Man in one person. For such is the debt of sin as no creature in heaven or on earth was able to discharge it. If Christ had not undertaken the discharge thereof our case would have been like the case of those angels who are reserved in everlasting chains under darkness unto the judgment of the great day.

Every Sin Being Mortal Is Yet Not Equal

QUESTION. What does the penalty whereby sin is made a debt import?

ANSWER. Sin is mortal. Yea, because this metaphor, "trespasses," being of the plural number, is indefinitely used and comprises all manner of sins under it, I may further infer that every sin is mortal. For that penalty which is due to these debts is death. Instance the first sin that was committed. And to show that the like holds true in every sinner, the prophet without any limitation, reservation, or exception at all says that the soul that sins shall die. If it is a sin, in that it is sin, it must be deadly be it great or small in thought, word, or deed. For the wages of sin (whatever that sin may be) is death. Being a sin it is a transgression of the law. For these two words sin and transgression are convertible and reciprocal terms. One imports as much as the other. Sin is a transgression. And all unrighteousness (or every transgression) is sin. But every transgression is deadly. For, "cursed is every one that continueth not in all things that are written in the law." And all unrighteousness is deadly, "for the wrath of God is revealed against all unrighteousness." And that is not without just cause. For all unrighteousness, every transgression, every sin is against the good will of God who is of infinite excellence and majesty, and in that respect it is of an infinite depravity and deserves an infinite punishment, eternal death.

OBJECTION. Thus all sins are made equal.

ANSWER. Nothing less. For neither does the same kind of punishment make all the crimes for which it is inflicted equal; nor does the same kind presuppose the same measure of punishment. Robbers and murderers are put to the same kind of death, yet murder is a more heinous sin than robbery. Besides, among such malefactors as are put to death the kind of death whereunto some are put is much more terrible than that whereunto others are put. Will any thence infer that all crimes that are capital are equal? Much more absurd is the inference of papists that all sins are made equal because all are made mortal. They themselves do not hold all the sins that they judge mortal to be equal. There are degrees of torment in hell. Though all such in their nature and kind (if they are not forgiven) plunge men into death and damnation, yet they do not plunge them into the same degree of torture.

The Distinction Between Venial and Mortal Sins

QUESTION. Are then no sins at all venial?

ANSWER. The distinction of venial and mortal sins rightly and wisely limited may safely be admitted, and that in four respects especially: in regard of the order that God has by His Word revealed; in regard of the subject or person in whom sin is; in comparison of one sin with another; and in regard of the church's manner of proceeding against sinners.

1. Concerning the order that by God's Word is revealed, there is an irrevocable decree passed upon the sin against the Holy Ghost, that it shall never be forgiven. However the secret decree of God is as inviolable against all the sins of every reprobate, yet because that determined doom is not revealed against any one sin but that of it only it is said, "There is a sin unto death." The sin therefore against the Holy Ghost is mortal. But in opposition to it Christ said, "All sins shall be forgiven," that is, they are remissible, pardonable, and in that respect venial.

2. Concerning the subject or person in whom sin is, after by faith the elect are grafted into Christ, though sin remains in them yet is it not imputed to them for condemnation. "There is no condemnation to them that are in Christ Jesus." All the sins therefore of true believers are venial. They shall be pardoned. But all the sins of unbelievers are mortal; they shall be punished with everlasting damnation. "The wrath of God abideth on him that believeth not." Besides, the true believer, though he may fall into many sins, will impenitently lie in no sin. So as such sins as in another would incur death and prove mortal, in him, by repentance become venial and are pardoned.

3. Concerning comparison of sins, it cannot be denied that some sins are very small, as a by-thought in a holy duty, an idle word, a little tap with the hand, and that other sins are very heinous, as blasphemy, perjury, murder, adultery, and such like. Therefore comparatively smaller sins may be called venial in relation to heinous and notorious sins that are called mortal in that they more apparently and more deeply plunge one into

death and damnation. Thus all ecclesiastical writers, both ancient and modern, have used this distinction.

4. Concerning the church's manner of proceeding against sinners, many sins daily pass from men that, though by ministers they are reproved and God's judgments are denounced against them, yet do not pass under the church's public censure. These have been called venial. There are other sins that even to men seem so intolerable as the church does not think the committers of them worthy to be admitted to the holy ordinances of God, but denounces against them some public censure of suspension, excommunication, or denunciation and anathema, till public repentance is manifested and satisfaction given to the church. Thus, because one of the church at Corinth had committed such fornication as is not so much as named among the Gentiles, St. Paul delivered him to Satan. These sins worthy of such censure have been called mortal.

But as our adversaries use the distinction of venial and mortal sins, it cannot stand with the forenamed nature of sin, implied under this metaphor of "debt." They say that many sins are venial because they are pardonable of their own nature and not worthy of damnation. They give these and such like instances of venial sins: Sudden motions of lust, anger, and envy, immoderate laughter, an idle word, deceit in a small thing worth no more than a half-penny, and so on. Their great champion Robert Bellarmine thus expresses the meaning of their church in this point: "Venial sin is, in its own nature distinguished from mortal; and without any respect to predestination, or to the mercy of God, or to the state of the regenerate, it is of that kind as it does not deserve eternal punishment." He inserts these phrases ("without respect to predestination, or to the mercy of God, or to the state of the regenerate") because orthodox divines have granted that the title venial may be applied to sin in regard of God's eternal predestination and purpose to pardon sin, and in regard of the mercy of God, which is greater than the desert of sin, and in regard of the regenerate, whose faith gains an absolution for sin. To show therefore that he and his heretical church, whose cause he maintains goes beyond the limits of all truth, he rejects the forenamed limitations wherein truth is bounded and will have venial sins to be of themselves in their own nature not worthy of damnation. In their sense these two terms, sin and venial, are contradictory. Sin is (according to the doctrine of the Scripture) worthy of damnation. Venial (according to their sense) is not worthy of damnation. To say therefore that sin is venial is to say that worthy of damnation is not worthy of damnation. But I demand, are their venial sins pleasing or displeasing to God? One of them they must be. A median cannot be given between these two contradictory terms that is neither of them. They dare not say that venial sins are pleasing to God. Then they must displease Him. If they displease Him they offend an infinite goodness, an infinite excellence, an infinite majesty, and in that respect are worthy of an infinite punishment.

As for their own instances of venial sins:

1. The most sudden motions that can be, though no consent should be yielded to them, are against the first and last commandments. Besides, the perfect law of God is spiritual. It requires integrity in the innermost parts, even in the spirits of men. The aforementioned thoughts are against spiritual integrity, and in that respect are against the law; they deserve the curse thereof. Yea, further, the most secret and sudden thoughts are acts and motions of the soul, as manifest to God as outward actions of the body. If therefore they are evil they are in His sight apparent transgressions. As for motions to lust, though never so sudden at the very sight of a woman, Christ accounts them a kind of adultery. And motions to anger He accounts a kind of murder. But adultery and murder are against the law and deserve the curse of the law.

2. Of idle words Christ said, "Men shall give account at the Day of Judgment." When the account is taken, shall idle words at the bar of that judgment be approved or condemned? To say they shall be approved were greatly to impeach the perfection of Christ's purity and justice. If then they are condemned, eternal death is their due. There is then no other penalty to be inflicted. All standing at that bar are either pronounced as blessed or denounced as cursed.

3. For stealing a half penny, does the law that says, "Thou shalt not steal," exclude half-pennies or not? If not, where is the exception? The words are indefinite, "Thou shalt not steal." He who steals a half-penny steals. In stealing a half-penny therefore he is a transgressor of the law and is guilty of the penalty and curse thereof.

To conclude, God shall bring every work into judgment with every secret thing, whether it be good or evil. The smallest things that can be imagined are comprised under these phrases, every work, every secret thing. If they are brought to judgment it is either to be rewarded or avenged. If they are good, they are to be rewarded. For even a cup of cold water given to a disciple in the name of a disciple shall in no wise lose his reward. But if they are evil, they are to be revenged. If at the Day of Judgment they are revenged, surely the revenge is eternal death. But venial sins are evil, not good. They shall therefore be brought into judgment, condemned, and punished with eternal death. I speak of sins not repented of, not washed away by the blood of Christ, of sins as they are in their own nature, in their own desert. For so stands the controversy between us and the papists.

Duties to Be Observed Because Every Sin Is Mortal

The knowledge of the nature of every sin, and of the due desert thereof, ought to make us diligent in searching into the law of God that thereby we may know what sin is ("for by the law is the knowledge of sin"), and knowing sin carefully and conscionably to avoid it ("for the wages of sin is death"). And in no way are we to make ourselves accessory to the sins of others (for so we bring the blood of others upon our own heads). And if we have committed sin ourselves, or made ourselves accessory to the sins of others, not to soothe our consciences with the smallness thereof, and thereupon remain secure, not caring to repent thereof ("except ye repent ye shall perish"). To work the more through repentance we ought thoroughly to search ourselves and from time to time strictly to examine our thoughts, words, and actions. And as we discern any transgressions or alterations in any of them, we are instantly to crave pardon for them. Yea, because we cannot be ignorant that many sins unaware pass from us, we are to desire a general discharge of all other sins (which two points are expressly noted in this fifth petition). As we crave pardon for all sins past, so ought we to be watchful over ourselves for the time to come, even so watchful as to abstain from all appearance of evil, not regarding the common scoffs against preciseness, as the world terms Christianity, careful and conscionable watchfulness over a man's self. Commonly the wickeder sort most justify themselves and the upright most judge themselves. The upright usually judge themselves for their very ignorance and negligence. And surely sins of ignorance or negligence would be better judged that they may be destroyed than excused, that they should be nourished. For everything must be brought to judgment, and of every idle word that men shall speak they shall give an account in the Day of Judgment. Let not therefore the small sins be slighted. Floods are made with small drops. Water soaks through small chinks, the ship is therewith filled, and if the pump is not plied the ship is drowned.

The Many Debts Wherein We Stand Bound to God's Justice

QUESTION. Why are debts set down so indefinitely in the plural number?

ANSWER. Our debts are many. Our sins are of sundry sorts, and of every sort there are many in number. First there is original corruption, which is the seed and spawn of all sins, and is a debt. Thereby forfeiture is made of that integrity wherein God at first created us, and which God's law, that is spiritual, requires of us. This David expressly reckons up among those sins and debts whereof he desired to be discharged. Besides all the sins that in our infancy and younger years, even before our calling, that of ignorance or weakness we committed, are debts, in which respect the High Priest offered for the errors of the people. These are so many that David was moved thereby to say, "Who can understand his errors?" Yet because they were debts, even the most secret of them, he desired to be cleansed from them. Much greater debts are the sins that we commit after we come to riper years, or after our calling, against knowledge and conscience, willfully and presumptuously. Earnestly therefore David prayed to be kept from presumptuous sins. So many are the sins whereby, as by debts, we stand obliged to the justice of God that they cannot possibly be all reckoned up. But the word "debts" being indefinitely set down in the plural number without restraint to any sorts of sins import all sins.

QUESTION. What instruction does this implying of many sins import?

ANSWER. Notice is to be taken of the manifold sins whereby we stand indebted to God. Surely those saints of old entered into a deep consideration hereof who acknowledged that their iniquities increased over their head, and grew up unto the heavens, and were a heavy burden, too heavy for them to bear.

By taking thorough and due notice of our many several sins…

1. Our souls will be the more wounded and humbled for them. The benefit whereof will be that God will be the more moved with pity and compassion towards us.

2. Our desire of discharge will be the more fervent. Whereby the Lord will rather be moved to grant our desire. "The effectual fervent prayer of a righteous man availeth much."

3. The long-suffering of God in bearing with so many sins, so many ways committed against Him, and from time to time heaped one upon another, will be the better discerned.

4. The riches of God's mercy in forgiving not a few pence, nor yet a few talents, but many thousand talents will be the more admired and magnified, and He Himself the more loved. She who had many sins forgiven loved much.

Little do they consider the necessity of this doctrine who never think of their sins, or of seeking any discharge, but when they have committed some heinous, notorious sin that brings them to some open shame, and then acknowledge that sin only, as if, that excepted, they were clean from all sin. I do not deny but that good use may be made of fastening the mind upon one principal sin that seems most horrible to the conscience and makes the party most ashamed, and whereby he conceives God's wrath to be most provoked, as the Israelites who said, "We have added to all our sins this evil," and Ezra, who said, "Should we again break Thy commandments and join in affinity with the people of these abominations?" David said, "Deliver me from blood-guiltiness." For by this means our corruption and vileness will appear in our sight much greater. Yet we are to rest only in acknowledgement of such sins alone. If we observe the fore-named confessions of Ezra and David we shall find many other sins reckoned up.

Let us therefore learn how to set our sins in order before God. To this purpose we have two excellent helps, one outside us and the other within us. That without us is God's law. That within us is our conscience. God's law shows what is amiss. Our conscience shows what we have done amiss. Apply your conscience to the law and you shall find yourself guilty of an innumerable company of heinous sins. These acknowledge, and having acknowledged what debts you can call to mind, and in particular craved pardon for them, then because many sins daily pas from you of which you take no notice, pray in general for pardon of all, and say as the psalmist, "Deliver me from all my transgressions." The burden of the least sin is too heavy for you to bear; it is sufficient to crush you down to the place of the damned. Were it possible to be eased of all but one, that one retained would hold you in everlasting chains under darkness. It is therefore necessary that a discharge of all sins be had.

Hitherto we have spoken of the thing acknowledged, debts. The appropriation of them in this word "our" follows.

The Appropriation of Sin to Ourselves

QUESTION. In what respect are the debts here mentioned called ours?

ANSWER. They are ours as they arise from ourselves, and as we are the true and proper cause of them, even the principal authors and practicers of them. This particle of relation "our" is here used in another sense than it was in the former petition. There bread was called ours because it was given to us of God, and by that gift we had a right to it. Here sins are called ours because they proceed from us, in which respect nothing is so properly ours as sin.

QUESTION. What do we learn from this application of debts to ourselves?

ANSWER. We are the proper cause of the sins that we commit. On this ground, the prophet says, "O Israel, thou hast destroyed thyself."

Sin is a voluntary action: and the will of man is free, so as it cannot be forced to sin, as we shall hereafter more fully declare. Only hereby learn that no man has cause to soothe or flatter himself. Of himself man is as bad as may be. Sin being yours, take that away which is your own.

The thing acknowledged (debts) and appropriation of them (our) being noted, the kind of discharge (forgive) is now to be declared.

God's Free and Full Discharge of Man's Debt

QUESTION. What does this word "forgive" import?

ANSWER. It means to freely and fully discharge a debt. Freely without any satisfaction on our part, fully without any reservation of any part of the debt to be exacted of us: but rather such an acceptance as if we never had been in any debt at all.

To forgive is so to pass by an offence as neither to exact nor to expect anything either in way of recompense or in way of punishment for it. Both recompense and punishment are counted a kind of satisfaction, which is directly contrary to remission. It is noted of the servant whose debt the Lord forgave that he had nothing to pay; no recompense therefore was given. Yet was he not imprisoned and no punishment therefore was taken. But that servant that imprisoned his fellow servant did not forgive the debt, and yet he received no part of the debt. For imprisonment is a punishment, and punishment is a kind of payment that he who is punished is said to pay.

Again, though a man actually exacts nothing for a debt or an offence, yet if he bears a revengeful mind or a grudging heart, he is not thought truly to forgive. Nay, if he is not as good friends with the debtor or offender as if he never had had ought against him he does not truly forgive him, but only appear so outwardly. But God's forgiving is as true, full, and in every way perfect as possibly can be. And therefore, as it expects no satisfaction, so it is accompanied with as gracious an acceptance as if no sin had been committed.

The Concurrence of God's Mercy and Justice in the Discharge of Man's Debt

QUESTION. Can it stand with strictness of justice to freely and fully acquit sinners?

ANSWER 1. It is not against justice that He who has an absolute and supreme power over all, and is to give an account to none, should freely forgive anything that is in any way due to Himself, whether it be duty or penalty. "I will show mercy on whom I will show mercy," says this supreme Lord. And again, "Is it not lawful for Me to do what I will with Mine own?"

ANSWER 2. Christ our Surety, in our stead and for us, has endured that penalty which we by sin deserved, and fulfilled all that righteousness which we owed.

QUESTION. Can satisfaction and remission stand together?

ANSWER. Yes, in three cases.

1. When the party that is forgiven neither does nor can make any satisfaction. Such are we in regard of that debt which we owe to God. No satisfaction therefore is exacted of us in our own person.

2. When His Son, who forgives, make the satisfaction. Such a Surety we have, who has made satisfaction for our sins, even the only begotten Son of God, who is true God. So that God has made satisfaction to God.

3. When He who forgives is no further bound to accept the satisfaction that He accepts than by His own promise. What other bond can be alleged to bind God than that whereby He has voluntarily bound Himself? So all on God's part is most free. Freely He gave His Son a ransom. Freely He imputes what His Son did and suffered to us. Freely He accepts us in

His Son. Freely He acquits our debt. Hereupon the apostle joins our redemption by Christ's blood, remission of sins, and the riches of God's grace altogether, implying thereby that neither of these cross the other, but that all of them may and do stand together. Christ's satisfaction is so far from impeaching the freeness of God's grace that it the more commends the same. For it is much more grace, and far greater mercy in God, not to spare His only begotten Son, but to give Him for sinners, than upon His absolute prerogative without any satisfaction at all to forgive sinners. Christ, the Son of God's love, is more highly esteemed of God than any satisfaction can be. But by the satisfaction that the Son of God has made there is manifested a perfect concurrence of infinite mercy and absolute justice. And the freeness of God's grace is clearly manifested and highly magnified thereby.

Man's Inability to Discharge His Debt

QUESTION. What doctrine does this word "forgive" imply?

ANSWER. Man is not able of himself to discharge the debt of sin. If he were, what need would there be of forgiveness? This is the reason why the psalmist desired God not to enter into judgment with him, because no man living can be justified in His sight, namely of and by himself. From God's forgiving of sin the apostle gathered that man is not justified by works, that is, by anything that he himself can do.

The recompense that is to be given for discharge of the debt of sin must be of infinite value and worth. For sin, being committed against an infinite majesty, provokes infinite wrath and so becomes an infinite debt. Can a finite creature as man is give a recompense of such worth? What shall a man give in exchange for his soul?

Nay, man has by sin utterly deprived himself of all manner of ability to do anything that in any respect might carry any show of recompense. He is dead in sin, insufficient of himself so much as to think anything as of himself.

But if it were granted that man was able of himself to do something, what is that to God unto whom the recompense must be made? "Can a man be profitable unto God? Is it any pleasure to the Almighty that thou art righteous? Or is it gain to Him that thou makest thy ways perfect? If thou beest righteous what givest thou to Him? Or what receiveth He of thine hand?"

Popish Satisfaction

Detestable in this respect are many positions of papists concerning man's satisfaction for sin by punishments voluntarily undertaken, imposed by priests, or inflicted by God, and concerning the merit of works whereby the guilt of temporal punishment for sin may be removed.

Some of the chief of those positions I will set down in the words of their great champion Robert Bellarmine, because the very expression of them is a sufficient refutation of them.

The Council of Trent teaches that God is satisfied three ways: By bearing patiently the punishments and scourges that are inflicted by God, by undertaking of our own accord laborious works, and by undergoing the penalty imposed by the censure of priests. According to them:

Our satisfaction is required so that the wrong done to God may be recompensed and the divine justice satisfied.

We must satisfy by those good works that are ours.

Satisfaction must be worthy, and it must keep such a proportion with sin as the offence may be truly recompensed by it.

By penal works satisfaction is made to God truly and properly for that guilt of punishment that remains to be expiated after the fault is forgiven.

God's grace assisting we may, after a certain manner, truly satisfy out of that which is our own, even to equality, and in that respect justly and of desert.

We have works of our own whereunto we are not bound, by which we may satisfy for wrong done to God.

Our works, as they came from the Spirit of Christ dwelling in us, have a certain infiniteness, and thereby also a certain equality with the wrong whereby we had troubled God by sinning.

Full remission of sin, so much as concerns all guilt of punishment, is the reward of those good works that are wont to be called satisfactory.

Laborious works are profitable for remission of sin and for deliverance from eternal death.

If by these and such like positions that which is due to the all-sufficient satisfaction of Christ is not attributed to man, let any indifferent reader judge. Can the things that in these positions are avouched of recompensing wrong done to God, of satisfying the divine justice, of a condign or worthy satisfaction, of satisfying truly and properly to an equality, justly, condignly, and that out of our own works whereunto we are not bound, of a certain infiniteness of our works, and a certain equality with the wrong whereby we have troubled God by sinning, of full remission of sin to be the reward of satisfactory works, of the profit of laborious works for remission of sin and deliverance from eternal death—can these things stand with God's infinite justice, with man's inability to any good thing, with man's unworthiness, and with the imperfection of man's best works? Then may light and darkness in their most extreme degrees, then may the Ark of God and Dagon, then may grace and works stand together. And yet the apostle says, "If by grace, then it is no more of works, otherwise grace is no more grace. But if of works, then it is no more grace, otherwise work is no more work."

They allege for grounds of the worth of men's works that:

1. They come from the Spirit of Christ.

2. Christ gives the virtue of satisfaction to men's works.

3. Man's satisfaction is not for the fault of sin, but for its punishment.

4. The punishment for which man satisfies is not eternal, but temporal.

To these I briefly answer:

1. Though the work of the Spirit is pure in itself, yet coming from us it receives a tincture, as water that comes from a pure fountain passes through a foul channel. Besides, the Spirit works according to the capacity of the object, not all fullness and perfection at the first, but in part, by degrees.

2. For Christ to give the virtue of satisfaction to men's works is to make men priests and saviors, which offices are His glory. But He will not give his glory to others.

3. The fault being discharged by Christ, the punishment is also thereby discharged. For the fault is the cause of punishment. Take away the cause, the effect follows and falls away. As God said to Adam of the forbidden fruit, "In the day that thou eatest thereof thou shalt die the death," so Nathan said to David, "The Lord hath put away thy sin; thou shalt not die." His sin being remitted, the punishment was removed.

4. That satisfaction which takes away the greater punishment, by just consequence takes away the lesser. If temporal punishment as well as eternal were not discharged by Christ's satisfaction it would not be a complete, but an imperfect satisfaction.

But papists, being pressed by our unanswerable arguments, to avoid them use the forenamed distinctions of satisfying for the punishment and not the fault, for the temporal and not for the eternal punishment, yet in their forenamed positions they apply man's satisfaction to the recompensing of wrong done to God, to divine justice, to remission of sins, and to deliverance from eternal death, and thereupon they attribute thereunto a certain infiniteness and equality to the wrong wherewith by sinning we have troubled God. Oh, blasphemy!

Humiliation and Self-Denial

As the greatness of the debt wherein man stand obliged to God, so also man's impotence and impossibility to discharge it, aggravates that wretched estate into which man by sin is plunged, and give him much more occasion and matter of humiliation. If there were just cause to weep much because no man was found worthy to open the sealed Book, how much more cause of weeping and mourning is there that no man is able to cancel the bills and bonds whereby we stand indebted to God, or in any way to discharge that debt?

Has not man in this respect just cause also to deny himself, and as a self-condemning debtor and malefactor to cast himself down before the Mercy Seat of God, and to crave mercy and forgiveness, as that servant in the parable did who had nothing to pay?

The Remissibleness of Sin

QUESTION. What doctrine does praying for pardon of the debt of sin afford?

ANSWER. Sin is remissible. If it could not be pardoned it would be altogether in vain to pray for forgiveness. Christ would never have directed and incited us to pray for that which is not possible to obtain. He stirs us up to ask, seek, and knock on these grounds, "It shall be given you, ye shall find. It shall be opened unto you."

The true reasons hereof are the free grace of God and the price that Christ has paid for this debt. The knowledge hereof:

1. Ministers good ground of much comfort to poor sinners who groan under the heavy burden of sin.
2. Emboldens sinners in faith to seek pardon.

3. Provokes and encourages them to turn from sin.

QUESTION. What doctrine may further be gathered from the application of forgiveness to debts in the plural number?

All the sins of the faithful are remissible. I say of the faithful because they who have right to say to God, "Our Father" (which the faithful who are sons of God alone have), are taught thus to pray, and because they, by the continual and powerful assistance of God's Spirit, shall be kept from falling into the only unpardonable sin, the sin against the Holy Ghost.

As the free grace of God and the price that Christ has paid are the causes that sin is pardonable, so the infinite riches of that grace and the all-sufficiency of that price are the causes that all manner of sins are likewise pardonable.

Let no sin therefore keep us from seeking pardon. Well note the gracious invitation of the Lord in Isaiah 1:18. He who has taught us to pray for pardon of sin has promised fatherly mercy and pardon to follow thereupon.

God's Prerogative in Forgiving Sin

QUESTION. To whom is this petition for forgiveness of sin directed?

ANSWER. To God, for every petition has relation to the preface, and to Him who is there described, which is God only.

QUESTION. What may thence be gathered?

ANSWER 1. God has power to remit sins.

ANSWER 2. God alone has that power.

As here, so everywhere in Scripture, we are directed to go to God for pardon, but nowhere throughout the whole Scripture to any other. The Jews so firmly held these doctrines as they accounted it blasphemy for any to arrogate that power to himself.

Every sin, as a sin, is a breach of God's law, and in that respect committed against Him, though it is also a wrong done to man. Now God being a supreme Lord over all, who can be imagined to have power to forgive transgressions against Him and His law?

This prerogative shows that Christ is true God. Had not Christ been God the scribes would have justly accused Him of blasphemy for taking upon Himself to forgive sin. Christ therefore in answering their slander does not deny their principle, that God only can forgive sin, but by a visible demonstration proves Himself to be the true God, and thereby reveals their misapplication of that true principle whereby they denied to Him who was true God His prerogative, and in accusing Christ of blasphemy they themselves were impious blasphemers.

Papists' Blasphemy in Giving Men Power to Forgive Sins

The Pope assuming this prerogative to himself thereby shows himself to be plain Antichrist. For as by his flatterers there is given to him, so he assumes to himself a power of granting indulgences, releases, and pardons for sins past, present, and to come; and of these some are full, some more full, and some most full releases. Yea, some of these releases and indulgences are often extended to more years to come than can be imagined that the world shall continue.

The power of absolution that is also given by the church of Rome is derogatory to the forenamed prerogative of God, and is in that respect blasphemous. For by the Council of Trent it is decreed not to be a ministerial declaration, but a judicial act of forgiving. Whereupon they infer that as wind blows out a flame and drive away clouds, so the absolution of a priest puts away sin, and that thereby both the fault and also eternal punishment is remitted, and that many are damned because they die before they are absolved by a priest. What is this but to make priests gods?

Confession of Sin to God and Man

The forenamed prerogative of God plainly shows that auricular confession, as papists enjoin it, is not absolutely necessary. For they hold that a particular confession of all a man's sins that he can call to mind is necessarily to be made in the ear of a priest, and that upon pain of damnation. We do not deny a necessity of confession. For without confession of sin no remission, no absolution can be expected. But this absolute necessity must be applied to confession unto God, whose prerogative it is to forgive sin. Yea, further, we acknowledge a necessity of confession to man, and that both publicly and privately, and both these either upon injunction by authority or upon a man's own voluntary motion. Public confession is to be made of sins publicly committed, whereby public offence is given or public detriment and damage made. In this case Joshua enjoined Achan to confess his sin and he confessed it. Because Saphira refused to make confession, being required of Peter to do it, she was suddenly struck with death. They of Ephesus that had been notorious sinners voluntarily made public confession of their sins.

Private confession is to be made also in three cases:

1. When one in authority requires it, as Elisha required his servant Gehazi to do it.
2. When private wrong is done, or offence given to one.
3. When a sin burdens the conscience, on which ground David made confession to Nathan and St. James exhorted all Christians to confess their sins one to another so that they may receive the more comfort by mutual prayer and direction. In this case choice must be made of such persons as are fit to have secrets made known to them, and able to help and ease a burdened conscience. Such are men of understanding, discretion, wisdom, and experience, yea, such as are faithful and pitiful and bear a loving heart toward the party that comes to them for comfort. Among others, ministers are in two respects most fit. One is because by their daily study and practice they are

most acquainted with the temptations of Satan, dispositions of people, and consolations of God's Word. The second is because by virtue of their ministerial function, being ambassadors for Christ, and having the ministry of reconciliation given to them, the patient may with more assuredness apply to his soul the promises that they pronounce.

But necessarily to tie every Christian, upon pain of damnation, to make confession of all the sins whereof he knows himself to be guilty to the priest under whose charge he is, be he never so ignorant or lewd, is without all warrant of God's Word, and against common sense and reason.

Confessing Sin to God and Seeking Pardon of Him

For the main duty that arises from the fore-mentioned doctrine concerning God's prerogative in forgiving sin, let us not dare to hide our sin from God as Adam sought to do, but humbly and penitently confess the same, as David and other saints of God from time to time have done. This duty is to be done not so much to make our sins known to God (for He knows them whether we confess them or not) as to show that we ourselves know them, take notice of them, feel the burden of them, are grieved for them, hate them, desire to be freed from them, and truly repent of them. Thus will God be moved to take pity on us and be merciful to our sins. God is not like man who takes advantage from the delinquent's confession, according to the proverb, "Confess and be hanged," but rather from thence takes occasion to show mercy. In relation to God this may well come into a proverb, "Confess and be saved. For "if we confess our sins He is faithful and just to forgive us our sins."

Going to God for Pardon

God's prerogative to forgive sin further emboldens us to go to Him, and to Him only for pardon of sin. In that sin is remissible and may be pardoned, we have encouragement to seek for pardon. In that it is God who forgives we are directed to seek pardon of Him. "I even I am He that blotteth out thy transgressions," says the Lord. And well we may be glad that He reserves this prerogative for Himself. For of whom can we with greater confidence expect to receive this gracious favor than of Him who is full of compassion, gracious, slow to wrath, and plenteous in mercy? Let us not therefore leave this Fountain of living water and go to broken cisterns that can hold no water. As we desire to be discharged of the debt of sin, so let us seek this discharge of Him who is able and ready to give it. Though we can make no satisfaction, yet His mercy surpasses all our offences.

God's Free and Full Discharge of Sin

QUESTION. What doctrine arises from the kinds of discharge implied under the word "forgive"?

ANSWER. The discharge that God gives is a free and full discharge. It must be free because in man there can be nothing to procure it. Nay, outside of God there is nothing to move Him to do it. "I blot out transgressions," says the Lord, "for Mine own sake." And again, "For My name's sake will I defer Mine anger." He does not retain His anger forever because He delights in mercy. That the discharge also that God gives is full is evident by the many metaphors used in Scripture to set it out. Such are these that follow.

1. "I am He that blotteth out thy transgressions, saith the Lord." This metaphor is taken from creditors who, when they purpose never to exact a debt, will blot it out of their books. After a debt is stricken out of a bill, bond, or book it cannot be exacted; the evidence cannot be pleaded.

2. "I have put away thy transgressions as a cloud and thy sins as a mist," said the same Lord. We know that the clouds that are driven away by the winds appear no more, nor the

mist that is dried up by the sun. Other clouds, other mists may arise, but not they that are driven away and dried up. Thus the sins that God forgives do not return again.

3. The same Lord says, "Though your sins be as scarlet, they shall be as white as snow; though they be red like crimson, they shall be as wool." Scarlet and crimson are double and deep dyes, dyes engrained, yet if the cloth dyed therewith is as the wool before it was died, if it is as white as snow, what has become of those dyes? Are they anymore? Is not the cloth as if it had not been dyed at all? Even so, though our sins, by reiterating them, by long lying in them, have deeply seized into us, yet by God's discharge of them we are as if we never had committed them.

4. "Ye are washed," says the apostle. By washing the filth of things is clean taken away.

5. "Thou hast cast all my sins behind Thy back," Hezekiah says to God. That which a man would not look on or regard, that he casts behind his back. The sins that God forgives He will have as out of His sight that He means no more to meddle with.

6. "Thou wilt cast all their sins into the depths of the sea," Micah says to the Lord. When a man would have a thing utterly gone he will cast it into the bottom of the sea, from whence there is no fetching it again. So the Lord deals with the sins that He forgives.

7. The psalmist pronounces him blessed whose sin is covered. A thing covered is not seen. So sin that is forgiven is before God as not seen.

8. The same psalmist pronounces him blessed to whom the Lord does not impute sin. A sin that is not imputed is as one that is not committed.

9. The prophet says of sin that is forgiven that it shall be sought for and not found. Is not that fully discharged that shall never be found, never appear?

10. God Himself says, "I will remember their sin no more." Surely that which God will not remember, He has fully discharged.

Finally, the man is pronounced blessed whose sin is forgiven. If the discharge were not full, how could the party discharged be by virtue thereof blessed?

Forgiveness being an act of God must be both free and full. For whatever God does He does freely for Himself, without any former desert, without expectation of any future recompense. No creature can deserve anything at His hands, much less can sinners and rebels. Neither can any creature give any reward or recompense to Him. As He needs none, nor expects any, so He can receive nothing that is not His own.

Merit of Congruity

The free discharge of God directly excludes all merit of man. For that which is done for merit is not freely done. Papists who maintain man's merit, not only for his salvation after this life, but also for his justification in this life, and for remission of sins, think to salve up all by a distinction of merit of congruity and condignity of desert and worth. They say that merit of condignity follows justification, but merit of congruity goes before it and merits and obtains both remission of sins and justification. Of that merit of condignity I have elsewhere spoken; neither is it pertinent to this place.

For merit of congruity:

1. Though it is taken in the fairest interpretation that can be, yet it cannot stand with free grace, with mere mercy; but it greatly impairs the same.

2. When they expound their own meaning, they acknowledge that remission of sins and justification is due as a recompense or reward to the said merit of congruity. For, they say, to every merit a reward answers; as there is a merit of congruity, so also a reward of congruity. And the merit of congrui-

ty is rather founded in some dignity of the work than in the promise of God. Does not their own exposition of congruity make it a plain condignity and desert?

3. When God first acquits and justifies a sinner, He finds in him no congruity, no fitness to receive mercy, but rather an enemy-like and rebellious disposition against Him. For when we were enemies we were reconciled to God. And "God, who is rich in mercy, for His great love wherewith He loved us, even when we were dead in sin, quickened us."

Popish Satisfactions for Sins Remitted

God's full discharge of sin excludes all remainder of punishment to be endured in this world, or elsewhere by way of satisfaction for the sin forgiven. For if any satisfaction remained to be done the discharge is not full. Derogatory therefore to the absolute fullness of God's discharge is the doctrine of our adversaries in this point. For they hold that after sin is forgiven there may remain a guilt of punishment to be satisfied for, sometimes in this life, sometimes in another life, namely in purgatory, sometimes in both. But by such punishments for sin, sin would again be called to mind and memory, to view and fight, to reckoning and account, which cannot stand with the fore-mentioned Scripture phrases of not remembering, not imputing, covering, casting behind the back, casting into the bottom of the sea, blotting out, and so on. We do not deny but that saints whose sins are forgiven may notwithstanding be punished in this life (as for the fiction of purgatory it deserves rather to be hissed at than refuted by arguments), but withal we say that those punishments are neither expiatory, nor satisfactory, nor yet vindictive for sin. If they were, Christ's expiation, satisfaction, and suffering might be thought insufficient. The punishments that are inflicted on them whose sins are forgiven are as a medicinal corrosive, but not a judicial revenge.

The Comfort that Arises from God's Free and Full Discharge

The free and full discharge that God gives of sin is a most sound and sovereign ground of comfort to such as by faith rightly can apply the same to their own souls. For so freely and fully does God remit all offence that neither by revenging it does He condemn us, nor by upbraiding it confound us, nor by imputing it the less love us.

A due consideration of our many heinous sins cannot but astonish us and make us ashamed to appear in the presence of God for pardon of them. But knowledge of the free grace of God (who of Himself, for Himself, and for His own name's sake pardons sin) and faith therein emboldens poor sinners to draw near to the throne of grace, and to cast themselves down before God's mercy seat for pardon, and to say, "We do not present our supplications before Thee for our righteousness, but for Thy great mercies."

Again, knowledge of the desert of sin, how the least sin deserves the wrath of God, and the least degree of God's wrath is an insupportable burden, cannot but frighten the soul of a sinner through the apprehension of any vindictive punishment to be endured for sin. What then can remain to satisfy the poor sinner but faith in God's full discharge? The promises of God being the ground of our faith, we have good ground to believe that, according to the forenamed promises, our sins, that we have humbly and penitently confessed, and for which we have craved pardon, are freely and fully discharged. If upon our own true humiliation and hearty supplication we believed this, what comfort, what peace might be brought to our souls thereby? Let us therefore often meditate on the fore-named grounds of faith that our faith thereby may be the more established and our consciences the more quieted.

The thing acknowledged, debts.

The appropriation of them, our.

The kind of discharge, forgive. These have hitherto been handled.

The parties to be discharged, us, are now to be considered.

Praying for the Pardon of Our Own Sins Especially

QUESTION. Who are comprised under this particle "us""

ANSWER. We ourselves and others. The first person includes ourselves. The plural number extends this petition to others.

QUESTION. What doctrine may thence be gathered?

ANSWER. Pardon is to be sought for our own and others' sins. Of seeking pardon for our own sins no question can be made. Holy men of God guided by the Spirit of God have done this in particular, even in the singular number, for themselves. "Put away mine iniquity, cleanse me from my sin, wash me, purge me," says the psalmist.

Love begins at home. If any duty of love is to be shown to ourselves, then this one especially above all others. For if sin is not pardoned what can be comfortable, what can be beneficial and profitable to us?

The application of this point concerns not only such as (through ignorance of that fearful estate wherein they lie by sin, or a profane neglect of this holy and heavenly duty of prayer) never call upon God for this or any other blessing on their own or others' behalf, but also, and that more especially, such as through some violent temptation and deep apprehension of God's indignation against them are afraid to pray for pardon of their own sins, and yet can heartily pray for the pardon of others' sins. These must be well instructed in this privilege that is here afforded unto us, and in that respect that God has to the particular prayer that is made by a penitent soul in his own behalf. God often hears one praying for himself when He does not hear him praying for others. But we never heard of any accepted for others that were not accepted for themselves. Everyone's prayer is most available for himself. Let the mind that such have to pray for others provoke them to pray first for pardon of their own sins. For until a man's sins are pardoned he cannot expect any blessing on others by his prayers.

Praying for Pardon of Others Sins

That prayer is to be made for others has been shown before. If for any other blessing we ought to pray in the behalf of others, then most of all for the pardon of their sins, the greatest blessing, if the extent of it is well observed, that in this world can be obtained for them. This was that for which Moses so earnestly prayed in the behalf of the Israelites, and for which Job offered up sacrifices in the behalf of his children. That express precept that the apostle gives of praying for others has special relation to their sins, as the reason imports in these words, "If he have committed sins they shall be forgiven him."

That reason is a reason of great weight, for by obtaining pardon of sin for another a soul is saved from death. What a privilege, what an honor is this to a Christian, that he should be a means of saving his brother's soul? What a benefit he thereby brings to his brother! The Scripture gives us many instances of the benefit of prayer in this kind, namely that it has been a means of obtaining pardon for many sinners and of preventing or removing many judgments from them. Witness the many prayers that Moses made for the Israelites when they had sinned against God, and in particular for Miriam. Witness also the prayer that Hezekiah made for the people who came unprepared to the Passover and the prayer that Job made for his friends who did not speak of God the thing that was right. No doubt but the prayer that Christ made on the cross for them who so evilly treated Him was a means through which many thousand Jews soon after His ascension were converted and had their sins pardoned. The like may be said of Stephen's prayer.

Not only to others may much good be brought by a conscionable performance of this duty, but to ourselves also. For our faith in the pardon of our own sins will be much strengthened thereby. By praying for the pardon of others' sins we shall the better acquaint ourselves with the extent of God's promises, which are the holy oil to make the lamp of our faith to continue her light.

We learn hereby to take notice of others' sins as well as of our own. Let us take notice of the public, open sins of the times and places where we live of those among whom we converse, but especially of those who are under our charge. And as we observe them we ought to be humbled for them, to make confession of them to God, and supplication for pardon of them. Hereof we have many excellent patterns in God's Word.

In performance of this duty let our minds be especially fixed on the sins of those who are under our charge and to whom we are by some special bonds linked, as Job who prayed for his children and friends, and Moses for the people under his charge. It is meet also to enlarge our prayer so as the inhabitants of the parish, town, city, and nation wherein we live may be comprised therein, as Daniel who confessed the sins of Jerusalem, Judah, and all Israel, and craved pardon for the same. Here we ought especially to be mindful of the sins of our governors and ministers, as the Levites were of the sins of their princes and priests. Finally, our prayers in this respect must be extended to our enemies, for which we have both the precept and pattern of Christ, and the pattern of the first Christian martyr, Stephen.

So much for the substance of the fifth petition. The condition annexed thereto follows.

Man's Forgiving Another

QUESTION. Which are the words wherein the condition annexed to the fifth petition is expressed?

ANSWER. "As we forgive our debtors."

QUESTION. What are the distinct points here to be considered?

ANSWER 1. The duty required, forgive.

2. The persons tied thereto, we.
3. The parties to whom it is to be performed, debtors.
4. The restraint thereof, our.
5. The resemblance, as.

In setting down the duty we are to note wherein it consists and when it is to be performed.

QUESTION. What is the main duty here required?

ANSWER. Men must forgive one another. Many precepts of Scripture tend hereunto, as, "resist not evil; avenge not yourselves; forbear one another; forgive one another; overcome evil with goodness." And answerable has the practice of the saints been from time to time. Instance Joseph, Moses, David, Paul, and others like them.

This is a special property of a saint and child of God in whom the wisdom that comes from above abides. For that wisdom is peaceable, gentle, easy to be entreated, full of mercy and good fruits. Hereby a manifest difference is discerned between that spirit that comes from above and that spirit that arises from the flesh, between a regenerate and a natural man. By nature man is exceedingly prone to revenge. The heathen who were guided only by the light of nature did not discern the excellence and necessity of this grace. Their philosophers, who were their divines, did not account it unlawful to revenge wrongs. Yea, they held it a bound duty and a glorious virtue to seek and take revenge insomuch as if any notorious wrong were done to a man and he was taken away before revenge was taken, and the surviving friends were negligent in revenging the same, they imagined that the ghosts of the deceased would never leave haunting and terrifying those surviving friends till they had taken revenge.

Many among us who are taught better divinity too much nourish this corruption of nature. If they are wronged by word or deed they think it dishonorable to put it up or pass it over without revenge, which is the cause of so many challenges as from time to time are given and taken, and of the many mortal and desperate duels that are daily undertaken; yea, and of many secret plots and practices for doing some notorious mischief and for taking away the very life of such as have done them wrong. If such as are able with better discretion and more moderation to temper their outward actions well observe and thoroughly try their inward disposition, they shall find this sprout of corrupt nature, revenge, too deeply fixed in them. Yea, they shall find many bitter fruits thence sprouting in revengeful thoughts and desires, wishing many mischiefs to fall upon them by whom they think themselves in any way wronged. What is this but inward revenge? Surely revenge is one of the most incurable sores of the flesh. It is most hardly subdued and mortified. It is a good sign therefore of a renewed nature it is to forbear revenge and forgive wrongs, if at least it is done in truth, from the heart, for the sake of conscience.

Far short of the Christian's goal they come, though they think they go far in the Christian's race, who are only mild, gentle, kind, and courteous till they are wronged, but then are implacable and will accept no reconciliation till they have taken revenge for that wrong. They think it a great glory that they can say, "I run into no man's debt. I wrong to no man. I ever have been and ever will be ready to do all offices of kindness that I can. But if any abuse me in any way and wrong me they shall know whom they abuse, and I will make them repent the wrong that they have done. My friend shall taste my kindness, but my enemy shall know what I am able to do."

The pretended goodness of such men lacks the substance of goodness; it has but a show and shadow thereof. That is sound, solid, pure gold that abides the flaming heat of the fiery furnace. A man's goodness cannot be proven to be found till it is tried by the fire of wrong or offence. Dogs, bears, tigers, lions, and the most savage beasts that be can be quiet and gentle until they are stirred and incensed. A proverb said, "The Devil is good while he is pleased." Behold then what kind of goodness it is whereof such men boast. No better than the goodness of the most cruel creatures, the Devil not excepted. Do what you can to a sheep, you cannot make it snarl or bite. Do but clap a dog on the back and he will be ready to fly in your face. He therefore that being provoked is stirred up to revenge retain his natural, doggish disposition. He who may justly be accounted a lamb or sheep of Christ's fold and has the Spirit of the Lamb of God in him will recompense to no man evil for evil, but will overcome evil with good. To this height of goodness the condition of this petition calls us.

This duty of forgiving one another being the main and principal point intended in this condition added to the fifth petition, which is the only by-clause in the whole Lord's Prayer, and which Christ thought not enough to insert in the prayer, but so soon as He had ended His form of prayer returned to this point again and again and again presses it both affirmatively and negatively, showing the advantage of forgiving and the damage of not forgiving. For a further pressing and enforcing of it I will endeavor to set out the excellence, utility, necessity, difficulty, and rarity of it.

1. For the excellence of it, it is one of those excellencies wherein God Himself glories, that He forgives sin. Therefore with great emphasis He says, "I, I am He that blotteth out thy transgression for Mine own sake." And with great admiration of this excellence the prophet says, "Who is a God like unto Thee that pardoneth iniquity?" They therefore who forgive wrongs show themselves like God in His excellence. Whereupon the apostle, having exhorted us to forgive, adds as a further motive to press the duty this clause, "Be ye followers of

God as dear children." Herein man shows himself a God to man, as on the contrary, by revenge, he shows himself a very devil. Many, like Lamech, boast and glory in taking revenge as a matter of great manhood, whereas in truth it is a part of much baseness and great cowardice.

2. For the utility of it, if this question is asked, "What profit is there in forgiving?" I answer as the apostle did of circumcision, much every way. Thereby assurance of God's forgiving our sins is obtained. We are made more capable of receiving mercy from God. We shall have much quietness in our souls. We shall appear more amiable before men, be the better loved of them, and receive more kindnesses from them. We shall avoid many mischiefs into which we might plunge ourselves by taking revenge, and that both God and man might bring us unto for taking revenge.

3. For the necessity of it, it is absolutely necessary for society with men and communion with God. In regard of society with men, there is no living in this world without a mind willing and ready to forgive wrongs, and that by reason of the wrongs that others from time to time will do to us and we to others. We live here among many and sundry sorts of people, and those of divers and different dispositions, some giving offence in one kind and others in another. If we are forward to take revenge of every wrong, and do not have a mind forward to forgive, we shall never have a quiet mind. Revenge will be as a poison continually working in our souls, exceedingly disturbing and disquieting them. And for ourselves, flesh is in us all; it abides in the best so long as they abide in this world. By reason of the flesh in us we are subject to many infirmities whereby sundry offences are given to others, sometimes on weakness and sometimes on willfulness; sometimes on sudden passion and heat of blood and sometimes again on deliberation and cold blood. By reason hereof we need that others should bear with us and forgive us. But if we do not forgive others, how can we look that

others should forgive us? Our example in taking revenge of others is a pattern to others to take revenge of us. It is just with the Lord to suffer men so to do according to that which Adoni-bezek said, "As I have done, so God hath requited me." So much is often expressly threatened. In regard of communion with God, there is no hope, no possibility of reconciliation and atonement with God for such as are ready to take revenge of men. Christ has set it down as a ruled case, as an inviolable law, more stable and unalterable than the laws of the Medes and Persians established by the king that, "If ye forgive not men their trespasses, neither will your heavenly Father forgive your trespasses." In the parable we read that the Lord who forgave his servants debt recalled his grant when he heard that servant would not forgive his fellow servant.

QUESTION. May then that remission that God grants be reversed?

ANSWER 1. That which hypocrites presumptuously assume to themselves, without due consideration of the conditions and qualifications of the gospel, may. For it is an absolution unjustly taken before it is fully given.

ANSWER 2. That circumstance in the parable is noted not simply to declare any reversing of God's grant, but to aggravate the heinousness of revenge, and God's hatred of and indignation against it. And it shows that though God in Himself is ready and forward to forgive, and could and would otherwise forgive such a debtor, yet if that debtor is hard-hearted to his brother and does not forgive him, neither will God forgive.

4. For the difficulty of it, wrath and revenge cannot easily be subdued. A combat and a conquest in that combat is requisite thereto. The combat must be with our own passions, and the conquest must be over them, which conquest flesh and blood can never get. He who rules his spirit is mightier than he who takes a city. Passions are exceedingly violent, very dangerous and pernicious. In us there is a great proneness to yield

unto them. Our flesh is very loath to strive against them. What hope then is there of any victory over them? Surely there must be more in us than flesh and blood to subdue them.

5. For the rarity or scarcity of it, I may justly in the prophet's sense use these words of the prophet, "Run ye to and fro through the streets, and see now and know, and seek in the broad places, if ye can find a man, if there be any that forgiveth wrongs and passeth by offences." View the world, observe such as are reputed to have a generous mind. Among them you shall find challenges sent and taken, and desperate combats undertaken for every slight wrong, for every disgraceful and displeasing word. Enter into the city, go about the country, mark the disposition of inhabitants in city and country, and you shall find among them, for petty injuries and ignominious speeches, complaints to justices, warrants, arrests, actions, imprisonments, and suits in law to the utter undoing of one another. Inns of Court, seats of justice, universities, yea, and pulpits are full of bitter invectives, spiteful maliciousness, and revengeful defamations for every offence, and that oftentimes when the offence is rather taken than given. Men, women, old, young, rich, poor, brothers and sisters, fellow servants, neighbors, friends, all of all sorts, are exceedingly given to revenge. If the thoughts of men could be ransacked, and the desire of revenge that therein lurks be discovered, it would then more evidently appear that this grace of forgiving wrongs, which is indeed rare in the excellence of it, is also exceedingly rare in the scarcity of it, hardly to be found anywhere.

If now the excellence of a thing in itself, if the utility and benefit that it brings to them who have it, if the absolute necessity thereof for communion with God or man, if the difficulty of attaining thereto, if the rarity of it, being such as very few attain unto it, are motives to stir us up diligently and earnestly to seek after it, then motives are not wanting to stir us up to use all means that may be to suppress revenge and to work in us a readiness and willingness to forgive.

This much of the duty here required. The time when it is to be performed follows.

Speedy Forgiveness

QUESTION. What time is limited for forgiving?

ANSWER. The present time. The word is of the present tense, we do forgive, which implies a present performance and a constant continuance. The time present has an opposition both to the time to come and also to the time past. He who in the present does a thing does not put it off to the future, contenting himself with a purpose to do it afterwards, as if it were enough to say, "I will forgive." Neither does he leave off to do it, contenting himself that heretofore he has done it, as if it were enough to say, "I have forgiven." But so soon as occasion of doing it is offered he does it; and so long as the occasion continues he continues to do it.

QUESTION. What doctrine may be gathered from the profession of forgiveness in the time present?

ANSWER. We must presently forgive. So soon as occasion of exercising this duty is offered it must be put into practice. As the shadow shows itself so soon as a body appears in sunshine, so must forgiveness show as soon as a wrong is discerned. "When ye stand praying, forgive." We may not dare to stand up to pray unless we forgive. Is it not then requisite that we forgive instantly? To this purpose tends this prohibition, "Let not the sun go down upon your wrath." His meaning is that we should not harbor heart-burning any whit at all. The phrase of not suffering the sun to go down on a thing is proverbial and implies a speedy redress. Contrary hereunto are they who suffer many sins to set on their wrath.

Revenge is a kind of fire, which if it is not presently quenched will soon prove unquenchable. Nay, it is a deadly poison that, if it once seizes on the soul, will soon destroy it. No fire, no poison is of a more increasing nature than revenge. Instance the revenge and wrath incensed in Cain against Abel, and in the scribes and Pharisees against Christ. It increased to blood. The longer revenge lasts the stronger it waxes. But forgiveness is the only means to quench that fire, to expel that poison. Can then forgiveness with safety be put off?

Assuredly Satan will take great advantage from the least delay. Whereupon the apostle advises us to give no place to the Devil. But by putting off revenge we give much place to him.

Hereby trial may be made of a mind rightly fitted and prepared for this duty of forgiveness. It manifests itself so soon as occasion is offered. So soon as the Lord had stricken Miriam with leprosy for the wrong she did to Moses, he, to show how ready he was to pass it by and to forgive it presently prayed for her.

But the deceitfulness of their heart is evidently discovered whose forgiveness consists only in a purpose to do it afterwards. That which is truly purpose will not always remain a mere purpose but, so soon as occasion is given, will prove a practice. Many think it time enough to forgive when they go to the Lord's Table; yet it may be that such go to that holy board but once a year. Surely that forgiveness which is then intended cannot be found. It may justly be suspected to be more on vain superstition than true devotion. What if they die suddenly before that time, and have no time, no thought to forgive? Can they think it safe to depart out of this world with a revengeful mind? I would gladly know of such whether they intend to pray before that time set for receiving the holy communion. If they intend so to do, can they think it well to pray in wrath? If men knew what a wolf, what a tiger, what a viper wrath and revenge were, they would at the first sight thereof be startled and get themselves as far from it as they could. If scorpions and asps were in men's houses, what pains would they take to cleanse their houses that they might dwell securely? But they keep anger, wrath, malice, hatred, and revenge, which are so many scorpions and serpents, and do not cleanse the house of God, which is their heart. Yea, such a perverse disposition have many as they use all the means they can to retain and nourish revenge, and to keep it in mind and memory. By oath, by imprecation, and other ways they will bind themselves not to forgive. They do not forbear to say, "I may forget the wrong, but I will never forgive it." Hereby they provoke God to keep their sins in perpetual memory and to bind Himself to execute vengeance on them.

Constant Forgiving

QUESTION. What other doctrine may be gathered from the profession of forgiveness in the time present?

ANSWER. Forgiveness must be a continued act. It must not, so long as we live, be reckoned among the things utterly past and no more to be performed. The time past has its date. The time to come may have no date at all. The time present is always in being. God therefore sets out His eternal being and abiding by the time present in this title, "I AM THAT I AM." He therefore who in truth says, "I forgive," must never be of another mind; he must never think of recalling what he has forgiven, or of waxing weary of forgiving though never so many wrongs from time to time are offered. Christ says, "When ye stand praying, forgive." And His apostle says, "Pray continually." If we must pray continually, and praying forgive, then must we forgive continually. Where Christ enjoined to forgive unto seventy times seven, He intended a readiness to forgive so often as we are wronged, be we wronged never so often. A set and definite number is put for an indefinite one.

Constant continuance in a good thing is that which sets the crown upon it and make it not to be in vain. But intermitting and omitting that which is well begun takes away the glory thereof. Revenging after wrongs provokes God to pass by without reward or regard our forgiving of former wrongs.

Let us not therefore be overcome of evil, but rather overcome evil with goodness. We have need, in regard of that extent of duty here required, to take unto ourselves an invincible resolution. For while we live in this world it cannot be but that we shall have wrongs offered unto us. It is not without cause that the apostle advises to "let patience have her perfect work." The perfect work of patience consists, as in the truth of it, whereby it is sound, not feigned, so in the extent of it, that it reaches to all kinds of wrongs and offences, and in the continuance of it, that it endures to the end. The notation of the word that the apostle uses implies this last branch of perfection, which is a persisting to the end, even to the end of this mortal life wherein we shall have use and need of exercising this duty of forgiveness. We may not therefore so much consider what wrongs and offences we have forgiven as how many more we may hereafter take occasion to forgive so that by our continual practice of this duty we may day after day say, "I forgive."

So much for the duty required. The parties tied thereto are next to be considered.

Dealing with Man as We Desire God Should Deal with Us

QUESTION. Who are especially tied to the condition of the fifth petition?

ANSWER. They who call God Father and crave forgiveness of Him. For this particle "we" in the condition, and the particles "our" and "us" in the preface and in the petitions, are all of the same number and person, and have a mutual reference to the same persons.

QUESTION. What doctrine hence arises?

ANSWER. Saints who crave and expect mercy of God are most bound to show mercy to man. This the Lord pressed upon His servant thus, "I forgave thee all thy debt because thou desiredst Me. Shouldest not thou also have had compassion on thy fellow-servant, even as I had compassion on thee?" This also the apostle especially presses upon professors as these reasons show, "There is one body, and one Spirit, even as ye are called in one hope of your calling: One Lord, one faith, one baptism, one God and Father of all."

By the mercy that saints who crave and expect mercy from God show, both God who forgives them and Christ, for whose sake God forgives them, are most glorified. The gospel also, and their profession thereof, are most graced and honored thereby; yea, and the mouths of such enemies as watch for occasions to disgrace professors of the gospel are stopped. Finally, the mutual good of the members of God's churches is hereby much promoted.

What great and just cause of complaint is in these respects given, by reason of the wrathful, revengeful disposition of many who in their profession of religion are very forward. Of those who in outward profession make their houses God's churches by the daily exercises of piety therein, constantly offering up their morning and evening spiritual sacrifices, who also by frequenting the house of public prayer, the ministry of the Word, the Lord's Table, and other services of God, make great show of much piety, have the name of saints, and seem to expect much mercy from the Lord, of those, I say, there are many who are full of envy, wrath and revenge, very quarrelsome and contentious, ready to arrest, to bind to the peace and good behavior, to cast into prison, to commence suits in law, and enter actions of trespass of defamation, and of other like petty matters upon very slight occasions. The prophet foretold the wolf should dwell with the lamb and the leopard lie down with the kid. But now such as profess themselves to be lambs and kids of Christ's flock can scarcely dwell quietly one by another. Many professors are as very firebrands as any others. Surely their profession and religion are vain. They mock God, they deceive man, and they lie against their conscience when they say, "We forgive." Their sin is the greater in that thereby they open the mouths of profane persons against the gospel of Christ and a profession thereof.

Let us who call God Father, who crave, who expect mercy of God, learn with what mind to do it, namely with a mind ready and willing to do for others what we desire to be done for us. Lift up pure hands without wrath, you who desire God to turn away His wrath from you. Show mercy, you who crave mercy of God. Be bountiful, you who long to taste the sweetness of God's bounty. Forbear with your brother, you who would have God forbear with you. So deal in every other respect as you pray God to deal with you. This is acceptable to God. This well becomes your profession. This will bring much comfort to your soul. Thus shall your prayer not be made in vain.

The duty and parties most bound thereto being declared, the persons to whom the duty is to be performed are to next to be set out.

The Several Kinds of Debts Whereby We Become Debtors to Man

QUESTION. Who are meant by "debtors"?

ANSWER. Such as in any way wrong man. For the apostle joins together these two phrases, wronged and indebted. So many ways as one wrongs another he becomes a debtor to him. But one may wrong another (according to those several, distinct heads of duties that the law enjoins to be performed to our neighbors) five ways.

1. In his place or dignity. Herein Aaron and Miriam, Korah, Dathan and Abiram became debtors to Moses. They spoke against that authority, eminence, and dignity that God had given him.

2. In his person or life. Herein Saul became a debtor to David by persecuting his person and seeking to take away his life. Herein also the Jews were debtors to Christ.

3. In his chastity. Herein Palti and Michal became debtors to David in that (Michal being David's wife) they two as man and wife lived and kept company together.

4. In his goods. Herein Onesimus became a debtor to Philemon by running from him and stealing his goods, which moved St. Paul to say, "If he have wronged thee, or oweth thee ought."

5. In his good name. Herein Shimei became a debtor to David by reproaching him and calling him a man of blood, a man of Belial.

All these wrongs God has expressly forbidden in His law so as they are double debts, one as transgressions against God, the other as injuries against men. The later of these kinds of debts is here meant in this condition. Of that kind are all the forenamed instances.

Making Satisfaction for Wrongs Done to Man

QUESTION. What doctrine does this title "debtors" applied to wrongs done to men imply?

ANSWER. Wrongdoers must make satisfaction for the wrong that they do. Every wrong is a debt. But a debt must be satisfied according to this charge, "Owe nothing to any man." God gave to the Israelites an expressed law for restitution or satisfaction of that wherein one had wronged another.

By satisfaction, as by a plaster, the wound that is made is healed and so wrong comes to be as no wrong.

The truth of repentance for the wrong that is done is also manifested by satisfaction. Zacchaeus hereby gave evidence of his unfeigned repentance. Were it possible to make satisfaction for the debts wherein we stand bound to God we ought to do it. But because by reason of the infiniteness of that debt we are not in any sort able to satisfy it, Christ, who is able, has undertaken it. He has become our Surety. He has discharged our debt. So as in regard of our debts to God, all that is expected of us for satisfaction thereof is by a true faith to apply the satisfaction of Christ. But because we may be profitable to man, and may make some recompense for that wrong we have done to him, we ought in this case to do to the utmost of our power what we can. He who is careful to make satisfaction shows that he is sensible of the wrong he has done and would, if it were possible, that it had not been done, which implies a penitent heart.

Besides, common justice and equity require satisfaction in what we are able. The heathen by the light of nature well discerned as much and have given many good directions thereabout. What a shame would it be for them who have the light of the gospel added to that light of nature live more in darkness and to love the works of darkness more than they did?

OBJECTION. They to whom men are indebted must forgive their debtors. Why then should debtors think of restitution or satisfaction?

ANSWER 1. That duty of forgiveness is required in case a debtor cannot, through disability, or will not, through obstinacy, make satisfaction. But it gives no liberty to him who is able to be willful in refusing to do what he is bound to do.

ANSWER 2. God's requiring mercy of one does not justify injustice and injury in another. Wherefore let everyone look to that especially which belongs to him and observe wherein he has wronged another, to do him the best right that he can, and that according to the wrong that he has done. If it is a wrong that is known, humbly to acknowledge the same to the party wronged. If an inferior has wronged his superior by any disloyalty, let him be the more loyal for the time to come. If one under subjection has been rebellious, let him be the more submissive and obedient. If one who owed service to another has been negligent or careless in his business, let him be the more industrious and diligent. Let him who has in any way dealt unmercifully with another take all occasions to show more mercy to him. He who has in any way defrauded another, let him to his utmost power make full restitution. He who has impeached the good name or credit of another, let him endeavor to right him whom he has discredited in his reputation. And so it must be in other wrongs. Thus will there be a healing of the wounds that have been made. And this is fruit worthy of repentance, which we are commanded to bring forth. Note this all you who by word or deed have offended any. Do not add obstinacy to injury. Do not persist in wrong. That is to make the sin sinful beyond measure. Your judgment shall be answerable to your sin.

As for such as having done wrong refuse reconciliation when it is offered, surely they have a devilish spirit. Such were they of whom the psalmist thus complains, "My soul hath long dwelt with him that hateth peace. I am for peace, but when I speak they are for war." These are firebrands in the societies where they are, more fit to live in hell among devils than on earth among men.

Departing from Our Rights

QUESTION. What other doctrine may be gathered from this metaphor "debtors" in relation to the duty of forgiving?

ANSWER. To forgive we must part with our rights. For a debtor to pay what he owes is a right due to the creditor. But a debtor must be forgiven. This cannot be unless the creditor lets go of his right and forbears to exact that which, were it not for this duty of forgiving, he might exact. Saul, having showed himself a professed mortal enemy against David, acknowledged that David, when he had him in his power, might have killed him; so in sparing him Saul acknowledged that David departed from his right. "Thou hast showed this day how thou hast dealt well with me; forasmuch as when the Lord had delivered me into thine hand thou killedst me not. For if a man finds his enemy, will he let him go well away?" The truth is that David was by all law bound to spare Saul's life and to forbear all revenge against his person because he was with his sovereign, which David well knew and accordingly professed as much. But in Saul's opinion he departed from his right, which he did in truth in Shimei's case. We have a worthy pattern for departing from one's right for peace's sake in the example of Christ, who though He was able to prove that He was not bound to pay tribute, yet paid it. So St. Paul did forbear to exact that of the churches, which he might have done.

If a man has no right to exact that which he seems to forgive, his forgiveness is no forgiveness. It is no work of mercy.

The common practice of men in standing to the uttermost for their rights cannot stand with the equity of that which is here professed, "we forgive our debtors." In all manner of wrongs to a man's place, person, chastity, goods, or good name, there is a kind of right for a man to take revenge, and such a right, as it may be, is not condemned, but rather justified by man's law. What kind of debt then can be forgiven if that which may be thought man's right is exacted to the uttermost? Quarrels, contentions, needless but harmful suits in law, disturbances of peace, and other mischiefs for the most part arise from men's overly strict standing to that which they conceive to be their right, from which they will not yield one hair's breadth. If the law gives a man advantage against his neighbor for a reproachful word, for a sudden though light blow, for a trespass on his land, for any forfeiture or the like, that advantage is taken by many; and therein they think they do what they may do, And yet for all that therein they may do much wrong; for often times extreme right is extreme rigor. Learn more to weigh what Christian equity and charity requires of us than what concept of our own rights or extremity of human law may egg us on to do. Thus will peace, unity, amity, and charity be preserved and continued among men.

Forgiving All Sorts of Debtors

QUESTION. What doctrine does the expressing of debtors in the plural number import?

ANSWER. All sorts of debtors must be forgiven. The debtors here have no limitation. Forgiveness therefore must have no restraint. Whoever offends, friend or foe, neighbor or stranger, great or mean, rich or poor, inferior or superior, in whatever any offend and wrong us, in our place, person, chastity, goods, or good name, yea, if one man shall in many offences, or often in one offence, becomes a debtor, and in that respect is as many debtors, forgiveness in all these and all other like cases must be granted. St. Paul required Philemon to forgive his inferior, his servant. David forgave his superior, his sovereign. Moses forgave the wrong done to his place and dignity. Stephen forgave the wrong done to his person and life. David forgave the wrong done to his chastity and his good name. The forenamed wrong that Philemon was required to forgive was in goods. Many were the wrongs that the priests, scribes, Pharisees, and other Jews did to Christ, yet He forgave them all.

Mercy has no stint set unto it. It is as a springing fountain that can never be dried up. Though never so much is fetched from it continually, yet it ever remains full. Charity is bountiful; it bears all things, believes all things, hopes all things, and endures all things. Forgiveness, therefore, being a work of mercy and charity, is of the same nature and condition.

As for the kind of debts, the greater they are, or the more it goes (as we speak) against the hair, against our corrupt disposition to forgive them, the greater is our glory in forgiving them. To forgive a small debt, a small wrong, is scarcely thankworthy. He is worse than a savage who can pass by nothing.

Hereby further trial may be made of the truth of forgiveness, whether it flows from the forenamed fountain of mercy and charity or is forced and performed on by respects. If it extends itself only to some debtors (whom for kindred or friendship sake, for hope of recompense, for fear of greater mischief, or for some other like by respects we are willing to forgive) and not to all sorts of debtors; or to small debts and wrongs (the forgiving whereof is scarcely thankworthy); or otherwise if it is drawn dry by the multiplication of debts, and after some debts forgiven it is no more to be found, surely it is not true forgiveness. It does not flow from the right fountain and head. By this note of trial many may be found faulty in the condition here required, the extent whereof, as it is to be applied to enemies who most incense the wrath of man, so to neighbors who, by reason of the many occasions of offence through their continual commerce, most often provoke; yea, and to friends also from whom offences are most unkindly taken. All must be forgiven.

After the duty required, the persons tied thereto, and the parties to whom it is to be performed, the restraint thereof in this word "our" follows to be handled.

Forgiving Our Own Debtors

QUESTION. Why is this particle of restraint "our" applied to those debtors whom we must forgive?

ANSWER. To distinguish them from God's debtors and to distinguish them from other men's debtors.

QUESTION. What doctrine arises from this restraint?

ANSWER. Everyone must meddle with his own debts. St. Luke makes this doctrine most clear by showing who are our debtors, namely everyone who is indebted to us. He says, "To us," not to others. Duly weigh all the places where this duty of forgiving is pressed on man and you shall find it limited with this restraint. God's Word lays no charge on man either to forgive God's debts or other men's debts.

True mercy, charity, patience, and wisdom is exercised in forgiving our own debts only; and thereby are these virtues best discerned to be sound and good.

It is intolerable presumption for man to take upon him to forgive God's debts, which are sins as we have before noted. One man may pray to God for such as sin (as Stephen did) that God would not lay their sin to their charge, and by that means sin may be forgiven. But no man can himself actually forgive any sin.

OBJECTION. Nathan forgave David's sin.

ANSWER. He only pronounced remission of his sin in the name of the Lord. His words are expressed, "The Lord hath put away thy sin."

OBJECTION. Christ gave power to His apostles to forgive sins.

ANSWER. He did not give them power actually of themselves or in their own name to forgive, but to declare, to apply in particular, and to assure the conscience of the penitent believer that God had forgiven him his sins.

As for other men's debtors, it is the part of a busybody to undertake the forgiving of them. Such remission may be an occasion of much contention, and thereby a man may bring himself into needless danger. He who meddles with strife that does not belong to him is like one who takes a dog by the ears. What does such a one get but a snap for his pains? Well therefore does the wise man brand him a fool who meddle with other men's matters.

It is further a note of hypocrisy for a man to be forward and earnest in pressing other men to forgive their debtors, and yet is himself hard-hearted to his own debtors. They are in some respects like those notorious hypocrites who laid such burdens on other men's shoulders as they themselves would not move with one of their fingers. The hard-heartedness of these men to their own debtors is so much the more offensive and inexcusable by how much more earnest they are with others to forgive. The apostle's severe reproach against such as did not themselves practice that which they taught others may fitly be applied to these hypocrites.

The last point observable in the condition annexed to the fifth petition is the note of resemblance, "as," that remains to be handled.

The Force of This Particle "As" in the Condition Annexed to the Fifth Petition

QUESTION. What does this particle "as" import, whereby the condition is limited to the petition?

ANSWER. A resemblance between God's dealing with us and our dealing with others. This resemblance does not consist in equality, quantity, or measure, but in equity, quality and manner; that as God, according to His surpassing greatness, is merciful, so we, according to our poor and mean ability, should also be merciful, though not in such a degree, yet in such truth, and that freely and fully, as God forgives.

This note of resemblance, therefore, is not here used as it was in the third petition, for...

1. There that from whence the resemblance is taken is more eminent. Here it is much meaner. It is there taken from those who are in heaven. But here it is taken from us on earth.

2. There it notes a pattern for doing. Here it notes an evidence of doing.

3. There it is used for direction, to show what we should do. Here it is for imitation, to declare what we endeavor to do.

QUESTION. Does not the manner of setting down this resemblance by way of condition import that our forgiving goes before God's?

ANSWER. No, for it has relation to our assurance of God's forgiving us, not to the act of forgiving as it is in God Himself. It is as if more amply we should say, "Lord, by that readiness that Thy Spirit has wrought in us to forgive our debtors, we have an evidence of Thy readiness to forgive us. In faith therefore we crave forgiveness of Thee." After this manner the apostle reasons in these words: "Hereby know we that we dwell in Him, and He in us, because He hath given us of His Spirit."

To forgive our brother is a fruit of brotherly love. Brotherly love sprouts from our love of God. But we love God because He loved us first. God's love therefore goes before our love. And God forgives us before we forgive our brother. But as the life of a tree that causes the fruit thereof is discerned by the fruit, so God's love in forgiving us, that causes us to forgive our brother, is discerned by our forgiving of our brother, and thereby also we come to have assurance thereof.

OBJECTION. St. Luke sets down this clause with a causal particle thus, "for we also forgive," whereby he implies that our forgiving one another is a cause that moves God to forgive us. And if it is a cause it must go before. For the cause is before the effect, at least, in order of nature.

ANSWER. That particle "for" does not always note the cause, but many times the effect, especially when the effect is a sign and evidence of the cause. As where Christ said of that deeply penitent women, "Her sins which are many are forgiven, for she loved much." That her love is there noted as an effect of God's forgiving her is evident by the question going before and the answer made thereto. The question was this: "A creditor had two debtors; the one owed five hundred pence and the other fifty. And when they had nothing to pay he frankly forgave them both. Tell me, which of them will love him most?" The answer was this: "He to whom he forgave most." Is not love in this question and answer expressly noted to be the effect of forgiveness? In the same sense respect and relation is love used in this application of that parable: "Her sins which are many are forgiven, for she loved much." Her much love declares that many sins are forgiven her. Thus is this Particle "for" ordinarily used as a note of the effect or sign in our common speech, as when we say things like, "There is fire for I see smoke. This tree has life for it sprouts. The sun is risen for, behold, sunshine."

True and Unfeigned Forgiving One Another

QUESTION. What doctrines does the resemblance between God's forgiving and ours import?

ANSWER. We must in truth forgive one another. Thus does God; thus may we forgive. Thus, as we say, must we be like God and forgive as He forgives. If we do not do so we lie in saying, "Forgive us as we forgive." We are expressly charged not to love in word or in tongue, but in deed and truth. But more particularly for this purpose, Christ expressly notes that forgiveness must be from the hearts of men.

Truth is a kind of perfection in this and all other duties, the best and greatest perfection that in this world we can attain to. It seasons and sweetens that little that we are able to do and makes it acceptable to God. Without this season and savor of truth all the show of forgiveness that we make is odious and detestable unto God; neither can it bring any comfort to our own souls. God is a searcher of the heart. He who would have his forgiveness acceptable to God must from the heart forgive. He who forgives with his tongue that which he retains in his heart forgives for man's sake, but does not respect God.

How many are there whose forgiveness, if it is tried by this touchstone of truth, will be found to be plain counterfeit, and so worth nothing? Counterfeit forgiveness is far unlike God's. It cannot be pleaded in prayer, nor can it give assurance of God's forgiving us. Yet the forgiveness of most is no better.

Some think they do very well if they forbear to take outward revenge, though they retain an inward grudge and secret hatred. This may be something to man, who does not know the thoughts of the heart; but to God, the searcher of hearts, it is as nothing. And if as nothing to Him to whom (if to any) it is pleaded in prayer, in what stead will it stand? Surely in no other stead, than to be as a witness against him at the judgment seat of God. For when a man outwardly restrains that which inwardly he retains, his outward forbearance shows that in his judgment he disallows that which he keeps in his heart. Thus he is made a witness against himself. Is not his secret corruption the more aggravated hereby? And shall not his condemnation be the more increased?

Yet greater shall their condemnation be who carry a fair face and make show of forgiveness when they retain a full purpose of taking revenge, only they put it off to some opportunity, as Esau put off the revenge he intended against his brother until the death of their father. This putting off of revenge until an opportunity arises show that it is no small revenge that they intend, as appeared by that which Esau said, "Then will I slay my brother." And it implies a settled resolution to do it, though for a time there was something that hindered them. What is this but settled anger, settled hatred, and settled malice? By these circumstances the sin is made much more heinous.

But what may be thought of them who make pretense of forgiving to be a means of taking revenge, as Joab did when he took Abner aside to speak with him quietly and smote him under the first rib; and when he took Amasa by the beard to kiss him and shed out his bowels; and as Absalom did who invited Amnon to a feast where he caused him to be slain. If such should use this petition they would thereby make a fearful imprecation against their own souls. A mere show of forgiveness without truth makes God to take the greater revenge on them.

Let men therefore forgive in truth as God does, or not seem to forgive at all.

Forgiving One Another Freely

QUESTION. What other doctrine does the resemblance between God's forgiving and ours import?

ANSWER. We must freely forgive one another. The word "forgive" applied to God implies as much. We therefore professing to forgive as God forgives must forgive freely, not on by-respects, not as forced, not for outward recompense, or advantage to ourselves, but for the Lord's sake, for love's sake, and for his sake whom we forgive. Where the apostle, before this duty of forgiveness, premises kindness and tenderness, saying, "Be kind one to another and tender-hearted, forgiving one another," he gives us to understand that it must be freely done; which is further enforced by the pattern of God that he sets before us in these words, "Even as God for Christ's sake forgave you." That which God does for Christ's sake He does most freely. This pattern the apostle himself exactly followed. For where he makes mention of his own forgiving another he says, "I forgave in the person, or in the sight of Christ, that is, freely heartily, approving myself to Christ therein, in whose presence I stood."

A kindness freely done is a double kindness, much more acceptable to God who loves him who does what he does cheerfully and willingly; and much more grateful to him to whom it is done. He who has a good eye, and thereby manifests willingness and cheerfulness in that good which he does, shall be blessed. But a man of evil eye makes the good that he does to be vomited up.

That in this particular we may indeed do as we profess to do, that is, freely forgive others as God freely forgives us, let us duly weigh the excellence of the pattern here set before us, the great difference between a free and forced kindness, the glory of this kind of forgiving (the more free it is the more divine it is), the great need wherein we stand of a free forgiveness (did not God freely forgive us we could look for no forgiveness at all), and the great benefit that thereby redounds to us. For that which is freely done brings much comfort to the soul of him who does it, makes other men the more to commend it, and moves God the more graciously to accept it and the more abundantly to reward and recompense it.

To show how ready we are freely for the Lord's sake, for conscience sake, not on by-respects, to forgive having to do with such wrong doers as are stout and will not ask forgiveness or seek reconciliation, we, even we who have received wrong must offer it, as St. Paul did to the Galatians and David to Saul. The phrases of seeking and pursuing peace imply as much. We seek things that are not offered to us and we pursue things that fly from us. The apostle presses this duty on us to the very utmost of our endeavor. "If it be possible," he says, "as much as in you lieth live peaceably with all men." God offers reconciliation to us, and beseeches us by His ministers to be reconciled to Him. If therefore we will be followers of God, and forgive as God forgives, we must not always stay until he who has done the wrong comes and asks forgiveness. Thus may we meet with such as we shall never forgive, and so deprive ourselves of the glory of this work of mercy.

A Full Forgiving of One Another

QUESTION. What third doctrine does the resemblance between God's forgiving and ours import?

ANSWER. Wrongs must be so passed over as if they had not been done. This is a full forgiveness answerable to God's, who so fully acquits us of our sins as if we had committed no sin at all. Our forgiveness therefore, by virtue of the foresaid resemblance, must extend itself not to some part only, but to the whole debt or wrong, and that with such a mind as if no debt had been due, no wrong done. Where the apostle to them who by starting from the gospel that he had taught had exceedingly wronged his ministry says, "Brethren, I beseech you, be as I am, for I am as ye are; ye have not injured me at all," does he not fully forgive the wrong, even so fully as if at all they had not wronged him at all? Thus much the same apostle requires of Philemon in regard of the wrong that his servant Onesimus had done him. So Joseph and Moses passed over the offences of their brethren. They so accepted and esteemed them as if they had done no wrong at all.

QUESTION. What if by the wrong a man does me I observe such infirmity, yea, and iniquity to be in him as by experience I find him to be a far other man than at first I supposed him to be. Ought I, notwithstanding, to make such account of him as I did before?

ANSWER. We must put a difference between a wrong done upon such an occasion as may afterwards be avoided, and that which is done upon an evil disposition, which remaining in a man may be a means to make him continue to do more and more wrongs. The wrong of the former must be so forgiven as the wrong doer is so accepted as if he had done no wrong at all. As for the latter, we are to try if he may be brought to sight of his evil disposition, and to repentance for the same. If he is, then we ought to esteem him as if he never had done us any hurt. But if he obstinately persists in that evil disposition and on all occasions again and again wrongs us, though we do, as we ought, fully forgive all the wrongs done, and neither take any present revenge nor keep them in mind and memory for any future revenge, yet we may in our judgment esteem him to be such a one as we find him to be. (Woe to them who call evil good, who put light for darkness and sweet for bitter.) For example, if I find one of whom I have had a very good account, and thereupon used him very familiarly, to have no command of his tongue, but on all occasions to be ready to blab out and blaze abroad whatever he sees or hears, if therein he has wronged me I may forbear to use him so familiarly as I did before, and take heed what secrets I communicate to him, though I fully forgive the wrong that is past. Or if I have accounted one to be an entire friend to me, but by experience find him to be hollow-hearted and maliciously minded against me, I ought wisely and warily to avoid his company, and to take heed of the snares that he lays for me (for which we have the pattern of David and Christ), yet so to pass by the wrongs done as if none had been done.

For attaining to this degree of forgiveness, that our forgiving may be as full as God's…

1. Revenge must be purged out of the heart. The heart is the fountain. If that is cleansed the streams will be clear.

2. Wrong must be put out of mind and memory so far as possibly can be. Things forgotten are as things not done.

3. No needful kindness must be denied to him who has wronged us.

4. Occasions of doing good to wrong doers must not only be taken, but sought. Readiness and willingness to do all offices of courtesy and charity to such as are ready to do all the mischief and injury that they can unto us shows that no revenge lurks in our hearts. Continual fruits of love cannot issue out of a revengeful heart.

The several points of the condition annexed to the fifth petition having been distinctly handled, for better clearing thereof sundry questions about proper debts, lawsuits, and execution of justice are to be resolved.

Requiring Proper Debts

QUESTION. May a Christian require debts of money or other like things due to him?

ANSWER. He may, for…

1. The law of God gives liberty to a creditor to take a pledge of the debtor for security of paying the debt in case the debtor is not very poor and the pledge is such a one as he cannot spare.

2. Debtors are commanded to pay their debts. Creditors therefore may take them.

3. God extraordinarily provided for a poor widow wherewithal she might pay her debt. Had it been unlawful for a creditor to require his debt, God would rather have provided means to restrain him from exacting the debt than for her to pay the debt.

QUESTION. How can requiring debts and forgiving debtors stand together?

ANSWER 1. Forgiveness here professed has respect rather to wrongs done than to commodities due. The word “debtors” is used metaphorically by way of resemblance. For he who does wrong makes himself, as a debtor, bound to some penalty for the wrong he has done. St. Mathew in his exposition of this condition uses a word that in relation to man signifies offences, wrongs, or injuries.

ANSWER 2. It restrains all revenge in exacting due debts. Whatever wrong we conceive to be done to us by not paying the debt must so far be forborne as we take no revenge thereof. We may not hate, revile, or evilly entreat our debtors for not paying their debts.

ANSWER 3. It keeps our exacting of debts within the compass of mercy. So that in case the debtor is in no way able to pay the debt we rather forgive it than by hard and cruel means utterly undo him by laying executions upon all he has or keeping him under perpetual imprisonment.

OBJECTION. It is Christ’s expressed charge to lend hoping for nothing again. How then may a debt be required if it may not be looked for again?

ANSWER 1. That, as other like precepts in Christ's Sermon on the Mount, is not simply, but comparatively to be taken. We should be so far from the cruel usurer's mind who is resolved to have both principal and interest or, rather than fail of either, to do what he can in strictest rigor of law against principal and surety, we should be so far from such a mind as not to look for anything, no, not for the principal again.

ANSWER 2. That precept is laid down as a rule of love and is according to the rule of love to be taken. Now love requires mercy to be shown to him who needs it. The rule of love is, on the one side, my brother's necessity, and on the other my own ability. This the apostle implies in this instance, "Who so hath this world's goods (there is a man's ability) and seeth his brother hath need" (here is his brother's necessity). On this ground, when a man lends he must be so mercifully minded that if his debtor falls into extreme poverty and is not able to pay what he has borrowed he will be willing to remit the whole debt, and in such a case not so much as to look for anything again.

ANSWER 3. Some restrain that general particle as if we should expect nothing of interest and surplus, as if he had said, "Lend, hoping for nothing above the principal, or for nothing by way of interest." In this sense it does not argue against the forenamed position of requiring a man's due debt, interest being no due debt, but forbidden by God's Word.

Going to Law

QUESTION. May a Christian by law exact his due debt in case his debtor is able, but willfull and refuses to pay it?

ANSWER. Yea, he may. For public magistrates and judges who have power to determine cases in law are of God. God has appointed them to force such as are willfull and obstinate to do that which is just and right, and to give to everyone his own;

yea, and He has commanded His people in matters of controversy to stand to the determination of the judge.

OBJECTION. St. Paul blamed the Corinthians for going to law one with another.

ANSWER. Going to law is not there simply blamed and forbidden, but sundry abuses thereof, such as…

1. Going to unfit judges (whom the apostle calls unjust and unbelievers) and bringing Christians before them.

2. Contending about small matters and mere trifles, even about words and light damages.

3. Too much forwardness to law, when law is the first remedy that is used for getting that which a man conceives to be his right. Many are so forward that secretly, without any notice given to the party sued, they will steal a judgment.

4. Doing wrong themselves. Even they who went to law were wrongdoers, as the apostle says, "you do wrong." Many who do wrong to others complain and commence a lawsuit against those to whom they do the wrong to color the wrong that they themselves do, and to get advantage for doing the greater mischief.

QUESTION. So in what cases may Christians go to law?

ANSWER 1. In matters of importance that are too hard for private Christians to decide.

ANSWER 2. When we have to do with obstinate persons who will be brought to nothing but what they are forced unto. St. Paul having to do with such was forced to appeal to Caesar.

ANSWER 3. After all private means that we can think of have been used. So law must be used in the last place, as the last remedy. After one has admonished a brother secretly, yea, and taken the help of some few friends, and yet he remains obstinate, Christ advises us to tell such as are in authority.

This may be done provided that all lawsuits are made in love. Let all your things be done in charity. Many are of the opinion that no man can go to law in charity, but they are grossly deceived. For he who justly and rightly goes to law at least supposes that he has right on his side, and that the party whom he sues did wrong in that for which he is sued. Now to bring a wrongdoer to do right is a duty and fruit of love.

Suing in law has respect only to that particular thing that is in question. But charity extends itself to all things wherein one may be profitable to another. The man who in one particular seeks to have from another that which of right belongs to him may in all other things be ready to do what good he can to that other.

The manner of prosecuting a lawsuit may be, as with all equity, so with much tenderness, mildness, and compassion and so that very particular is done in love.

ANSWER 4. In a doubtful case questioned in law a man may be so willing to stand to the sentence of law as to be content either way, whether it goes with him or against him. Yea, if it appears that right is on his adversary's side, to be glad that the law has discovered right even against himself. Does not this show much love? Wherefore though by the apostle's prohibition we are taught as much as may be to forbear law, to suffer some loss, to bear with some wrong, and in some things to part with our rights, yet on the forenamed grounds, and with the forenamed proviso, it is both lawful and expedient to seek the help of law, the ends whereof are very good: To defend the innocent, to relieve the oppressed, to punish the evil doers, to decide doubts, to determine rights, and to give everyone their own.

Magistrates Punishing Wrong

QUESTION. May wrong done to a man be punished?

ANSWER. Yea, by such as have authority. The Lord has given to magistrates, and such as are in authority, the power that of right belongs to them for this end, to punish evil doers. They who have so done have been commended for it. They who have been negligent therein have themselves been punished of God. He to whom the wrong is done may forgive the wrong done, and yet the magistrate punish him.

QUESTION. May magistrates punish wrong done to themselves?

ANSWER. Yea, also, for the office of a magistrate may be distinguished from his person. The wrong is done to his person; the punishment is taken by virtue of his place and office. The wrong for which Solomon commanded Adonijah to be slain, and Abiathar to be removed from the priesthood, was against himself. And the particular occasion that he took of putting Joab to death was conspiracy with Adonijah against himself.

QUESTION. How then are magistrates tied to forgiving their debtors?

ANSWER. By being restrained from private revenge. In which respect David blessed God for keeping him from revenging himself with his own hand. We must distinguish between public justice and private revenge. That arises from judgment, this from wrath. That is accompanied with love, this with hatred. That is done in God's name; this is a man's own. All private revenge, though no outward hurt or wrong is done thereby, is a sin in the revenging party because of the inward corruption whence it arises. Much hurt may fall on a delinquent by public justice and yet no sin in the execution thereof because it may stand with equity, pity, mercy, and charity; and it may aim at the good of the party punished, yea, and turn to his good also. A malefactor may be accused, condemned, and punished with stripes, fine, imprisonment, banishment, excommunication, death, or otherwise, and yet the bonds of mercy and love not be transgressed. Thus may lawsuits be made, and obstinate or negligent debtors cast into prison, as these are parts of public justice, and yet the condition of the fifth petition not be violated, if anger, hatred, malice, revenge and such like corruptions do not taint the foresaid execution of justice.

The distinct points of the forenamed condition having all been handled, the main scope and just consequence thereof is further to be considered.

Imitating God in Forgiving Wrongs

QUESTION. Why is the condition annexed to the fifth petition?

ANSWER. To move us to forgive one another and to give us assurance of God's forgiving us.

It must be a strong motive in that all the evidence that we can have of God's mercy in forgiving us arises from our ready mind and forward disposition to forgive others. If we forgive men, God will forgive us. If we do not forgive men, God will not forgive us. Our Lord therefore enjoins us to make this profession, "as we forgive," that we, knowing and believing God's indulgence and readiness to forgive us, might be moved to do the like for others; and might not dare to approach the mercy seat of God to crave pardon of Him unless our conscience can and does bear witness for us that we are on all occasions ready to grant pardon to such as wrong us.

QUESTION. What doctrine does the first end of the condition added to the fifth petition afford?

ANSWER. God's mercy to man is a powerful motive for man to show mercy to man. Therefore God's practice is often set as a pattern before men. Forgive one another as God has forgiven you. Be merciful as your Father is merciful. Walk in love as Christ has loved us. Be followers of God. Be perfect, as your Father in heaven is perfect.

Two special things there are in God's pattern that are of great force to move us to imitate Him.

1. The infinite difference that is between Him and us.

2. The infinite debt wherein we stand bound to His justice.

Such is the surpassing excellence of God, such the brightness of His majesty, such the absolute supremacy of His sovereignty, such the omnipotence of His power, such His all-sufficiency, that man compared to God is but dust and ashes, vile, wretched and miserable. Yea, all nations before Him are as nothing, and they are counted to Him as less than nothing. What man is, he is of God. God is our Creator, we the work of His hands. He is our Sovereign, we His subjects. Between man and man there is no such difference. All, in relation to God the high Lord, are fellow servants. Though in a mutual relation one to another there are some differences, as between magistrates and subjects, masters and servants, parents and children, yet those differences are but external and temporal. They are external, in the affairs of this world, for outward order and government (in Jesus Christ all are one). They are temporal, for the time of this world (after this life the servant is free from his master). All are as angels, yea, all children of Adam, as in the points of their humiliation they are from the same mold, of the same corrupt nature, subject to the same infirmities, at length brought to the same end, so in the points of their exaltation they are all (I speak of the several sorts and kinds of men, not of every particular person), they are all made after the same Image, redeemed by the same price, partakers of the same grace, and heirs of the same inheritance. If then God, the Creator of all, and Supreme Lord over all, who stands in no need of anything that man can do, nor can reap any benefit from man, who never wronged any nor needs forgiveness, if God can forgive man, shall not man forgive man, one creature another, one fellow-servant another, man who needs man's help and may reap much good by mutual agreement and reconciliation with man, who often wrongs another, and needs to be forgiven of others—shall not man forgive man, man who daily sins against God? As the difference between God in relation to man, and man in relation to other men, is beyond comparison, so also is the debt that man owes to God and that which one man owes to another. In the parable the debt due to the Lord is said to be ten thousand talents and the debt due to the servant a hundred pence. Among men there is some difference between talents and pence and between ten thousand and one hundred. So that parable sets out a great difference between the debt wherein we stand bound to God and that which one man owes to another.

And this difference greatly enforces the motive taken from God's example. If God forgives talents, shall not we forgive pence? If God forgives ten thousand, shall not we forgive one hundred? But this difference is only in a parable. In truth there is infinitely more difference between the sins that we commit against God and the wrongs that one man does to another in weight than between talents and pence; and in number than between ten thousand and one hundred. Our sins for weight are infinite, being committed against an infinite Majesty. The penalty due to them is God's infinite wrath, the infinite curse of the law, eternal damnation. No such wrong can possibly be done to man. As for the number of our sins, it is innumerable. They are more than the hairs of our head. No man can do so many wrongs to us as we daily commit sins against God. On these and other like grounds might the Lord well say to his hard-hearted servant, "I forgave thee. Shouldest not thou also have had compassion on thy fellow-servant, even as I had pity on thee?" Considering the great things we receive for small, let us not be slack to forgive one another.

This pattern of God is duly to be weighed, and often to be meditated on. Good patterns and precedents, as they give good directions, so they are great inducements to stir us up to do a thing, especially when they are the examples of such as we have just cause highly to esteem. Now who is more highly to be esteemed than God? What more worthy pattern can there be? It is a high honor to be like God and to do as He does. God's example is a perfect pattern, and in that respect is to be followed; yea, so much the rather because it takes away all those pretences that men allege for justifying their revenge and not forgiving such as wrong them.

Their pretenses are such as these:

1. He who has wronged me is a base fellow.

ANSWER. What is more base to you than you are to God?

2. The wrong done is insufferable.

ANSWER. What is more insufferable than your sins against God?

3. It is not the first time that he has wronged me.

ANSWER. Did you never but once sin against God?

4. He may wrong me again and again if I put up with it.

ANSWER. Why do you think so uncharitably of your brother? But might you not sin again and again against God?

5. It is not becoming my place and honor to put up wrongs.

ANSWER. Is your place and honor greater than God's?

6. I shall be counted a coward if I do not revenge wrongs.

ANSWER. Is God so accounted for bearing with your sins?

If God does thus, why are you so greatly incensed with wrath when any does any wrong to you? You should rather behold yourself, how you have carried yourself against God. If anything will make you forgive, surely this will.

Praying Without Revenge and Praying for Revenge

QUESTION. What other doctrine does the said end of the condition added to the fifth petition import?

ANSWER. Prayer may not be made for pardon with a revengeful mind. For we are bound to make profession of forgiving our debtors so often as we pray for pardon of our sins. The charge of lifting up pure hands without wrath tends to this purpose. So also does the charge of leaving the gift before the altar and being first reconciled if we remember that our brother has ought against us. This phrase, "hath ought against thee," is a legal term and implies a lawsuit or a difference. So is it used by St. Paul in his apology before Felix. "They ought to have been here before thee and object if they had ought against me." So the reconciliation required is in a variance whether we have done or received wrong. Satisfaction must be made for the wrong that a man does. Remission must be granted to the wrong that is done to a man. He who refuses to do the one or the other, if he says the Lord's Prayer, makes a fearful imprecation against himself, as we shall hereafter more distinctly show. "Let not therefore that man think that he shall receive anything of the Lord." The God of peace does not accept the sacrifice of him who is at variance.

OBJECTION. Is prayer then to be omitted when by a wrong done passion is moved?

ANSWER. A double sin would so be committed, one by omitting a bound duty, he other by persisting in a hateful sin. The only warrantable and comfortable course in that case is to subdue passion, to cast off desire for revenge. Breach of charity gives no dispensation for neglect of piety. Christ's charge is this: "First be reconciled, then come and offer thy gift." Let this be well noted of such as forbear to come to the Lord's Table because they are not in charity, an unchristian practice.

On this ground, as at all times, so especially when we draw near to the throne of grace, we ought to keep a narrow watch so that anger, wrath, envy, malice, and revenge do not enter into us. Yea, then especially we ought thoroughly to search and examine ourselves whether those or any other like evil qualities have been bred in us or have entered into us, and still remain lurking in us. First purge them out before you pray. God prefers mercy before sacrifice. He who comes to offer a sacrifice, being at variance, God calls away from His altar. Those who fast for strife and debate God does not regard; neither will He hear the many prayers of those whose hands are full of blood. For "the wrath of man worketh not the righteousness of God."

What now may we say or think of such as pray for vengeance to fall upon others? Surely their prayers are odious in

God's sight, and thereby they pull vengeance on their own heads, which they do much more who by prayer, vow, and sacrament bind themselves to do mischief and take revenge, yea, and that upon their sovereign and kingdom where they live, as Jesuits and other papists often do. It is probable that they whose blood Pilate mingled with their sacrifices did so and that that kind of punishment as a just recompense was by the divine providence inflicted on them. As a man loves cursing, so shall it come unto him; as he clothes himself with cursing, so shall it come into his bowels like water, and like oil into his bones.

The Assurance That Our Forgiving Gives of God's Forgiving Us

QUESTION. What doctrine does the other end of the condition annexed to the fifth petition afford?

ANSWER. Man's forgiving his brother gives assurance of God's forgiving him. This is one main end of adding this condition of our forgiving our brother to our desire of God's forgiving us, as is evident by that causal particle "for," which St. Luke sets before it thus, "For we also forgive." The reference that Christ makes immediately after this prayer makes the point most clear. His inference is this: "If ye forgive men their trespasses, your heavenly Father will also forgive you." Does He not thereby imply that by forgiving men we gain assurance of God's forgiving us? On this ground Nehemiah in his prayer to God pled the kindness that he had shown to the people of God.

OBJECTION. Many heathen and other mere carnal men who could have no assurance of the forgiveness of their sins have forgiven many wrongs done to them.

ANSWER. Their forgiving is not true forgiving because it arises from by-respects to themselves, and not from brotherly love, much less from conscience and due respect to God. For if their kind of forgiving is duly weighed it will be found to be:

1. Either in some slight matters that do not much provoke wrath or greatly need forgiveness, or

2. To some friend, kinsman, or such like person, who in some outward respect they like and love, or

3. For hope of some recompense and advantage to themselves, or

4. For fear of greater mischief that might ensue if they should manifest any thought of revenge, or it may be

5. By reason of a heavy and dull disposition that makes them insensible of wrongs, like him that is brought in thus speaking, "They have stricken me and I was not sick; they have beaten me and I did not feel it."

True Christian forgiving is a part or branch of that wisdom that comes from above, a fruit of that Spirit that resides in Christ, an effect of God's forgiving us. Sons of men are by nature wrathful and revengeful. They are wrathful in that they are very soon, upon every small and slight occasion provoked to wrath, as dry tinder is ready to be fired by the least spark. They are revengeful in that, being provoked, they are as it were, on fire with revenge, like gunpowder, that as soon as it has taken any fire is instantly all aflame. The apostle, among other properties of a natural man, reckons these: maliciousness, envy, debate, malignity (whereby all things are taken in an evil part), implacableness, and unmercifulness. And in another place to the same purpose he said that we are hateful, hating one another. In regard of this wrathful and revengeful disposition, men are resembled to wolves, leopards, bears, lions, asps, and dragons. Unless this nature is altered it is no more possible for a man in true brotherly love to forgive than for one of the forenamed savage creatures to be quiet and do no hurt when they are stirred up and provoked. Nature must be altered before a wrong can be thoroughly and rightly passed by and forgiven. This alteration of nature proceeds from an apprehension of God's love to us in Christ, and that in pardoning our sins.

For the love of God shed abroad in our hearts by the Holy Ghost is as fire that warms our hearts, thawing out the hard frost of hatred and revenge, and making them pliable to God's heart and affection to us, merciful as He is merciful, kind, gentle and patient as He is, forbearing wrongs and forgiving debts as He does. Hence then it follows that if our disposition is inclined to forgive, and if according to that inclination we in truth actually forgive, we may be assured that God has forgiven us, even as when we find a cold thing hot we may infer that it has been heated.

Learn hereby how to know God's mind towards you. You need not climb up to heaven there to behold the face of God whether He frowns or smiles, whether love or anger is seated in His eyes, but dive into your own heart and there observe what is your mind towards your brother. No looking glass can give a truer representation of your face than your own heart, a demonstration of God's heart towards you. We love because He first loved us; and we forgive because He first forgave us.

Well may we hereby comfort our souls in the day of temptation when the conscience is perplexed with doubting your pardon. If you find in yourself a readiness to forgive your brother, you may conclude that God has forgiven you. To strengthen your faith herein, duly weigh the infinite disparity between God's goodness and yours. This is as an ocean that has no bottom, no bounds; yours is but as a drop. If then you for His sake out of your drop of goodness can afford forgiveness answerable to the wrongs done to you, may you not infer that God out of His bottomless ocean will afford forgiveness answerable to the sins that you have committed against Him? When your conscience is burdened with the heavy weight of your sins, think of your willingness to forgive your brother, and from thence as from a sign, effect, or evidence learn to quiet your conscience and settle your faith, and in faith say, "Forgive me as I forgive," or, "Forgive me, for I forgive. It is indeed but little mercy that I have shown, for my nature was capable of no more. But Thy bounty is not hindered by want of power. Thou canst grant as much as Thou wilt." Thus may the heart be enlarged in craving pardon, and faith settled in obtaining it.

And because this is such a special means to resolve your soul of the pardon of your sins, be the rather moved to subdue your passion when you are provoked to cast out wrath and readily to forgive. Seeing it is requisite that we offer up prayers to God for mercy and pardon, let us by the testimony of our conscience get to ourselves that we may make our carriage an advocate to our prayers and truly say, "We also forgive our debtors." They who feel the weight of sin would give all they have, and do what possibly they could, to be eased thereof. If you never felt the burden of sin on your own soul, inquire after such as are wounded in conscience; and, because things seen are more sensible, and make a deeper impression, go to them, mark their agonies and their outcries; thereby judge what a heavy burden sin is when the soul feels the burden of it. Once you feel the weight of it, I make no question but that, if Christ should ask you, as once He asked a blind man, "What wilt thou that I should do to thee?" you would answer, "Lord, that I may be eased of the burden of sin." Behold here how you may be eased. As any occasion is offered, forgive. Thus in doing goodness to man you do the best and greatest goodness to yourself, in that God (whose goodness infinitely surpasses yours) is moved thereby to do good to you. This is a great encouragement, a ground of much comfort, to such as can and do forgive men. Though they have no recompense from man, though they are laughed at for it, yea, though they are worse dealt with (as David was) and more wronged because they are so ready to forgive, yet God's gracious acceptance thereof and His merciful dealing with them for it is recompense enough.

The Revenge That Revengeful Persons Bring Upon Themselves

QUESTION. What doctrine follows as just consequence from the forenamed condition?

ANSWER. They who do not forgive men are not forgiven of God. Bring that which is here intended by Christ into a true, logical, syllogistic form and the consequence will appear to be most just. The form is this: "Forgive us as we forgive others. But we do not forgive others. Therefore do not forgive us." The proposition is expressed in the Lord's Prayer. The assumption is deduced out of the inward disposition and outward practice of the revengeful person. The conclusion flows from the premises by just and necessary consequence. Yet further to confirm this conclusion, and to show that it is not wrested, let it be noted how Christ immediately after this prayer expressly infers as much in these words, "If ye forgive not men their trespasses, neither will your Father forgive you your trespasses." In the parable you find as much verified. For the Lord delivered that servant who would not forgive his fellow servant to the tormenters till he should pay all that was due to him. Thereupon Christ makes this inference, "So likewise shall My heavenly Father do also unto you, if ye from your hearts forgive not everyone his brother their trespasses."

It is God's usual manner to deal with men according to their dealing one with another. These proverbial speeches import as much: "With what measure you mete it shall be measured to you again. Whatsoever a man soweth that shall he reap. He shall have judgment without mercy that hath showed no mercy." Dives, who denied to Lazarus the crumbs that fell from his table, was denied a drop of cold water to cool his tongue. For man is to man in God's stead. By our carriage to man God takes trial of our disposition to Him. Whereupon St. John says, "Whoso hath this world's goods, and seeth his brother hath need, and shutteth up his bowels of compassion from him, how dwelleth the love of God in him? For he that loveth not his brother whom he hath seen, how can he love God whom he hath not seen?"

God's mercy is operative as fire: it warms that heart in which it abides, and works mercy therein. Where therefore no mercy to man can be found, there is just cause to suspect no mercy of God has been shown. The soul of an unmerciful man is no fit receptacle of the mercies of God. It abuses and perverts them.

Behold here the folly of cruel, hard-hearted, and revengeful persons who, like the unmerciful servant, deny that to their brother that they crave of God. What can they look for of God but such measure as was meted out to the said servant and to Dives? They therefore who deal unmercifully with others do most harm to themselves because thereby they provoke God to deal unmercifully with them. Consider this, O wrathful and revengeful persons. The time may come when you will as earnestly desire one drop of God's mercy as Dives desired a drop of water to cool his tongue; and yet you shall have your desire no more satisfied than his was.

This consequence of God's retaining their sins who do not forgive their brethren much enforces the fore-mentioned exhortation to forgive. As there was shown the great advantage of forgiving others (which is assurance of God's forgiving them), so here is declared the great damage of not forgiving, which is a strict exaction of the utmost penalty for all that debt wherein we stand bound to God's justice. He who from his heart does not forgive his brother who has offended him, by this petition procures to himself not absolution, but condemnation, and by his own profession causes himself to be more severely judged. For he turns his petition for himself into a fearful imprecation against himself; and whatever his words may be, in effect he prays that God would not forgive him. He turns the sense of this word, "forgive," to be, "do not forgive." Is not this the ready way to pull vengeance upon his own head for all the sins whereof in any kind he stands guilty before God? Woeful in this respect is the plight of those who are so possessed by revenge that they cannot forgive. How insensible of their good or hurt are they on whom these motives work nothing at all! Oh, be moved, even for avoiding this great mischief, to forgive; and take heed that by not forgiving your neighbor some small and light wrongs against you, you keep yourself from obtaining pardon of your heinous sins before God.

Deprecation Against Evil

QUESTION. What is to be observed about the order of the fifth petition?

ANSWER. That which it has in common with the sixth, and that which is proper to itself.

Two things are common to them both: the distinct kind and the general matter of them both is the same. The distinct kind wherein these two last petitions differ from all the rest is deprecation, that is, prayer for the removal of evil. In the fifth petition we pray to be freed from the guilt and punishment of sin. In the sixth we pray to be freed from the power and bondage of sin.

QUESTION. What do we hence learn?

ANSWER. Deprecation must be added to petition. We must be careful as well to pray against those evils which do or may annoy us as for those good things that may or do help us. This kind is expressly mentioned among the other warrantable kinds of prayer, and on all occasions it has been used by the saints. Accordingly it may and must be used by us, and that in regard of God's glory and our own good.

1. The glory of God's pity and power is much magnified hereby. Of His pity in that by going to Him in all our miseries we acknowledge Him to be a God of compassion, moved with our miseries; else we could have no heart to go to Him. The

servants of the King of Syria persuaded their lord, being overthrown in battle to go with sackcloth upon their loins and ropes upon their heads to the King of Israel on this ground: "We have heard that the kings of the house of Israel are merciful kings." Were we not persuaded that He to whom we go is pitiful and merciful, scarcely would we be moved to lay open our sores before Him. Well, mark the prayers of the saints and you shall find the mercy, pity and compassion of God much pleaded in them. The glory of God's power is also magnified by deprecations in that He is acknowledged to be for all turns able to do and able to undo. He is able to do that good for us that He sees to be needful for us, and able to undo that knot of misery wherewith through our own folly we are bound, and to break those snares wherewith we are entangled.

2. Our need requires that being in misery we should be delivered out of it, or else all the good that can be bestowed upon us will be but as a show or shadow of goodness; no sweetness thereof can be tasted; no benefit can be reaped thereby. Abraham, conceiving it to be a great misery to be childless, when God graciously promised him to be his shield and exceeding great reward answered, "What wilt Thou give me, seeing I go childless?" This supposed evil took away the sweetness from that exceeding great reward that was offered to him. The Israelites, being in grievous bondage, when Moses came to them in the name of the Lord to comfort them, did not hearken to him for anguish of spirit. All the delights that the heart of man can desire are as nothing to him who is sick at heart, or tortured with tormenting diseases, if he is not freed from that sickness and eased of that pain.

In what a desperate case may we now think them to be who, being in misery, either seek no help at all or, which is all one, seek help of such as can afford them no true help.

Of the former sort are...

1. Such as through a blockish stupidity, like beasts, lie under that evil that lies upon them and do not seem to be moved therewith, as those Jews of whom the prophet thus complains, "O Lord, Thou hast stricken them, but they have not grieved."

2. Such as through willful obstinacy are so far from praying to have the evil that is on them removed that, by continuing in sin, they bring more and more evil upon them. They are like Ahaz, who therefore is thus branded, "This is Ahaz."

3. Such as through a malicious impudence, when they are pinched and pressed with the evil that lies on them, blaspheme the name of God, as the profane King of Israel, and they who were tormented at the pouring out of the fourth vial, did.

Of the latter sort are…

1. Such as trust in means without God, as Asa, who did not go to the Lord, but to the physicians, and the Israelites who went down to Egypt for help, but did not seek the Lord.

2. Such as seek help of such things as have no power or virtue at all to help them in that for which help is sought; as they who, being troubled in conscience and wounded in soul, seek to ease themselves by merry company, music, gaming, and the like. So Saul, when the evil spirit came upon him, must have music; and the Baalites, when their request was not granted, leaped upon the altar and cut themselves with knives and lancers; and papists to like purposes whip themselves. Yea, also they seek to drive the devil away with holy water, holy oil, crucifixes, crossing themselves, and other like foolish toys.

3. Such as seek help of him who will take all advantages against them, and work them the more mischief for trusting him, even the Devil himself. All who go to witches, conjurers, sorcerers, and such instruments of Satan, for help in any need seek help of Satan. They are as Saul who went to the witch at Endor and Ahaziah who sent to Beelzebub.

All these, and other like helps, are no better than a reed, whereupon if a man leans it breaks, and rends his flesh who leans thereon.

For our part, therefore, let us take notice of the evils whereunto we are subject, and of the remedy warranted and sanctified for removing them, and wisely and conscionably use the same.

This deals with deprecation, which is the distinct kind of the two last petitions. The general matter of them both follows.

Taking Care for Our Spiritual Welfare

QUESTION. What is the general matter of the two last petitions?

ANSWER. Spiritual, such as concerns our souls. As in the fourth petition we were taught to pray for such temporal blessings as were meet for our bodies, and for our outward estate in this world, so in the fifth and sixth petitions we are taught to seek such spiritual blessings as concern the good of our soul, that he who is fed of God may live in God.

QUESTION. What are we taught hereby?

ANSWER. We must take care of our spiritual welfare. Care must be had for the good of our souls as well as of our bodies. Where Christ moves us to moderate our immoderate care for the things of this world He presses us earnestly to care for our souls. And that is not without just cause, for...

1. Our happiness consists in the spiritual welfare of our souls. "Blessed is the man unto whom the Lord imputeth not iniquity, and in whose spirit there is no guile."

2. Herein lies a main difference not only between reasonable and unreasonable creatures, or civil and savage men, or professors of true religion and idolaters, but also between all natural and spiritual men. The natural man, whether he lives in the church or out of it, minds only the things of this life. The things of the Spirit of God that concern his soul and the

spiritual good thereof, he does not receive for they are foolishness to him. Only the spiritual man, who is both in the church and of the church, enlightened and guided by that Spirit which is in the church, and in every part and member thereof, well discerning the things of the Spirit of God, tending to the happiness of his soul, carefully seeks after them.

The folly of most men is hereby discovered. For their care is wholly and only for the things of this life. They neglect their souls, as if they had no souls at all to care for, or did not care what became of them. Their own proverb verifies as much against them, which is this, "Let God take care for my soul, and I will take care for my body." This is a cursed proverb. In both the parts thereof it savors rank of atheistic profaneness. The latter part implies a desperate casting off of God's care for their bodies; the former, a presumptuous thrusting of their souls on God against that course that He has expressly prescribed.

Let us learn wisdom from this ground of wisdom taught by Him who is the wisdom of God. Let us not disjoin the care of these two sweet companions that God has so nearly linked together, our body and soul. Let both in their place and due manner be cared for. Let spiritual things be provided for the soul, which is a spiritual substance, as well as earthly things for the body that is of the earth. By that care that nature moves us to take for the temporal good of our bodies, we ought to be so far from resting therein as we ought rather to be raised up thereby to seek how we may procure good to our souls. Surely Christ, by inferring the petitions for our soul's good, immediately upon that which concerns the good of our bodies, intends thereby that by sense of our bodies need we should be made sensible of the soul's need.

For this end, let us…

1. Take notice of our spiritual needs. Ignorance of need makes men negligent of providing things that are needful.

Laodicea, not knowing that she was wretched, miserable, poor, blind, and naked, did not regard the gold that might make her rich, the white raiment that might cover the shame of her nakedness, and the eye salve that might make her see.

2. Inquire after the means of help. The wise man often greatly presses this duty of seeking and searching after the things that are needful and useful.

3. Conscionably and carefully use the means that are afforded for help. This was the counsel that Christ gave to the forenamed church of the Laodiceans, to buy gold tried in the fire, and white raiment, and to anoint her eyes with eye salve.

Doubling Our Care for the Good of Our Souls

QUESTION. Why are there two petitions for our spiritual good?

ANSWER. 1. The things concerning our spiritual estate are far more excellent, as the soul is more excellent than the body, and as things concerning eternal and heavenly happiness surpass such as concern only a temporal and earthly contentment. The merchant who sold all that he had to buy the treasure hidden in the field and the pearl of price was not ignorant hereof.

ANSWER 2. They are more absolutely necessary. We may want the temporal things of this world and yet not be miserable. God can turn that want to our advantage. But the want of spiritual blessings makes us extremely miserable. True happiness consists in the fruition of these. Yea, the happiness of our temporal welfare consists in our spiritual welfare. No benefit, no comfort can be received from all that this world affords unless sin is pardoned and we are freed from the power thereof.

ANSWER 3. We are by nature more dull and backward to seek after spiritual things than temporal ones. These are visible, and the sweetness of them is more sensible, sooner discerned, and more easily tasted. The other, being invisible, is more insensible. So we have more need to be the more earnest in seeking of them.

QUESTION. What are we taught hereby?

ANSWER. Our care for spiritual things must be double. With much more earnestness must we seek spiritual blessings over temporal blessings. It is of spiritual good things that Christ says, "First seek, etc." Both before and above all other things seek them. First, this not only notes out the order, but also the manner of seeking. It is of spiritual blessing that St. Peter says, "Rather give diligence, or give the more and greater diligence, to make them sure. Our mind must with the utmost of our endeavor, even with full bent, be carried that way.

A due consideration of this point manifests the blindness, and aggravates the folly, of them who prefer temporal before spiritual blessings. They are like the Gadarenes, who made more account of their swine than of Christ. Into this ship of fools may the following well be thrust:

1. Who put of the time for seeking the good of their souls, but will lose no time for advancing and increasing their temporal estate. They who put off their providing of oil until the hour wherein the bridegroom came are called foolish virgins.

2. Who put by the opportunities that by God's providence are afforded for doing good to their souls. Felix, who when by Paul's preaching his heart was so smitten as he trembled, said, "Go thy way for this time," and yet watched all opportunities for a bribe.

3. Who so eagerly pursue the things of this world wherein they take delight, or from whence they expect profit, as they neglect the care of their souls. Such a one was profane Esau, who followed the profits and pleasures of the field till he fainted, and then sold his birthright for a mess of pottage.

4. Such as seek the spiritual things of their soul, but so loosely and carelessly as if they did not care much for them.

These are like the lukewarm Laodiceans who can expect nothing but to be spewed out of the mouth of Christ.

Let us be otherwise minded: and for that end discern well between things that differ. Until the understanding is thoroughly informed in the difference of matters, and know which are the most excellent, the will cannot incline itself to one more than to another. This therefore the apostle prays for in the Philippians' behalf, to discern things that differ.

Wisely prefer the more excellent things. As David, who when others said, "Who will show us any good?" (meaning temporal goods) thus prayed to God, "Lord, lift Thou up the light of Thy countenance upon us."

Stir up the gift of God. That desire, that love, that delight that in any measure is in you towards the spiritual good things of your soul, nourish and increase that they neither decay nor die in you.

Help the weakness of nature. When the spirit is ready, the flesh will be backward. And when one would do good, evil is present with him. A law in the members wars against the law of the mind. This often makes us dull, heavy, and sluggish. Wherefore (as the wise man advised), when the iron is blunt, put to more strength.

Thus we have dealt with the general matter common to the two last petitions.

The Blessings That Pardon of Sin Brings

QUESTION. What proper thing is to be considered about the order of the fifth petition?

ANSWER. The inference of it upon the fourth and the precedence of it before the sixth.

QUESTION. What doctrine does that inference afford?

ANSWER. By pardon of sin the things of this world are made true blessings. All the things that in this prayer we are taught to crave are so to be craved as blessings. But sin is as deadly poison to daily bread. While it remains upon us unpardoned, nothing that this world affords can be a true blessing, for sin brings a curse upon every creature that we use. But pardon of sin takes away that curse, and so makes all that we use to be true blessings. That man therefore is pronounced blessed whose transgression is forgiven.

Learn hereby in the use of all temporal blessings to seek for pardon of sin. It is one end of grace before meat (according to the ancient and commendable custom of God's people) to have the curse taken away from the creatures we use, and to have them turned into a blessing. Do the same. Crave pardon of sin before you go about the work of your calling, before you take a journey, before you go to any recreation though you know it to be lawful and proper, before you go to bed, when you rise up, in all things, at all times seek remission of sin. Never think yourself well or safe, no, not in your greatest abundance or best prosperity, until you have assurance thereof. Sin that is not remitted lies as a bondage at the door and keeps all God's blessings from entering. Sin, like a cloud, hides from us the bright sunshine of God's favor. Sin, like the accursed thing that Achan stole, makes us a prey to our deadliest enemies. Sin, as the wild gourds, brings death with it, and that into such things as are otherwise wholesome and good. Sin, like that handwriting that on a wall appeared to Belshazzar, in the midst of our greatest jollity, will change countenance, trouble thoughts, loose joints, and make knees to smite one against another. Is there not then great and just cause in all things at all times to seek pardon thereof?

This was the inference of the fifth petition on the fourth.

The Precedence of Justification Before Sanctification

QUESTION. What doctrine does the precedence of the fifth petition before the sixth import?

ANSWER. Justification goes before sanctification, for the former of the two last petitions concerning our spiritual good set out our justification, the latter our sanctification. This precedence is to be applied rather to order than to time. For at that very moment that Christ pardons sin He conveys His Spirit into us whereby sin is mortified. St. Paul therefore, where he sets down these two together, sets righteousness before sanctification.

Justification causes sanctification, in which respect the apostle says that we are sanctified by faith in Christ, that is, faith uniting us to Christ, by whom we are justified, receive grace for grace, a further grace to sanctify us.

Sanctification declares justification, in which respect St. James says that we are justified by works, that is, declared so to be. As by virtue of our justification we are presented blameless before God, so by virtue of our sanctification we are declared to be righteous before men.

As the cause therefore goes before the effect, and as the effect follows the cause, so are justification and sanctification in their order one to another.

This order affords one sound argument against justification by works. All good works are parts of sanctification. If by the merit of them we are justified, sanctification must go before justification.

This order proves our justification to be free because in order of nature it goes before any good thing that we can do.

It also demonstrates the precedence of faith before acceptable repentance in order of nature. Faith is the instrument of our justification, repentance a principal grace of our sanctification.

It lays down the ground of pardon of sin, which is nothing in ourselves, but the mere free grace of God, which is to be pleaded for obtaining pardon.

Thus much of the order of the fifth petition. The particular good things to be craved are next to be declared.

Graces to Be Prayed for in Regard of the Pardon of Our Own Sins

QUESTION. What are the particular good things for which we are taught to pray by virtue of the fifth petition?

ANSWER. Such as concern the petition itself and such as concern the condition annexed to it. The things that concern the petition itself have respect to the pardon both of our own and of others' sins. For we are taught to say in the plural number and first person, "Forgive us our trespasses."

QUESTION. What are the things that concern the pardon of our own sins to be prayed for?

ANSWER. 1. Knowledge of the nature of sin, how horrible a thing it is, into what a woeful plight it brings the creature, making it a debtor to the revenging justice of God. For this end the law distinctly sets down the curses that by sin are pulled on man.

ANSWER 2. Knowledge of a man's own sins. How he himself, being guilty of sin, is a debtor to God, and in that respect in a most woeful estate. This David well knew when he said, "I know mine iniquity," and Job who said, "Behold, I am vile."

ANSWER 3. Sense of the burden of sin. All the knowledge that can be had of the horribleness of sin, and of the multitude and heinousness of the sins whereof we stand guilty, will not sufficiently move us to be eased of the burden of them until we feel the weight thereof lying on our own souls, and even oppressing them. This made David so earnestly desire God not to rebuke him in anger, for of that earnest plea he renders this reason, "Mine iniquities are gone over mine head, as a heavy burden they are too heavy for me."

ANSWER 4. A broken heart and contrite spirit. A man may feel the heavy burden of sin and yet not seek to be eased, but lie under it as a beast or as one who despairs of all help. But if the heart is truly broken and touched to the quick with the sense of sin, it will not let a man rest until he has obtained pardon. In that psalm where David most earnestly craves pardon, he shows that he had a broken heart.

ANSWER 5. Humble confession of sin, for this petition is a plain acknowledgement thereof. Without confession there is no hope of pardon; but promise of pardon is made to him who confesses his sin.

ANSWER 6. Earnest desire of pardon, that we may be freed from the guilt and punishment of sin. To confess sin and not to desire pardon is but to put in evidence against ourselves. This is that which is most distinctly expressed in this petition, and which ha ever been performed by all the saints.

ANSWER 7. Knowledge of God's free grace and rich mercy. Without this, though a man never so much feels the burden of sin, he has no sure ground, nor can he have any heart to seek pardon. It appears that David was well instructed therein, in that he so much pleads and presses it.

ANSWER 8. Understanding the sacrifice of Christ, what that sacrifice was, the pure and precious blood of the Son of God; by whom it was offered up, by Himself through His eternal Spirit; for whom, even for us miserable sinners; to what end, to be a ransom for our sins so that satisfaction might be made to God's justice for the same. This sacrifice added to God's mercy shows how perfectly God's mercy and justice meet together in man's redemption. No marvel then that St. Paul desired to know nothing but Jesus Christ and Him crucified.

ANSWER 9. A right discerning of the perfection, even of the active obedience of Christ, and of the end thereof, how He fulfilled all righteousness and how we are made righteous thereby. Thus we may see how the debt of obedience that we owe, and are not able to perform, is performed by our Surety, and we by reason thereof are accepted as righteous.

ANSWER 10. A high esteem of Christ. For Christ, the great things that He has done and suffered, and the many great benefits that issue from thence are not for hogs, that as vile things will trample them under feet. St. Paul accounted all things but loss and dung in comparison of Christ.

ANSWER 11. Hungering and thirsting after Christ and His righteousness. These are they who shall be satisfied and filled, and in that respect are blessed.

ANSWER 12. Faith in the pardon of sin. All the fore-named points without this will but aggravate a poor sinner's misery. This is what brings a full discharge with it. In the disease and distress of the soul through sin, Christ will say as He did to such as were afflicted in body, "As thou hast believed, so be it unto thee. Thy faith hath made thee whole."

ANSWER 13. Peace of conscience. This follows faith and gives good evidence to the soul of the discharge thereof from sin.

These are special graces that respect the pardon of our own sins.

Graces to Be Prayed for in Regard of the Pardon of Others' Sins

QUESTION. What things in regard of the pardon of others' sins are to be prayed for?

ANSWER. Compassion by reason of them. Considering the woeful plight into which sin brings men, our bowels ought to be moved thereat. It is noted of Christ that He grieved for the hardness of the Jews' hearts. Was there not great compassion in him who thus prayed for others, "Oh, this people have sinned a great sin; yet now if Thou wilt forgive their sin, and if not, blot me out of Thy book"? This compassion will make us as earnest for the pardon of the sins of others as of our own.

ANSWER 2. Humiliation for them. Good Ezra was so dejected and humbled for the sins of others that he rent his garment and mantle and plucked off the hair of his head and beard, and fell down dazed.

ANSWER 3. Confession of them. It was usual with the saints to confess unto God the sins of others. For which purpose the confessions of Moses, Ezra, Nehemiah, the Levites, Daniel, and others are worthy to be observed. Humiliation and confession of others sins is evidence of a holy zeal of God's glory. Fear of the just vengeance of sin may make us humble ourselves for our own sins and penitently confess them to God. But to be so affected for others sins shows a brotherly fellow-feeling, and so a holy indignation against sin, as it is a sin offensive to the divine Majesty.

ANSWER 4. Supplication for the pardon of them. This is the main duty expressly taught in this petition. It is a special means of obtaining pardon for others' sins. But it is not in our own power to do it. It is a gift of the Spirit, and a gift promised. We may therefore, yea. and we must pray for it. And having it, then say to God as Moses did, "Pardon, I beseech Thee, the iniquity of this people," and as Christ did, "Father, forgive them," and as Stephen did, "Lord, lay not their sin to their charge."

These are principal graces to be prayed for by virtue of the main petition.

The Graces That Are to Be Prayed for by Reason of the Condition Annexed to the Fifth Petition

QUESTION. What graces are to be prayed for by virtue of the condition annexed to the fifth petition?

ANSWER. In general, such a mind to our brother as we desire God to bear to us. This Christ implies under this one word, "merciful," where He says, "Be ye merciful as your heavenly Father is also merciful." Hereby as in a looking glass we shall set out God's mind to man and show forth the praises of God, yea, and gain good evidence of God's good mind to us.

In particular, pray for such graces as these:

1. Love. This is a duty that has been required from the beginning; and it is the ground of all goodness, kindness, and forgiveness. Where the apostle exhorts us to forgive, he adds this direction, "Walk in love," showing thereby that love will make men forward to forgive.

2. Meekness. This is in the sight of God of great price. It is of special use to keep a man from being provoked, and from desire of revenge. Christ being of a meek spirit, when He was reviled, did not revile in return. Moses was commended for being a very meek man, and this is given as evidence and proof thereof, that he was not provoked to wrath by the wrong that Aaron and Miriam did to him.

3. Compassion or, to use the Scripture phrase, "bowels of mercy." This makes us pity such as wrong us. And because in doing wrong to us we know they do themselves the greatest hurt, a compassionate spirit will work in us more pity towards them than revenge against them, and in that respect to pray for them even when they are wronging us, as Christ and Stephen did.

4. Long-suffering. This the apostle adds to the forenamed meekness and bowels of mercy. This keeps a man from being overcome with multitudes of wrongs. God Himself is said to be a God of long-suffering in that He continues to pass by many wrongs time after time without executing judgment and revenge upon the doers thereof. In regard of the many wrongs whereunto, while we live in this world, we are subject, long-suffering is necessary.

5. Power over wrath. Hereby, though it so falls out that anger is stirred up in us by the injuries of wicked men, yet by

holding it in, as it were, with bit and bridle, we may be kept from excess, and from sin, according to this intimation of the apostle, "Be angry, but sin not." Herein lies a main difference between natural men and regenerate men. Because in natural men there is only flesh; when anger is kindled it burns more and more. But because in regenerate men there is spirit as well as flesh, by that spirit the lusts of the flesh are suppressed and quenched, as is evident in the case between David and Nabal.

6. Forgetfulness of wrongs, that we do not allow them to abide continually in our mind and memory. Thus God deals with trespasses committed against Him. "I will remember their sin no more," He says. It is a part of the renovation of memory to let slip, forget, and not to hold and retain evil things, and in particular revenge. Remembrance of wrongs increases desire for revenge, but forgetfulness thereof causes fullest forgiveness.

7. Readiness to forgive. This is the main thing intended in this condition. All the other graces before mentioned are but preparations hereunto.

8. Truth in the act of forgiveness. Herein lies the liveliest and best resemblance between God's forgiving and ours. This is especially intended in this particle of resemblance.

Hitherto we have dealt with the good things that by virtue of the fifth petition, and the condition annexed thereto, are to be prayed for.

The Things for Which Thanks Is to Be Given by Virtue of the Fifth Petition

QUESTION. What are the particular good things for which by virtue of the fifth petition we are to be thankful?

ANSWER. Such as concern God's forgiving us our trespasses and such as concern our forgiving other men their trespasses.

Those that concern God's forgiving us are such as follow:

1. God's free grace, in that for His own sake, without any desert of ours, He passes by and pardons our sins. In this respect the prophet magnifies Him and says, "Who is a God like to Thee, that pardoneth iniquity? He retaineth not His anger forever, because He delighteth in mercy."

2. God's rich mercy, in that notwithstanding our many, foul, and heinous sins, the spring of His grace is not dried up, but He is pleased to forgive them all. This incited Paul to make known his thankful mind to God.

3. God's long-suffering, in that He has not taken that advantage against us that we from time to time have given Him, but rather by His patience has led us unto repentance. The person who duly considers how many just occasions he has given to God to cut him off, and to give him his portion with the damned and devils in hell, being brought to some assurance of the pardon of sin, cannot but heartily bless God for His good and great patience towards him.

4. Christ Jesus. It is He who saves people from their sins. This is the greatest matter of thanksgiving that ever was or can be given to sons of men. The Virgin Mary, therefore, at her first conception of Him, magnifies the Lord. The angel that first brought the news of Christ's birth, proclaims it to be glad tidings of great joy. Yea, a choir of heavenly spirits sang praise thereat, saying, "Glory to God in the highest."

5. The obedience that Christ yielded to the law. It was for our sakes; unto us He is made righteousness that we might glory in the Lord.

6. The ransom that He paid for us. Among many other blessings for which the apostle gives thanks, the blood of Christ by which we have forgiveness of sins is one. And well may it be one, for by it eternal redemption is obtained.

7. The intercession that Christ continues to make for us. Herein the apostle, after a holy manner, triumphs, which is a special kind of glorifying God. Great cause have we so to do,

for hereby all the virtue and efficacy of Christ's sacrifice is applied to us.

8. The gospel whereby all the forenamed blessings are revealed. The apostle expressly gives thanks for this. All the rich treasures of the mystery of godliness would be of no use to us if by the gospel they were not opened to us.

9. The sacraments, whereby remission of sins is sealed up, and so ratified and assured unto us. When the eunuch and the jailer were baptized they rejoiced, which being done spiritually in the Lord includes a praising of God. And to show that the holy communion is a matter of thanksgiving the apostle calls it "the cup of blessing." And from the primitive times of the church under the gospel it has been called "the Eucharist," that is, a grateful commemoration of a thing.

10. Sight and sense of sin, and sorrow for the same. These are preparing graces, needful for such as expect pardon of sin. The apostle rejoiced and thanked God for these graces in the Corinthians. They are evidences of remission.

11. Understanding of the mysteries of the gospel. The gospel is a light that reveals those mysteries. But what is light without sight? A blind man in the brightest sunshine receives no benefit by the sun. The apostle therefore who preached the gospel to the Corinthians thanked God that they were enriched in all knowledge.

12. Faith in the Lord Jesus. By it pardon is obtained. Concerning it thus says the apostle, "After I heard of your faith in the Lord Jesus, I cease not to give thanks for you."

13. The fruits of faith, like a quiet conscience, a joyful heart, and comfortable spirit and such like. These being kindly wrought give evidence of our discharge of sin.

14. Means and evidences of pardon given to others. As we pray for the pardon of others' sins, so we must be thankful for the evidences that we see thereof. In this respect the church of the Jews glorified God for repentance to life granted to the

Gentiles. Their repentance was evidence of God's mercy in pardoning their sins.

These are good things for which God is to be praised by virtue of the fifth petition.

The Things for Which Thanks Is to Be Given by Virtue of the Condition Annexed to the Fifth Petition

QUESTION. What are the particular good things for which thanks is to be given to God by reason of the condition annexed to the petition?

ANSWER 1. All the evidences of God's indulgences toward us in pardoning our sins. For to this end is our profession of forgiving others here expressed. Where therefore there is such an evidence as we may boldly make profession thereof we ought to be thankful for it. Thus St. Paul gives thanks, as for faith in the Lord Jesus so for love to all the saints, an evidence thereof.

ANSWER 2. The means whereby we are kept from taking revenge. Thus David blessed God for sending Abigail to keep him from avenging himself with his own hand.

ANSWER 3. The alteration of our wrathful and revengeful nature. We could not in truth make this profession, "We forgive," if our nature were not altered.

ANSWER 4. That measure of brotherly love that we have. Without love all show of forgiving is but a mere show.

ANSWER 5. A spirit of meekness and patience. These and other like graces make us ready and willing to forgive. This Spirit comes from above and is one of those spiritual blessings for which God is to be blessed.

ANSWER 6. A heart seasoned with truth, by virtue thereof we are emboldened, even in relation to God's forgiving us, to say, "as we forgive."

Hitherto we have dealt with the matter of thanksgiving that the fifth petition affords.

Duties Required in Regard of Desire of Pardon of Our Own and Others' Sins

QUESTION. What duties are we to endeavor after by virtue of the fifth petition?

ANSWER. Both such as concern the petition itself and also the condition annexed to it.

In regard of the petition we ought...

1. To acquaint ourselves with the law of God. This is needful because by the law is the knowledge of sin. Thereby therefore we shall know what sinners we are and in how great need we do stand of pardon. By the law is man's soul humbled, pricked, and broken, and thereby prepared to seek pardon. By the law man is stripped of all self-conceit. Every mouth is stopped and all the world made guilty thereby.

2. To be well instructed in the gospel, and in the promises thereof, as Theophilus was. For by the gospel the grounds of pardon are revealed. By it faith is wrought. By it the conscience is quieted.

3. To partake of the sacraments, for they are seals of our discharge.

4. To confess our sins to God. "For if we confess our sins, God is faithful and just to forgive us our sins."

5. To ask pardon. This is the duty here expressly set down.

6. To believe pardon, for faith is a duty required of all to whom the gospel is preached.

These are duties that concern the pardon of our own sins.

Duties required in regard of the extent of this petition for the pardon of other sins as well as our own are these that follow.

1. To take notice of the sins of others so that we may better discern what great cause there is to pray for them. For this end they who spied the great sins of the Jews told Ezra thereof.

2. To make known to other men sinning their sins. Thus may they be brought to be humbled and to find mercy for them, as David was humbled and found mercy.

3. To make confession of them to God, as Ezra, Daniel and others did and procured pardon.

4. To pray for pardon for them as the forenamed saints did. For by a faithful and fervent prayer of the righteous, if one has committed sins, they shall be forgiven him.

These duties the petition itself requires.

Duties Required by Reason of Our Profession to Forgive Others

QUESTION. What duties are required by virtue of the condition annexed to the fifth petition?

ANSWER 1. To take notice of God's merciful dealing with us. For this is the ground of the kind of profession here made, "As we forgive." Joseph taking notice of God's good providence towards him made him the more kind to his brethren.

ANSWER 2. To follow God in His goodness, a point expressly enjoined by the apostles. They who do not imitate God cannot make this profession, "As we forgive."

ANSWER 3. To put on such graces as may make us ready to forgive. These are bowels of mercy, kindness, humbleness of mind, meekness, long-suffering, forbearing one another, etc. Without these a man will not be brought to forgive wrongs.

ANSWER 4. To put away revengeful passions. As water extinguishes sparks of fire, so a revengeful humor puts away all good motions and intentions of forgiving.

ANSWER 5. To accept all means of atonement offered, as David accepted the means that Abigail used to pacify his wrath. This will bring us to forgive.

ANSWER 6. To offer reconciliation, as Abraham did. There are some of so crabbed a disposition as they will never be reconciled, though they are the wrong doers, unless they be sought unto. Except therefore we seek them there will be no reconciliation; and if there is no reconciliation, how can it be thought that we can say in truth, "We forgive"?

ANSWER 7. Not to yield to such as incite us to revenge. Hereof we have a worthy pattern in David. If we hearken to such as stir us up to revenge we may be brought even against our own mind and disposition to take revenge.

ANSWER 8. Actually to forgive. This is it that we plainly profess. We mock Him who will not be mocked, and the truth is not in us if we utter this condition and do not indeed forgive.

ANSWER 9. To make peace between others. For we profess in the plural number of others as of ourselves that we forgive; we must therefore endeavor that others may do so. And herein shall we be blessed. Blessed are the peacemakers.

So much for the duties that both the petition itself and also the condition annexed thereto require.

The Matter of Humiliation that the Fifth Petition Affords

QUESTION. What are the things to be bewailed by reason of the fifth petition?

ANSWER. Such as are against the petition itself and such as are against the condition.

Against the petition are such as these:

1. Adam's sin. Thereby did man first come to be indebted to the revenging justice of God. On this ground the wise man thus complains, "Lo, this only have I found, that God hath made man upright; but they have sought out many inventions."

2. The guilt of Adam's sin. This justly is imputed to us because he was a public person and bore in his loins all who shall come from him to the end of the world. This therefore the apostle complains of where he says, "By the offence of one,

judgment came upon all men to condemnation. And by one man's disobedience many are made sinners."

3. The many offences of our forefathers. By them we are the more deeply indebted to God. These therefore the people of God bitterly bewail.

4. Original sin, even that corruption of our nature wherein all are conceived and born. This contains in it the seed and spawn of all sin and so defile us throughout as in every power of soul and part of body we are made loathsome, odious, and abominable in God's sight. This therefore David with much compunction of heart acknowledged.

5. All our actual sins. These are plain, palpable debts which the most ignorant that are cannot deny to be so. Under the burden of these the saints in all ages have much groaned. The more in number, or the more heinous they have been, the more grieved and perplexed the saints have been for them. Mark David's bitter complaint in this kind: "There is no rest in my bones because of my sin. For mine iniquities are gone over my head; as a heavy burden they are too heavy for me."

6. Our being an accessory to the sins of others. Thus we add to the heap of our own debts the debts of others whereby the heap is made much greater. The blood that David with much grief acknowledged was that which at his appointment Joab had caused to be shed. By his direction he made himself accessory thereto. So Eli by his too great indulgence and lenience towards his wicked sons made himself accessory to their sin, and liable to judgment for the same.

7. Our disability to discharge our debt of obedience. God gave us power at first to fulfill all righteousness. But now there is, while we live in this world, an impossibility thereto. Of this St. Paul thus complains, "To perform that which is good I find not."

8. Ignorance of the gospel. By the gospel the only means of discharging our debt is revealed. How then can they be dis-

charged who do not know it. In this respect the apostle with great grief thus sets forth the doom of such ignorant persons. "If our gospel be hid, it is hid to them that are lost."

9. Hardness of heart. This makes men senseless both of the burden of sin and also of God's wrath and vengeance against sin, which makes God to think of greater and greater vengeance. When Christ observed hardness to possess the hearts of the Jews, He mourned for it.

10. Infidelity. This makes all the means of pardon prepared and offered on God's part to be void on our part. In regard of this the prophet thus complains, "Who hath believed our report?"

11. Evidences of God's wrath upon us. These are signs of the debt of sin lying on our account as not discharged. This was the ground of the prophet Jeremiah's lamentation.

12. God's wrath on others, especially for our sin. We who pray for the discharge of others' sins have cause to mourn when we see the wrath of God lying on them for sin, especially if we ourselves have been any cause of procuring it. This humbled David and made him say, "Lo, I have sinned, and I have done wickedly; but these sheep, what have they done? Let Thine hand be against me."

These are things to be bewailed by reason of the fifth petition.

Against the condition vices to be lamented are such as these:

1. The touchiness of our nature whereby it comes to pass that passion is soon stirred up, and every small wrong makes us think of revenge. Small was the occasion that Joseph's brethren took to execute revenge upon the youth.

2. The violence of our passion. If passion is once moved (as soon it is moved) it is very ready to exceed and to grow into extremity. Among other natural corruptions of men the apostle

reckoned that they are fierce. How fierce was Saul against David?

3. Our implacableness. After men are once provoked they are hardly pacified again. This is another corruption of natural men reckoned up by the apostle, that they are implacable. Though the debtor in the parable fell down at his creditor's feet and sought him, saying, "Have patience with me and I will pay thee all," yet he would not. But after he had laid hands on him, and taken him by the throat, he cast him into prison till he should pay the debt.

4. Our insatiableness in taking revenge. No revenge seems sufficient to a revengeful spirit (such are all our spirits by nature). So much the apostle implies in this description of natural men, "Their throat is an open sepulcher; the poison of asps is under their lips; their feet are swift to shed blood; destruction and misery are in their ways." Haman, only because Mordecai refused to bow to him, thought it a light matter to lay hands on Mordecai alone, but thought to destroy all the Jews throughout the whole kingdom.

To these vices, touchiness, fierceness, implacableness, insatiableness in revenge, we are all by nature exceedingly prone. There are few that, as occasions are offered, do not in some way or other manifest as much. Very hardly, if it all, will all maliciousness be rooted out of us while flesh remains in us. These vices therefore afford us much matter of grief and humiliation, and that both in regard of ourselves and others also.

7
The Sixth Petition

The Sum and Several Parts of the Sixth Petition

QUESTION. Which is the sixth petition?

ANSWER. And lead us not into temptation, but deliver us from evil.

QUESTION. What is the sum of this petition?

ANSWER. Our sanctification, for as the former set out our justification, so this sets out our sanctification, under which two headings all our spiritual good to be expected in this world is comprised.

QUESTION. Of how many parts does this petition consist?

ANSWER. It consists of two parts. The first is in these words, "and lead us not into temptation," which imports a preventing of evil feared. The other is in these words, "but deliver us from evil," which implies a recovering from evil fallen out. So as our desire in this petition is that God would be so far from giving us over, like a just and severe judge, into the power of the executioners of his wrath, that rather, like a pitiful and merciful father, if at any time we are overtaken by them He would rescue and deliver us.

QUESTION. What points are to be considered in the first part?

ANSWER. The matter whereabouts it is made, temptation.

The action that is prayed against, lead not into.

The Person to whom the deprecation is directed.

The parties on whose behalf it is made, us.

Temptation and Tempters

QUESTION. What is temptation?

ANSWER. In general it is a proof or trial, as the notation of the word in both the original languages shows. David therefore joins these two words together, tempted and proved, which the apostle translates by two distinct words, whereof one signifies to tempt and the other to prove. And another apostle applies the word commonly put for temptation to that proof and trial that is made by fiery persecution. 1 Peter 4:12: "Think it not strange concerning the fiery trial which befalleth you for temptation which is to try you."

Temptation then, generally or indefinitely considered, is of an indifferent nature, neither simply good nor simply evil, but good as it is well used and evil as it is ill used. It is therefore in Scripture attributed to God, from whom nothing but that which is good can come, and to the Devil, from whom proceeds nothing but that which is evil, and also to men who sometimes are guided by the Spirit of God and sometimes by the spirit of Satan.

Temptation, when it is attributed to God, is to be taken in the best sense, and that to prove, discover, and make known what is in man. As Moses said to Israel, "Thou shalt remember the way which the Lord thy God led thee to tempt thee (or to prove thee) to know what was in thine heart." It is not as if God were ignorant thereof, for He understands our thoughts afar off (Psalm 139:2), but that He might make known to them what indeed was in them. Now God, by tempting men, makes known sometimes such graces as are in them (so He tempted Abraham), and sometimes such corruptions as lurk in them (so He tempted Hezekiah). Neither of these temptations can be thought to be unjust or in any way evil.

Temptation, when it is attributed to Satan, is always to be taken in the worst sense that can be, for his temptations and his intentions are as bad as may be. The devils are unclean, evil spirits, spiritual wickednesses. Satan is the wicked one. He ever tempts men to sin, endeavoring by his temptations to draw men into sin. And because he never ceases so to tempt, by a kind of property he is called the Tempter. For he tempts sometimes immediately by himself (so he tempted Christ), sometimes mediately by his messengers (for a messenger of Satan was sent to tempt Paul). His messengers are of several sorts. Some tempt with siren songs, and "Delilah delights" lull men asleep (as Samson was lulled) and bewitch them (as the Galatians were bewitched). Others are tempted with thundering threats, and boisterous buffets terrify men, as many of the Jews were kept from making open profession of Christ by reason of the terrible edicts that were made against such. Many Christians forsook Paul by reason of the fierce persecution raised against him. Hence has risen the distinction of temptations on the right hand and on the left, all enticing allurements to wickedness being counted temptations on the right hand, and all violent discouragements from goodness being counted temptations on the left hand. Thus Satan, as he thinks may most make for his advantage, either insensibly like a wily serpent winds himself into men, or violently, like a roaring lion, bears all before him. Not unfitly is he called the Creator's maul, His maul for the whole earth. He knocks the elect for their profit and he knocks down the reprobate unto their perdition.

Temptation attributed to men must be examined according to their different kinds and accordingly censured.

Men tempt God, themselves, and other men, all which may be well or ill done.

They may tempt God well by making proof of His power and truth for strengthening their faith when they are called to an extraordinary work (as in this case Gideon did) or have some extraordinary promise made unto them (as in this case Hezekiah did) or have some special warrant, in which case because Ahaz refused to tempt God he is blamed.

Men may evilly tempt God by presuming too much, when they have no good ground and sufficient warrant for their presumption (as the Devil would have had Christ to have done and as the Israelites did when they carried the Ark into the army), or by an undue doubting and despairing of God's help in time of need (as the Israelites often did in the wilderness). In both these ways the Israelites tempted God after the spies returned from searching the land of Canaan. For first, through despair, they thought of returning back again to Egypt and, being blamed for that, they fell into another extreme and presumptuously would go against the Canaanites without the ark, and without Moses their guide.

2. Men tempt themselves well when they search and examine themselves to find out the secret corruptions of their souls or the truth and strength of grace in them. Hereunto they are expressly exhorted. But they evilly tempt themselves when by presuming too much upon their own strength they cast themselves into unnecessary dangers (as Peter did) or when, by the inward corrupt motion of their own soul they are enticed and drawn unto any evil. "Every man is tempted when he is drawn away of his own lust and enticed."

3. One man tempts another well when on just ground they try to find out some excellence in them (to which end the Queen of Sheba came to Solomon to tempt him) or else some hidden corruption in them. Thus the Church of Ephesus tempted them who said they were apostles but were not, and so found them to be liars. But one man tempts another evilly when he entices him to sin (whereunto Joseph's mistress tempted him) or when he tries to ensnare him and to bring him into any danger. Thus the ministers of the Pharisees tempted Christ.

These are the several kinds of temptation mentioned in the Scripture.

The Kind of Temptation Meant Here

QUESTION. What kind of temptation is meant here?

ANSWER. Temptation unto sin, whether it arises from Satan, ourselves, or other men.

QUESTION. Is temptation to sin simply evil?

ANSWER. No, not in the party tempted, if he does not yield thereto but resists it. For Christ, who was free from all sin, was tempted unto sin.

QUESTION. Why then are we taught to pray against it?

ANSWER. The principal thing against which we are here taught to pray is the power of that temptation, as is evident by this particle "into." Yet there is great cause why we should also pray against the very act of temptation, that we are not tempted to any sin at all, both because the act itself is evil in them who tempt to sin, and also because by nature we are as prone to yield to every evil whereunto we are tempted as dry tinder is apt to be set on fire by every spark that falls upon it. For every imagination of the thoughts of man's heart is only evil continually. Herein lies a main difference between the quality of Christ's human nature and ours. His was so perfectly pure as no temptation could fasten upon it. It was to temptation as a sea of water to sparks of fire that soon extinguishes them. Ours is as dry tinder, yea, as dry gunpowder.

Man's Subjection to Temptation

QUESTION. What observation may be gathered from the mention of temptation in this deprecation?

ANSWER. Men in this world are continually subject to temptations. These complaints of the apostle ("I find a law that when I would do good evil is present with me," and, "O wretched man that I am, who shall deliver me from the body of this death?") verify as much. So also does woeful experience in all men. If there is a man who does not find this true in himself, his case is desperate; for either he is deprived of all spiritual understanding and sense, so that he is not able to discern a temptation, or his whole course of life is so full of temptations, and he is such a slave to them, they so frequent on him, and he so free towards them, as he cannot see the wood for the trees. He cannot tell when he is tempted because he is never but tempted. Temptations are not as enemies to him to be resisted, but as his best friends to have the best entertainment that he can afford unto them. Thus a man, accounting temptations to be no temptations, may in his own imagination be free; but indeed no man is free.

This is thus ordered partly by God's wise providence (to manifest His own divine properties, to make known the graces that are in His children, to discover their weaknesses, to prevent secret corruptions, and to declare a difference between this present life and that which is to come) and partly by the malice of Satan, both to deface the image of God in men and also to bring them to eternal destruction. For he is a professed enemy both of God's glory and also of man's salvation.

A due consideration of our condition in this world to be so subject unto temptations may well move us to be strong in the Lord and in the power of his might, and to put on the whole armor of God, that we may be always well prepared to stand against all temptations. Yea, also (according to Christ's direction) to watch and pray that we do not enter into temptation and (according to St. Peter's direction) to be sober and vigilant; for Satan takes great advantage both from intemperance and also from security. Witness Lot's incest for the one and David's adultery and murder following thereupon for the other. And because of the continual danger we are in by reason of the manifold temptations whereunto we are subject while we are on earth, we ought to aspire after heaven and to say with the apostle, "O wretched man that I am, who shall deliver me from the body of this death?"

This much for the matter of temptation. The action deprecated is, "Lead us not into."

Leading into Temptation

QUESTION. What is meant by leading into?

ANSWER. Giving one over to the power of that whereunto he is brought. In this sense the psalmist, making by divine instinct imprecation against a reprobate enemy, says, "Set a wicked man over him, to do with him at his pleasure." Our English makes a manifest difference between "unto" and "into," which is worth noting in this place. The latter implies a degree further than the former. A man who cannot swim may be led *unto* a deep pool and yet be safe enough; but if he is led *into* it he is in great danger of drowning unless he is pulled out again. They who translate it, "cast us not into temptation" well express the sense.

Being in the Power of Temptation

QUESTION. When are men in the power of a temptation?

ANSWER. When thereby they are brought into sin. For sin is the downfall of the soul into the tempter's pit. It is therefore in the Greek called a slip or a fall. The word most properly signifies the very act of falling. The apostle said of covetous men that they fall into temptation and a snare, and into many foolish and hurtful lusts, that drown men in perdition and destruction. The first sin that Adam committed, whereby he apparently fell into Satan's snare, is often termed a fall. In regard of this power that temptation has over a man, St. James said, "Every man is tempted when he is drawn away of his own lusts."

The action being declared, the person to whom it is directed is to be considered. The person is He to whom all the other petitions are made.

God's Leading into Temptation

QUESTION. How can God be said to lead into temptation?

ANSWER. Both in regard of those who tempt and those also who are tempted. In regard of those who tempt, it is by permission and instigation. Not Satan nor any other, be they never so mighty or malicious, can tempt a man unless God permits them; instance Job's case, yea, instance the case of the swine into which unclean spirits entered and forced them into the sea. And when they are permitted, they cannot go beyond those limits that the Lord appoints for them. Instance again the case of the said Job. This made much to the glory of Job. Besides this permission, the Lord also makes those who tempt men executioners of His wrath and justice, and in that respect He may be said to instigate and stir them up. For God deals with obstinate sinners as judges do with convicted malefactors. They give them over to the power of the hangman. Now God has many executioners of His wrath. The chief of all is the Devil. Among others may be reckoned up a man's own lusts. In this respect therefore it is said of the Gentiles that God gave them up to uncleanness through the lusts of their own heart; and again, that God gave them up unto vile affections.

In regard of those who are tempted, God may be said to lead them into temptation partly by leaving them to themselves and partly by withdrawing His grace from them. Man, in regard of spiritual strength, is as weak as water that cannot uphold itself but runs all about. Without grace he can neither think, will, affect, or do any good. If therefore he is left to himself, how can he stand against a temptation? God leaving Hezekiah, he soon fell. Yet God's grace is able to establish us against all temptations, even the most violent that can be. "My grace is sufficient for thee," says God to St. Paul, when a messenger of Satan was sent to buffet him. Now in that God permits and instigates tempters to tempt men, and withdrawing His grace that is sufficient for them, leaves them who are not able to stand of themselves, He is said to lead them into temptation.

Freeing God from Being the Author of Sin

QUESTION. Can God be an Author of sin?

ANSWER. No, verily. It is the greatest blasphemy that can be to avouch or think any such thing of God. There is no one thing so contrary to another, not white to black, not darkness to light, not death to life, as sin to God. That which is said of lying may more generally be said of sin. It is impossible (and that in the strictest and absolute kind of impossibility that can be) that God should sin or be a cause or Author of sin. This we ought to believe and profess...

1. Because His supreme and absolute power is such as it ought not to be called into question. Is it fitting to say to a king, "You are wicked"? and to princes, "You are ungodly"? How much less to say such to Him who does not accept the person of princes?

2. Because the perfection of His purity is such that it admits no mixture. God is light, and in Him is no darkness at all.

3. Because He is the original Fountain of all goodness, so that if this principle (does a fountain send forth at the same place sweet water and bitter?) is infallibly true of any fountain, it is without contradiction most true of this original Fountain. On these and other like grounds we may well know that God has power to give, withhold, or withdraw what He will and when He will, and to support or forsake whom He will. Also, He is not bound to that law which He has set to His creatures, nor to give an account to any. Yea, we ought to acknowledge God to be as most pure in His nature, so most just in all His counsels, words, and works; and if we cannot fully and clearly understand how the forenamed actions concerning leading into temptation can be attributed unto God, and yet God be freed from all accessary to sin, to lay our hands upon our mouths, and to ascribe it to the shallowness of our own apprehension. But in no way are we to charge God with folly or sin.

Among the principles that without all gainsaying ought to be believed, this is one of the prime, that the Lord is a God who has no pleasure in wickedness. He can in no way be accessary thereto. But besides this absolute sovereignty and perfect purity of God, other particular reasons of God's dealing with men in this kind may be given, and those so clearly just and equal as anyone but such a one as is blinded in his mind by the god of this world may discern the justice and equity thereof. For…

1. Where God permits tempters to tempt men it is for good and just ends, as to try and prove men's faith, courage, wisdom, patience, and other like graces, all which were by this means proven to be found and great in Job, or else to discover their weakness and secret wickedness that they may neither be too secure nor overbold and self-conceited. By this means and for these ends Peter's weakness was discovered.

2. Where God bids, sends, or instigates tempters to tempt men, as in the cases of Ahab, of the Gentiles, and of antiChristians, it is as a just judge to punish former transgressions so as these tempters are therein executioners of God's justice.

3. Where God leaves men to themselves and withholds His assistance, it is to give evident demonstration that man without God is nothing, no more able to stand of himself than a child that is newborn. Now there is great need that man should be evidently convicted hereof lest he be too presumptuous of his own strength and neglect God.

4. Where God withdraws His Spirit, or any grace from man, it is as a just punishment for abuse thereof. In this respect God took away His Spirit from Saul. Compare 1 Samuel 10:9 and 11:6 with 1 Samuel 16:14.

To conclude this point, so far is God from being in any way an accessory to sin by leading into temptation as, contrarily, He turns the evil thereof unto good. For as at first He brought light out of darkness, so ever since by His almighty power, unsearchable wisdom, and perfect purity He has brought good out of evil—good to Himself by making the glory of His justice in punishing, of His pity in succoring, of His power in supporting, of His faithfulness in delivering, of His wisdom in catching the subtle in their own craftiness and disappointing their plots and practices, and of other of His properties to shine forth the brighter. He brings good also to His saints, as Joseph said to his brethren, "Ye thought evil against me, but God meant (or disposed) it unto good." Thus, though the temptation is evil, yet God is good even in leading into temptation.

Man's Inability to Resist Temptation

QUESTION. What doctrines does praying unto God to not lead us into temptation teach us?

ANSWER 1. Man is not able of himself to stand against temptations. If he were, what cause of fear would he have of being led into temptation? The prophet well knew this who said, "O Lord, I know that the way of man is not in himself; it is not in man that walketh to direct his steps." The apostle said, "We are not sufficient of ourselves to think anything of ourselves." If man cannot direct his steps, nor of himself think anything, can he withstand all tempters and keep himself from all temptations?

This inability has come upon us by sin, which has deprived us of all that spiritual strength that God at our first creation gave us. For God made man righteous, even after His own image, by virtue whereof man had power to remain steadfast in that estate and to withstand all tempters so as not to be overcome with any temptation. Only that power was left to his own power and free will that he, abusing, voluntarily yielded to the temptation of Satan and deprived himself of all spiritual strength and life and now by nature is dead in sin. He is now in no way able to resist any temptation further than God gives him grace and strength so to do. Therefore He does not say, "Without Me ye can do little," but, "nothing."

Hereby the vanity of such as are presumptuous in their own strength (wherein Peter failed too much), and of such as arrogantly boast of anything that is in man, is discovered. St. Paul forewarned Christians to take heed hereof, and very emphatically thus enforces this point, "What hast thou that thou didst not receive? Now if thou didst receive it, why dost thou glory as if thou hadst not received it?"

Hereby also we are taught both humiliation for this natural impotence that man has brought upon himself, and abrogation of all goodness and confidence in ourselves. If John saw cause to weep for mans inability to search into the records of God's counsel, how much more cause have we to weep and be humbled, even in dust and ashes, for our natural impotence to withstand temptations that are so dangerous to our soul and in denial of ourselves to say, "I know that in me dwelleth no good thing."

God's Overruling Power in Temptations

QUESTION. What other doctrine may be gathered from this deprecation directed to God?

ANSWER. God has an over-ruling hand in all temptations. The Lord who has taken away your sin and pardoned your offences can preserve and keep you from the wiles of your adversary the Devil. He can either keep us safe from all or He can give us over into the power of everyone. Otherwise there would not be such cause of flying to Him in time of temptation, as in this petition is implied. But that is true what St. Peter says, "The Lord knoweth how to deliver the godly out of temptations." And this of St. Paul is true, "God is faithful, who will not suffer you to be tempted above that you are able."

As the supreme sovereignty and absolute power that God has over all creatures evidently proves the point (For who has resisted His will? If He says to a tempter, 'go,' he goes. Or if He says, 'come,' he comes; or, 'do this,' he does it.), so the care that He takes of His church to provide for it, to protect it, to keep it safe from all dangers, and to bring it to rest and glory in heaven, shows the reason why He retains an over-ruling hand in all temptations. Though in wisdom He allows tempters to assault His children, yet He will order the assault so as it shall not prevail against them, no, nor turn to their damage, but rather to their advantage; for the effecting whereof He holds the reins in His own hands to let them loose or hold them in as He sees cause. That which God said to Sennacherib, "I will put My hook in thy nose and My bridle in thy lips," He does to all the tempters of His church. This care of God over His church the psalmist thus excellently sets forth in these words, "He suffered no man to do them wrong, yea, He reproved kings for their sakes, saying, 'Touch not Mine anointed, and do My prophets no harm.' "

We learn hereby in all temptations, and in all straits whereunto thereby we are brought, to look unto God (as Jehoshaphat did when by reason of the multitude of his mighty enemies he knew not what to do), and to fear God more than them who tempt us; for on this ground we may with confidence say, "The Lord is my helper, I will not fear what any tempter can do." For there may be sure and safe defense from all those evils that Satan plots and practices against us if God delivers us.

The Restraint of the Power of Tempters

QUESTION. What third doctrine does the direction of this deprecation unto God teach us?

ANSWER. The power of such as tempt us is limited. This is evident by the restraint of the arch-tempter Satan, who sets all on work. Even he, when God pleased, was bound a thousand years. And though he desired to have the disciples, that he might sift them as wheat, yet he could not, as he desired, prevail over them. He did something, but he came far short of his desire.

By this means the Lord gives evident proof that His power extends itself over the most mighty and malicious enemies that His church has, and forces them to say, "This is the finger of God." Yea, by this means His church even in this world is kept safe so as the gates of hell cannot prevail against it. For if Satan and his instruments had power to do what they will, the whole church would soon be devoured. Her adversary, the Devil, like a roaring lion, walks about, seeking whom to devour.

We all who are members of the true church, though even in that respect we are the more tempted and assaulted, have just cause to rejoice, and to comfort and encourage ourselves against the many temptations of Satan and other tempters. Though they desire and seek our utter ruin, yet they are restrained; they cannot achieve what they desire and seek. They are like a fierce, nasty dog that is chained and can go no farther than to the length of his chain. On this ground the Lord gives this advice, "Fear none of those things which thou shalt suffer. Behold, the Devil shall cast some of you into prison that you may be tried, and ye shall have tribulation ten days, etc." The particular number (some of you, not all), the kind of persecution (cast into prison, not, put to the sword), and the determinate time (ten days, not perpetually) all imply a restraint. And thereupon He infers His exhortation, "Fear none of these things," on the same ground. Christ, having foretold His disciples that in the world they would have tribulation, adds this encouragement, "Be of good cheer, I have overcome the world."

This restraint of the power of tempters further ministers just occasion of praising God and saying, "Blessed be the Lord who has not given us as a prey to their teeth. Our soul is escaped as a bird out of the snare of the fowlers. The snare is broken and we are delivered." Fitly, to enforce the equity of this duty, I may apply to our present purpose that which Christ said of the fierce persecution of the Jews, "Except the tempter's power were limited, there should no flesh be saved; but for the elect's sake it is restrained."

Next we come to the Person leading. The parties led into temptation are to be considered. They are comprised under this particle "us," which being a word of the plural number includes more than ourselves; and it being of the first person has relation to the preface.

The Extent of Our Desires for Others' Freedom from Temptation

QUESTION. What instruction does this particle "us," being of the plural number, teach us?

ANSWER. Our desire must be for the spiritual freedom of others as well as of ourselves. This desire made St. Paul send to know the faith of the Thessalonians, lest by some means the tempter had tempted them. This also made him jealous over the Corinthians, and zealous against those tempters who had crept in among the Galatians.

Tempters seek to deface God's image in His saints which, if they do, they impeach His glory. Yea, if they get any of the saints into their snares they will continually blaspheme the name of the Lord and say in scorn and derision, "These are the people of the Lord."

The snares also that tempters lay drown men in perdition and destruction if they are fast held thereby. And if they prevail against some they will be the more bold to set on others, as Senacherib, who by the victories that he got against other nations was so fleshed that he thought God could not deliver Jerusalem out of his hands. Thus by the advantages that Satan gets against others we ourselves are in great danger.

The zeal therefore that we ought to have for God's glory, the love we owe to our brethren, and the care that lies on us for our own safety require that we seek others spiritual freedom as well as our own.

Whenever you feel the burden of any temptation, or discern the danger thereof, think of others who have the same common enemies that you have, and by reason thereof are in the same common condition; and think not all is well enough when you have found some assistance against them or freedom from them. Remember how mindful of others Christ was in the hour of His trial and temptation. It is expressly said of Him in that He Himself has suffered being tempted, He is able to succor those who are tempted. Though we have not such power to succor, yet, according to our power, we ought to have such a mind.

That Subjection Wherein Saints Are to Temptations

QUESTION. What instruction does the relation of this particle "us" to the preface teach us?

ANSWER. God's children are not exempt from temptations. They who call God "Father," and who testify their due respect to Him, are taught to pray against temptations, which would not be needful to be taught if they were not subject thereto. Run through the Scripture, observe the lives of those saints that are there recorded, and you shall find the doctrine abundantly proven. Take one example that may be representative of all. Christ, the dearest of God's children, the Son of His love, in whom His soul delighted, was often sorely tempted both by Satan himself and also by his instruments. If hereupon it is demanded what the privilege of saints over and above the wicked is in regard of temptation, I answer, very great, both in that they are assured of sufficient strength so as they shall not be vanquished by any, and also that every temptation shall in the issue turn to their good.

The love that God bears to His children, and the fatherly care that He takes of them, moves Him to prove them, to exercise them, to scour them, to keep them upright, to make them wise, watchful, and ever well prepared by temptations. Besides, Satan's greatest malice is against them.

It is therefore no good inference that many make that God is angry with them and does not love them, that He is not their Father, nor they His children, because He allows them to be tempted. This was the inference that the friends of Job made of his trials and temptations. But God's own censure of their disputation shows the non-consequence thereof. The truth is that they who find themselves wholly freed from temptations have most cause to doubt God's fatherly love to them and care over them. The apostle pronounced such to be bastards and not sons. If we well consider the estate of the church we may soon find that such as are spiritual are much more fiercely assaulted than such as are carnal. The more sure Satan is of any, the more quiet and secure he allows them to be. A lion runs and roars after that prey that is out of his clutches; but that which he has brought into his den and is sure of he can allow to be still and quiet until he means to devour it. So it is with Satan. While a strong man armed keeps his palace, the things that he has are in peace. Woe to them who are in such peace within Satan, that strong man's palace.

The Freeness of Man's Will in Sin

QUESTION. What may be observed from the relation of the parties tempted to the action of leading into temptation?

ANSWER. Man is not forced to sin. For it is implied that if man does not yield the tempter can have no power over him. He that is led goes along with him who leads him. "Every man is tempted when he is drawn away of his own lusts and is enticed." This phrase ("own lusts") implies a voluntary yielding. On this ground are the exhortations in Scripture made to men to resist the Devil and to give no place to him. Whereby is implied that if we stand against him he cannot prevail against us.

Many like exhortations are given to withstand and not to yield unto other tempters, such as the world and the flesh.

Sin is of the will, which cannot be forced. Though the will by Adam's fall has lost all that liberty and freedom to good that it had by creation, and by corruption is made a slave to sin, yet as the mind retains understanding so the will retains freedom. For freedom is as essential to the will as understanding is to the mind. Indeed, the corrupt will of man can will nothing but that which is evil; yet the evil that it wills it wills freely and is not forced thereto. Freedom of will is not opposed to restraint in one kind, but to constraint in that kind, to compulsion and coaction. The will of devils is restrained to evil; they cannot will good, but evil only. Yet the evil that they will they will freely and willingly; they are not constrained and compelled thereto. Yea, God's will, which is most absolutely free, is restrained to one kind, which is good. He does not have in His will a liberty to evil. To will evil is against the perfection of His will. Wherefore though the will does not have a liberty to choose either of the contrary parts, good or evil, yet a freedom and willingness it retains in that whereunto it yields. It neither is nor can be constrained thereto. All that Satan does or can do is by some means or other to move men to yield to that whereunto he tempts them. Whereupon the apostle says, "I fear lest by any means as the serpent beguiled Eve through his subtlety, so your minds should be corrupted, etc." To affect this the old wily serpent has many and manifold means, some inward, some outward.

Inward means are such as delight or frighten men. He works delight by stirring up their corrupt humors and so inclines their will to his temptation. Thus he stirred up the corrupt humor of pride in David, and thereby provoked him to number Israel; and the corrupt humor of covetousness in Judas, in which respect he is said to enter into him. The means that in this kind Satan uses are drawn to three headings:

1. The lust of the flesh, which is voluptuousness, whereby the flesh is so tickled and delighted that it draws the will to anything. Such persons the apostle calls lovers of pleasures more than lovers of God.

2. The lust of the eyes, which is covetousness. A covetous man is even ravished at the sight of wealth. When Achan saw silver, gold, and other precious things in Jericho, he coveted them and took them, though they were accursed. There is not a thing of price that a covetous man casts his eye upon but instantly he covets it, and so dotes thereon that he will do anything to have it.

3. The pride of life, which is ambition, and vain affectation of the honors and promotions of this life. This puffs up above their mortal condition, as is evident in the examples of Haman, Nebuchadnezzar, Tyrus, and Herod. Such, through their pride, will not seek after God.

As by these pleasing temptations Satan allures, so, by inward fears, frights, and terrors he draws others to yield to him as he tried to draw Job, and as he prevailed with many of the people in Christ's time.

The outward means that he uses are such external objects as he conceives to be agreeable to their humor, and therefore sets them before them as he set before Christ all the kingdoms of the world and their glory, or such as he conceives to be of force to terrify them, as are all manner of troubles and afflictions. Thus it is said that the devil cast some of Smyrna into prison. Whether the means that are used to draw men to sin are fair or foul, by none of them is the will forced, but only moved to yield itself to the temptation.

This point affords two useful directions. One is in regard of sins past, to judge ourselves for them, and upon ourselves to lay the whole blame, and not to think it a sufficient excuse to lay the blame upon any other. Many will say when they are taken in some notorious sin, "The devil owed me a spite, and now has paid it to me," thinking thereby to extenuate their sin. This conceit Eve had when she said, "The serpent beguiled me." And if any man has been the occasion of their sin they will lay the blame upon them, as Adam did upon Eve. But had they been resolute in their own will, neither Satan nor any of his instruments could have made them to sin. They who thus think to shift off sin bring the greater load upon their own souls. For this keeps them from that degree of humiliation and contrition that would move God to pity them. When men in truth lay loads on themselves, God is ready to ease them. For to such as labor and are heavy laden Christ says, "Come unto Me and I will give you rest." But on such as by the shifting of sin think to ease themselves, God will lay loads. What loads of woe did Christ lay upon the hypocritical scribes and Pharisees who put off all burdens from themselves? What a load was laid on Saul, who by mincing his sin sought to ease himself? And what ease was given to David who laid the burden of sin upon himself? Now whether it is safest so to shift off sin as to provoke God to lay the burden of it on us, or so to burden ourselves as to move God to ease us, you be the judge. Is there not now more need of true confession than false justification?

The other direction is in regard of such sins as we are tempted unto, but have not yielded unto, that we take courage and boldness to ourselves and with a resolved purpose never to yield resist the temptation. Man's will, if he stands stoutly and does not yield, is an impregnable fort. Satan must by some means or other, fair or foul, bring a man to yield up his fort before he can enter into it. What stronger motive to resist, to stand out, to hearken to no parley, to endure the utmost assault than this? Wherefore in this spiritual combat against temptations watch, stand fast in the faith, act like men, and be strong.

Thus far of the meaning of the first part of the last petition, and of the instructions thence arising. The second part follows.

"But deliver us from evil"

The Extent of this Word "Evil"

QUESTION. Wherein does the latter part of the last petition differ from the former?

ANSWER 1. In that the former part respects especially evil to come, to prevent it, this latter evil, past or present, to redress it.

ANSWER 2. In that it notes out the cause of sin, which is temptation. This notes the quality and effect of sin, which is evil.

QUESTION. How many things are to be considered in this latter part?

ANSWER 1. The thing prayed against, evil.

ANSWER 2. The thing prayed for, deliver.

ANSWER 3. The Person to whom the one and the other is directed.

ANSWER 4. The persons for whom they are made.

QUESTION. What is comprised under this word "evil"?

ANSWER 1. Satan, the principal author of evil.

ANSWER 2. All other kinds of evil.

Satan is thus in other places called "the evil one," and this word evil is often put for everything that is contrary to good, and that with the article prefixed before it. Now as this title "good" is of a large extent, so on the contrary is "evil." The greatest evil of all is sin. Judgments also for sin, and those both temporal and eternal, are called evil. In this large extent is the word here to be taken. And because it comprises under it all manner of evils, it is fitly set in the last place.

Evil Is the Only Thing to Be Prayed Against

QUESTION. What doctrine arises from the expressed mention of evil in this deprecation?

ANSWER. Evil is the only thing to be prayed against. Observantly mark all the deprecations mentioned in Scripture and by a particular induction of them you shall find this general position abundantly proved. Take one instance that may be representative of all, because it is the best of all, that which Christ made a little before His death, "I pray not (says Christ to His Father) that Thou shouldst take them out of the world, but that Thou shouldst keep them from the evil."

Evil is the venom, the poison, the sting, that makes anything to be hurtful. It is evil that makes so great a difference as there is between angels and angels, men and men, actions and actions, temptations and temptations; some are good some are evil. No opposites are more directly contrary one to another than good and evil. As nothing therefore but that which is good is to be prayed for, so nothing but that which is evil is to be prayed against.

Learn hence wisely to observe what is evil in anything and accordingly pray against it; yea, as it is more or more evil, so more instantly and earnestly pray against it. Of all evils sin is the greatest—greatest in the kind and nature of it, greatest also in the effects and fruits of it. It is the cause of all evils. Nothing but that which is affected or infected by it is evil. The Devil, the world, wicked men, and other creatures of God that are called evil, are infected therewith. All manner of punishments and pains that are indeed evil, whether temporal, spiritual, or eternal are caused by it. Of all other evils this ought most of all to be prayed against. All things also that are causes hereof, or occasions hereto, are to be prayed against as being in this respect evil. Thus temptations and afflictions are to be prayed against, not simply and absolutely, for St. James wills us to account it all joy when we fall into divers temptations. And the apostles rejoiced in their sufferings; yea, Job expressly blessed God for taking away as well as for giving. For by the good and wise providence of God temporal crosses often turn to our good and profit. "It is good for me that I have been afflicted," says the psalmist. "God chasteneth us for our profit," says the apostle. In regard of this fruit that by the over-ruling providence of God arises out of afflictions they are indeed matter of thanksgiving when God so orders them; and therefore they are not simply and absolutely to be prayed against. Yet because through the weakness of our flesh they often cause discontent, impatience, and other sins (in which respect they are evil), so far forth as they cause any such evil effect they may be prayed against—at least we must pray that they do not bring forth any sin in us.

Thus are we to pray against company keeping, against feasting, against pleasures and pastimes, and against all other things that are usual occasions of sin, yea, against the abuse of every good thing. For the abuse of a good thing is evil. And because wicked men are often made Satan's instruments of working much evil, we may also pray against all their evil plots and practices, not against their persons. They are to be prayed for (unless we know them to have sinned against the Holy Ghost, or to be utterly rejected of God, or have some particular warrant, as the prophets often had, not to pray for them). More directly we are to pray against all spiritual judgments that are not only punishments of sins, but sins themselves, as hardness of heart, error of judgment, inordinate lusts, despair, and such like. These are directly evil. Thus are we to pray against eternal damnation, a dreadful evil. Finally, though Satan is not the only evil here meant, yet he is a special and principal evil one.

The Respects Wherein Satan Is Called the Evil One

QUESTION. How is Satan a special evil one?

ANSWER 1. He is the primary author of evil.

ANSWER 2. His disposition is only to evil.

ANSWER 3. His temptations are all to evil.

ANSWER 4. His continual practice is in evil.

ANSWER 5. All evildoers are of him.

ANSWER 6. He has his hand in all evils, as may be exemplified in these particulars: outward mischiefs done by men, bodily diseases, vexation of spirit, extraordinary judgments from heaven, evil thoughts of the heart, evil words, evil actions, dissuasions from good, hindrances of good, and provocations to evil.

Satan therefore may not be excluded out of the evils here intended, but our deprecation rather is especially to be directed against him.

Thus much of evil prayed against. That which is prayed for is in this word "deliver."

The Many Ways of Delivering from Evil

QUESTION. How may one be delivered from evil?

ANSWER 1. By keeping away that evil which is ready to fall upon him. Thus were the Israelites delivered from the host of the Egyptians who eagerly pursued them.

2. By assisting him on whom the evil is fallen so as he is not overwhelmed and overcome therewith. For this purpose read Psalm 69:14–15.

3. By altering the nature of the evil and turning it to a man's good. Thus God turned Joseph's abode in Egypt to much good. Herein this proverb is verified, "I would have perished if I had not perished."

4. By taking away the force of the evil, as the force of the fire was taken away so that it did not burn Shadrach, Meshach, and Abednego. This deliverance Christ promised to His disciples.

5. By removing the evil clean away. Thus God delivered Israel from the devouring pestilence.

6. By taking one away from the evil to come. Thus the good son of wicked Jeroboam, thus the good King Josiah, thus many righteous men have been delivered.

The Hope of Recovery That Remains to Those Who Fall

QUESTION. What doctrine may be gathered from praying for deliverance?

ANSWER. There is hope of recovery to such as are fallen. For deliverance from evil presupposes a fall into evil, and prayer for this deliverance implies that we may be recovered out of it. This is verified as by manifest experience of many saints who in all ages have been recovered, so by this approved proverb, "A just man falls seven times and rises up again," which, though it is principally intended of affliction, yet may also be extended to sin.

The ground of this hope arises from God Himself, even from His mercy whereby He is moved to pity His children in all their miseries, whereupon the prophet says, "It is of the Lord's mercies that we are not consumed, because His compassions fail not," and from His power whereby He is able to help them whom He pities. Upon this the apostle of the Jews says, "They also, if they abide not still in unbelief, shall be grafted in; for God is able to graft them in again." Hope arises also from His truth, for "He that is faithful and will do it" has made many promises of deliverance.

This point concerns such as stand and such as are fallen. In regard of this hope of recovery they who stand ought to comfort the feeble-minded who are troubled with fears of utter desertion, as if God were implacable and irreconcilable towards them who are at any time overcome by any temptation. The caveat that Christ gave to Peter is to be practiced by all who have any spiritual strength, "Strengthen thy brethren." Yea, also they ought in the spirit of meekness to restore such a one.

As for those who are fallen, they are taught not to despair, but to say as the Spirit teaches them, "Come, let us return unto the Lord; for He hath torn and He will heal us. He hath smitten and He will bind us up." Withal they are not to continue in

Satan's snares, but to do what they can to come out of the same according to that pithy persuasion of the Lord, "Remember from whence thou art fallen, and repent, and do the first works."

As for the rash and peremptory censure of Novatians on such as fall, it is the less to be regarded because it is directly contrary to the main scope of this latter part of this last petition. It is not without cause judged heresy by the ancients.

Having noted the things prayed against and prayed for, we are further to consider to whom our desire herein is to be directed.

God Is the Only Deliverer

QUESTION. What doctrine may be observed from directing this part of the petition to God?

ANSWER. God is a deliverer from evil and God is the only deliverer from evil.

Were not God able and willing to deliver, why should this petition be directed to Him? But He who has taken away our sins is able to keep us from the snares of Satan. Could anyone else deliver, why should that other one be left out in this perfect platform?

Among other titles, Deliverer is often attributed to God: and hereby is the Lord proven to be God.

There is just cause therefore that in all evils we should fly unto the Lord and call upon Him in the day of trouble. And when we do not know what to do, fix our eyes upon Him and in faith expect deliverance from Him. It is good that a man should both hope and quietly wait for the salvation of the Lord. And as we have deliverance from any evil, give all the praise thereof to this Deliverer.

Is not their folly hereby evidently discovered who in their trouble do not look to the Holy One of Israel, nor seek the Lord, but look and trust such as cannot deliver? Some look to weak flesh, others to wicked friends, others to false gods. Much like these are our adversaries the papists, who in several evils have several saints to fly to, as in danger of shipwreck to Saint Nicolas, in time of war to Saint George, in captivity to Saint Leonard, in infection of plague to Saint Rochus, in fear of fire to Saint Laurence, in travail of childbirth to Saint Margaret, in the fit of a fever to Saint Petronil, in toothache Saint Rombal or Saint Apollonia, and in other distresses to other saints. Yea, in Our Lady's Psalter, they have turned all the petitions made to God for deliverance to the Virgin Mary: "Deliver me, O Lady. How long dost thou forget me, and dost not deliver me in the time of trouble? To thee, O Lady, do I lift up my soul, let not the snares of death prevail against me. In thee, O Lady, have I hoped, let me not be confounded forever. O thou blessed Lady, in thy hands our salvation is laid up." Have we not now just cause to cry out against them, as the Prophet Jeremiah did against the idolatrous Jews, and say, "Be astonished, O ye heavens, at this, and be horribly afraid; for My people have committed two evils: They have forsaken Me, the Fountain of living waters, and hewed them out cisterns, broken cisterns that can hold no water."

Thus much of the person of whom is sought deliverance from evil.

The last point concerns the parties for whom it is sought.

The meaning of the petition being opened, the order is next to be considered.

Sanctification Accompanying Justification

QUESTION. What may be observed from the connection of this petition with the former?

ANSWER. Sanctification accompanies justification. As the sum of the former is justification, so the sum of this latter is sanctification, and in our prayer we are taught to join them together as this particle "and" imports. For proof of the indissoluble connection of these two read Romans 6:1–2 and 1 Corinthians 6:11.

The grounds hereof are:

1. The manifestation of mercy and purity in God.

2. The cleansing virtue that accompanies the merit of Christ's sacrifice.

3. The operation of the Spirit immediately issuing from our incorporation into Christ.

4. The efficacy of the gospel.

5. The virtue of faith.

All these are evidently set out by the conjunction of sanctification with justification.

1. Justification commends the rich mercy of God in acquitting sinners freely and fully of all that debt wherein they stand obliged to His revenging justice. And sanctification sets out His purity, showing that that God who pities sinners will not bolster up sinners in their sins. His pity moves Him to justify them and His purity moves Him to sanctify them.

2. That blood of Christ that is shed for the remission of sins purges our conscience from dead works to serve the living God. This double use of Christ's sacrifice was manifested by that blood and water that issued out of Christ's side while He was on the cross. They therefore who are justified are also sanctified.

3. By the Spirit of sanctification we are united unto Christ; and this Spirit by virtue of that union is conveyed into every of the members of Christ's mystical body. Now if any man does not have the Spirit of Christ, he is none of His. But if His Spirit is in any, it sanctifies them.

4. The grace of God that brings salvation, that is, the gospel teaches us that, denying ungodliness and worldly lusts, we should live soberly, righteously, and godly. That word therefore whereby we are justified gives no liberty to any licentiousness, but both directs us in the way of righteousness and also gives us

ability to walk in that way. Hereby it appears that the gospel is as pure and incorrupt as the law. Indeed the law is so perfect a rule of righteousness as it curses everyone who in the least degree swerves from it. This the gospel does not do, but offers pardon to the transgressor. Yet it no more tolerates or countenances the least sin than the law does; nay, rather it brings the sinner who has gone astray into the way of righteousness again and enables him to walk in that way, which the law cannot do. So herein the gospel has an excellence over the law. But if the gospel in showing mercy should bolster up a sinner in any one sin the law would triumph over the gospel, yea, and condemn it. It is therefore necessary for justification of the gospel that sanctification continually follow justification as a handmaid does her mistress; or rather that, as two sworn friends and fellows, they always keep company together.

5. Faith purifies the heart. For that man who in truth believes his sins to be pardoned will not like a swine wallow in the mire. A true apprehension of God's fatherly love works a filial love in man's heart, which love makes him as truly to desire and endeavor after sanctification as justification.

They therefore who boast of their justification and are not truly sanctified sever God's purity from His mercy and the virtue of Christ's sacrifice from the merit thereof, yea, the operation of His Spirit from the union of His members unto Him. They turn the grace of God into wantonness and proclaim their faith to be a fruitless and a lifeless faith, and in sin give too just cause to suspect that their pretence of justification is a mere pretence.

We learn then both to gain sound assurance to our own souls, and also to give good evidence to others of our justification by our sanctification.

Man's Proneness to Sin After Forgiveness

QUESTION. What may be observed from the inference of the sixth petition on the fifth?

ANSWER. After pardon men are prone to fall again. Otherwise there would be no need for such as have assurance of the pardon of sin to pray against temptation, or for deliverance from evil. As woeful experience in all saints, even the best that ever lived, verifies the truth hereof, so do also the daily sacrifices that under the law were appointed. For every propitiatory sacrifice gave the believer assurance of a full discharge for his sins, yet after one was offered up, another and another, time after time was to be offered. He who is washed only needs to wash his feet. His feet therefore needed to be washed. And why should he who is justified need to wash his feet if he were not subject to fouling them again and again?

The grace of justification does not utterly root out all remainder of sin. The flesh abides in the best so long as they abide in this world. Witness the complaint of that justified apostle St. Paul. Wickedness remained in all the apostles notwithstanding they were truly sanctified.

There were of old a certain sect called Puritans who indeed were plain heretics, and so judged by the church, who professed themselves to be perfectly holy and pure. Their heresy is plainly confuted by this petition. Yet is it again revived by Familists, yea, and by papists too. For they hold that some are so righteous in this life as they need no repentance, but keep the Law of God, and by their righteousness free themselves from the curse thereof. If these are not Puritans, I do not know who is.

[EDITOR'S NOTE: Gouge is here referring to the fact that when the term "Puritans" was first used to describe the late sixteenth and seventeenth century divines whom we now freely call the Puritans that term was a play off of the word "Cathari" from the Greek Katharoi for "pure ones." The Cathars were a dualist, medieval, twelfth-century, religious sect of Southern France that challenged the authority of the Roman Catholic Church. Consequently, the early Puritans, such as William Perkins, viewed the term "Puritan" as a "vile term" charging them to be mystical heretics who thought of themselves as being very holy. The term "Puritans" stuck, however, and some generations later the Puritans accepted it more freely as they acknowledged that they indeed were seeking to promote purity in every area of life.]

For our part, let none boast of a pure and immaculate heart. Seeing no man is without sin, whoever says he is without fault is either proud or foolish.

Let us even after we have good evidence and assurance of the pardon of our sin remain watchful against all enticements and temptations to sin, and well remember that caveat that Christ gave both to him that he healed at the pool of Bethesda, and also to her whom, notwithstanding she was taken in the act of adultery, he absolved, "Sin no more." This caveat does not imply that a man may keep himself pure from all sin, but that he ought, with the best care and greatest watchfulness that he can endeavor to be so pure. Care therefore must be taken to prevent sin to come as well as to seek redress for sin past; otherwise sin will soon creep upon us again. If Satan is cast out of a man, he will endeavor to return into the house from whence he was cast out; and if he finds it empty he will soon take his opportunity and enter with seven other spirits more wicked than himself. They who take notice of Satan's subtlety in this kind by woeful experience find that after their most frequent prayers, strictest observation of the Sabbath, sincerest participation in the blessed Sacrament, solemnest humiliation of their souls on a day of fast, in and by which holy duties they have obtained great assurance of the pardon of their sins and much comfort to their souls, Satan has been very busy in tempting them afresh and drawing them to wallow in the mire of sin. Though therefore Christ Himself should say to us at once He did to the man who was brought on a bed to Him, "Be of good cheer; your sins are forgiven you," yet we have no cause to be careless and secure, but rather to be the more watchful lest Satan by a re-entry make our last estate worse than the first. We have need therefore of daily sanctification so that we who sin daily may cleanse away our sins by continual sanctification.

Man's Answering God's Mercy by Duty

QUESTION. What other doctrine may be observed from the inference of the sixth petition on the fifth?

ANSWER. The mercy of God to man requires duty of man to God. The fifth petition noted out God's great mercy in discharging our debt; and the sixth our bound duty in avoiding that which displeases and dishonors Him and, by the rule of contraries, in endeavoring after that which pleases and honors Him. It is said of them to whom God says, "It is My people," that they shall say, "The Lord is my God."

Equity and gratefulness require as much. It is most just and equal that the goodness of a Sovereign should be requited with all the duty that a subject can perform, and not to do it is a great point of ungratefulness.

The unrighteousness therefore and ungratefulness of man to God is too manifestly declared. Though man has rebelliously risen up against the Lord and taken part with His enemy, yet the Lord has graciously offered pardon to man; and, notwithstanding His gracious offer of pardon, man will not be drawn from the enemy's side, but as a sworn slave continues to fight under his colors. God greatly complains hereof.

Let us be better advised and first take notice of the kindness of the Lord to us, and then endeavor to walk worthy of the Lord. Let us therefore be as conscionable in performing duty to

God as we are desirous to receive mercy of God so that we may manifest a true childlike disposition to God and show we respect Him as well as ourselves in our desires and endeavors.

Avoiding Temptations

QUESTION. What may be gathered from the connection of the latter part of the sixth petition with the former part?

ANSWER. For avoiding evil temptations must be avoided. To this purpose tend the many dissuasions in Scripture from temptations, such as these: "Walk not in the way. Refrain thy foot. Come not nigh the door. Avoid. Pass away. Touch no unclean thing. Have no fellowship with the unfruitful works of darkness. Come out from among them."

Temptations to sons of Adam are as fire to dry stubble, dry tinder, yea, and dry gunpowder. A little spark soon causes a great flame. Temptation first brought man, even in his innocent state, to evil. If then corrupt man does not avoid temptation, how can he be free from evil? Observe the great evils into which the saints in any ages have fallen, and you shall find them to be occasioned by temptations. Noah's drunkenness, Lot's incest, David's adultery, Solomon's idolatry, Peter's denial of Christ, were all evil effects of temptations.

Be wise now therefore, O sons of men, especially you who indeed desire to be free from evil. Do not dally with temptations but rather, as Christ did, resist them manfully and put them away as far from you as you can. Men will not bring barrels of gunpowder near the fire, but lay them in places far from fire. Shall they be more careful for their earthly houses than you for your heavenly souls? Do not boast of your ability to quench the fire of all temptations. Your ability in this kind must then be greater than Peter's, or Solomon's, or David's, or Lot's, or Noah's, yea, or Adam's in his innocence. For a man to cast himself into temptations, and to receive no evil from those temptations, is as great a miracle as was the preservation of

Shadrach, Meshach, and Abednego in the midst of the hot fiery furnace was.

Calling on God For All Things

QUESTION. What may be observed from directing all the petitions that in any way concern our good to God?

ANSWER. God is all in all. The fourth petition sets Him out a Giver of good things, the fifth as a Forgiver of debts. The former part of the sixth sets Him out as a Preserver from danger whereunto we are subject, the latter part of the sixth as a Deliverer from evil into which we are fallen. On this ground might the psalmist well say, "Whom have I in heaven but Thee? And there is none upon earth that I desire besides Thee."

They who know and believe God to be as He is, all in all, cannot but detest that heathenish and blasphemous distinction of white and black gods, the former of which they made bestowers of good things, the latter deliverers from evil things. But to us there is but one God, the Father, from whom are all things and we in Him. Of Him we ought to seek every good thing we want. To Him we ought to fly for succor against all evil. So we are here taught, and so let us do.

The General Points for Which We Are Taught to Pray in the Last Petition

QUESTION. What are we to pray for by virtue of the last petition?

ANSWER. Such things as concern the whole petition in general, or the distinct parts thereof in particular:

1. In regard of the whole, we ought to pray for sanctification. Thus St. Paul prays for the Thessalonians, "The very God of peace sanctify you wholly." As our own happiness moves us to pray for justification in the former petition, that we may be acquitted of sin, for which we would otherwise be damned, so

the honor of God should move us to pray for sanctification. For this is the will of God, our sanctification, and thereby is the holy God much honored.

2. In regard of the manner of setting down this petition negatively, we are taught to pray for freedom against the power of sin, as the psalmist does where he says, "Cleanse me from secret faults; keep back Thy servant also from presumptuous sins. Let them not have dominion over me." For in sin there is a guilt that makes us liable to God's vengeance (this is prayed against in the fifth petition) and a power that holds us in bondage and makes us such slaves thereto that we cannot serve God.

3. For this end we are taught to pray for participation of the power of Christ's death.

4. And we are also to pray for participation of the Spirit of Christ. For in Christ's death there is distinctly to be considered a merit and a power. The merit thereof frees from the guilt and punishment of sin. The power thereof frees from the dominion, yea, and by degrees from the very act of sin, which in the saints after the death of their body shall utterly cease. Of this power of Christ's death thus speaks the apostle, "We are buried with Christ by baptism into death." And again, "Our old man is crucified with Him that the body of sin might be destroyed, that henceforth we should not serve sin." This power of Christ's death is conveyed to us by the Spirit of Christ. For we are dead in sin. But if the Spirit of Him who raised up Jesus from the dead dwells in us it will quicken us. Wherefore that we may partake of the power of Christ's death, we must pray for participation of the Spirit of Christ. David well knew how requisite this Spirit was to keep down the power of sin, and therefore, having prayed for pardon of sin, he further prayed that God would not take His holy Spirit from him.

These are the general things that by virtue of this whole petition we are to pray for. We will further note out such particulars as concern the distinct parts.

The Particulars for Which We Are to Pray by Virtue of the First Part of the Last Petition

QUESTION. What are the particulars to be prayed for under the first part of the sixth petition?

ANSWER 1. Knowledge of our spiritual enemies. Without knowledge of them there will be no fear of them, no desire of help and succor against them, or of freedom from them. The people of Laish, not knowing that the Danites were their enemies, or that they had any purpose to surprise them, were secure and made no preparations for their own defense and so were utterly vanquished. Such ignorance makes most in the world as secure as they are. Experience shows that the more ignorant any are the more deeply they are plunged into Satan's snares and the faster held thereby. Here therefore we must pray for knowledge of the distinct kinds of our spiritual enemies, of their number, might, malice, subtlety, and diligence. That we may the better know all these, the apostle largely and distinctly describes them in Ephesians 6:12.

ANSWER 2. Sight of the danger wherein we are by reason of them. To know that there are enemies, pernicious and dangerous enemies, little moves them who see no danger they are in by reason of such enemies. When Elisha's servant saw the host of Aram that compassed the place where he was, then he cried out, "Alas, my master, what shall we do?" Thus will they be affected who are able to discern the danger wherein they are by reason of their spiritual enemies. They will inquire what to do. But the danger that is not seen is not feared. Wherefore God sends ministers to people to open their eyes that they may come from the power of Satan to God.

ANSWER 3. Wisdom to discern their wiles, their many cunning strategies and kinds of assaults, and to find out where their strength lies and how they may be withstood. Thus shall we be kept the more safely from them that we do not fall into their temptations and be overcome by them. David, who obtained such wisdom, undoubtedly prayed for it.

ANSWER 4. Understanding our own weakness. How unable we are to stand of ourselves; much more unable to withstand such enemies as we have that are not, as we, flesh and blood, but spirits, yea, principalities and powers. When the spirit is ready, the flesh is weak. How much more weak will it be when the spirit is secure? Such as do not know their own weakness will be so overly bold and presumptuous as they will not fear to cast themselves into temptations.

ANSWER 5. Knowledge of the almighty power of God. Thus the apostle expressly prays in behalf of the Ephesians that they may know what is the exceeding greatness of His power towards them who believe. Knowledge of the enemy's power and of our own weakness cannot but frighten us and make us faintingly fall into their temptations unless withal we know the power of God to be able to make us stand, to subdue our enemies, and clean to free us from all their temptations. Knowledge hereof will raise up our hearts to God in all dangers.

ANSWER 6. Restraint of Satan's power. This the angel intended when he said to the devil, "The Lord rebuke thee." So malicious and audacious is Satan that he will not stick to assault the best if the Lord does not restrain him. It is most likely that he could not be ignorant that Christ was the Son of God, and yet he ventured to set upon Him. Now when God has given us understanding of His own power, of our own weakness, and of Satan's might and malice, then shall we see just cause to pray to God to rebuke Satan.

ANSWER 7. Assistance from God. For though Satan is restrained yet we cannot stand of ourselves, but shall fall even through our own weakness. The consideration of his own weakness made the psalmist seek help of God. For if God is for us, who can be against us? There is great reason therefore to seek assistance of God.

ANSWER 8. Confidence and courage in God. This is what the apostle intends where he exhorts us to be strong in the Lord. For none of them who trust in God shall be desolate. He is their buckler. He saves them. It is therefore most requisite to pray for confidence in Him.

ANSWER 9. Sufficient grace to bear our assaults when we are tempted. For sometimes it is needful for us to be tempted. Then our request ought to be that that which is needful may prove useful and profitable, which cannot be without God's grace. This therefore God gave in the time of temptation to His apostle, teaching us thereby in the like case to pray for the like grace.

ANSWER 10. Power over the flesh. The flesh is a secret inward tempter whereby Satan gets great advantage. It continually lusts and fights against the Spirit. If it prevails we are gone. Now in that this flesh is ever in us so long as we retain flesh upon us, who does not have cause to pray and cry as the apostle did, "O wretched man that I am, who shall deliver me from the body of this death!" (Romans 7:24) We can neither fly from nor put to flight this cruel enemy. We cannot but carry it about with us because it is bound to us. And, which is more miserable, we are forced to nourish this enemy; we cannot destroy it.

ANSWER 11. Contempt of the world. The world is another tempter that has sundry baits of pleasures, profits, and promotions to allure us unto it; and through five gates, the five senses, it wounds us. If they are opened, and our hearts attentive to the allurements thereof, we are in great danger to be overtaken therewith; death may enter by those windows. So there is great need we should pray as the psalmist did, "Incline not my heart to covetousness. Turn away mine eyes from beholding vanity" (Psalm 119:36–37).

ANSWER 12. Patience under all crosses. Crosses are a kind of trial and temptation. By impatience we are brought to faint and sink under them, which is to be overcome. This is what Satan watches for. For as soon as he observes any to faint and fall, he presently seizes upon them. Not without cause therefore did the apostle pray for the Colossians that they might bee strengthened with all might unto all patience. Under this heading are comprised hope, comfort, joy, and glory in afflictions, all to be prayed for and withal an invincible courage against persecution for the name of Christ.

ANSWER 13. Moderation of all afflictions. Though we have some patience, yet if afflictions increase they may so try our patience as to bring it to naught. For they who have the greatest measure have but their own measure; and afflictions by continuance and increase may exceed that measure, which the prophet well knew when he prayed, "O Lord, correct me, but with judgment." By judgment is not there meant vengeance and indignation (for it is opposed to wrath), but wisdom, discretion, and moderation. Hereby we are kept both from fainting when we are chastened and also from murmuring against the rod.

ANSWER 14. Preservation from a reprobate sense. For if we are once given up thereto then Satan has fast hold of us. God has utterly forsaken such. Every temptation is to them as a snare to hold them fast and as a hook to pull them down to destruction. Most fitly may that which the apostle says of them who will be rich be applied to such as are of a reprobate sense, "They fall into temptation and a snare, and into many foolish and hurtful lusts, that drown men in perdition and destruction." For men of a reprobate sense are such as, being deprived of all judgment and conscience, run headlong into such evils as are against the instinct of nature. Because blindness of mind, hardness of heart, deadness of conscience, perverseness of affection, pride, presumption, self-conceitedness, idleness, carelessness, security and such like vices are forerunners unto a reprobate sense, we ought also earnestly to pray against them all.

The Particulars for Which We Are to Pray by Virtue of the Second Part of the Last Petition

QUESTION. What are the particulars to be prayed for under the second part of the sixth petition?

ANSWER 1. Recovery from being fallen into sin. This is one main point desired in David's penitential psalm, especially in this phrase, "Renew a right spirit within me." Repentance is that grace whereby such as are fallen recover themselves, as is evident by this advice that Christ gives, "Remember from whence thou art fallen and repent." Repentance therefore is here to be prayed for. Satan is as much disappointed by repenting of sin as by not yielding to sin.

ANSWER 2. Dispossession of Satan. Satan is that evil one who has his finger in every evil thing. So long as he abides anywhere freedom from evil cannot be expected. If he therefore has really entered into any, as he did into the woman of Canaan's daughter, we must pray, as she did, to have him dispossessed. For by prayer and fasting he may be cast out. If otherwise he seizes on us by putting into us evil thoughts, stirring up corrupt humors, setting before us evil objects, frightening us, or vexing us any way in soul or body, we are taught to pray for deliverance from him.

ANSWER 3. Alienation of heart from the world. They who have been bewitched by the world, so as they have loved the same, and have been entangled therein, which is a great evil, ought to pray to be pulled out of it and to have their hearts turned from it, as the heart of Amnon was from Tamar. So that the hatred wherewith they hate it may be greater than the love wherewith they loved it. This we ought to pray for in regard of lewd company, unlawful games, undue honors, unjust gain, immoderate pleasures, or any other like thing wherewith we have been bewitched. Until our hearts are alienated from the world we shall never be thoroughly delivered from the evil of the world.

ANSWER 4. Suppression of all the lusts of the flesh after they are risen up. Prevention of them is implied in the former part of this petition. If that is not obtained, but the flesh rises up and lusts and rebels against the Spirit, our desire ought to be to have those lusts beaten down again, and we freed from the thralldom of them. St. Paul reckons up 17 particular lusts of the flesh together. Those and other like those are all simply evil, such evils as if they are not beaten down and we delivered from the bondage of them, will bring us to eternal death.

ANSWER 5. Removal of judgments. Such afflictions as come from the wrath of God, and so long as they lie upon us, manifest His indignation against us, are as evils to be prayed against. In which respect thus prays the church, "Turn us again, O God, and cause Thy face to shine. O Lord God of Hosts, how long wilt Thou be angry?" Such a judgment was that plague for the removal whereof David built an altar and offered sacrifice. Among these spiritual judgments are most earnestly to be prayed against, such as were mentioned previously. If the prevention of them is to be prayed for, much more is deliverance from them, for they are doubly evil as they are sins, and as they are punishments of sins and effects of God's wrath. To this heading may be also referred all manner of crosses, such as war, famine, plague, poverty, captivity, imprisonment, reproach, sickness, pain, and such like afflictions, for removal whereof we may pray as was shown before.

ANSWER 6. A blessed departure out of this world. So long as we are in this world we are subject to many evils that lie and press sorely upon us. But by death we are delivered from them all, at least if our death is in the Lord, for they only are blessed who die in the Lord. They who do not die in the Lord are not delivered from evil, but like the fish that leaps out of warm water into flaming fire go from the lesser evil into the greater by many degrees.

QUESTION. May a man thus pray for death?

ANSWER. Not simply and absolutely, with desire to have the time appointed by God prevented, but with submission to the good pleasure of God. Concerning our departure out of this world two things are here intended. First, that we are willing to depart, and, second, that our departure is in the Lord. Both these are manifested in old Simeon's swanlike song where he shows his willingness to depart and his desire to depart in peace. So much also is evident in St. Paul's desire. "I have a desire to depart." This was not an absolute prayer for death. It was a manifestation rather of what he could willingly have wished in his own behalf than of what he peremptorily or absolutely would desire. Now where he adds, "and to be with Christ," he shows what kind of death he desired. And this we must absolutely desire, that when we die we may die the death of the righteous, a happy death, which is a final delivery from all the evil whereunto in this world we are subject.

ANSWER 7. Resurrection of the body. For death in itself is an evil, holding the body in the grave as in a prison where it rots and is consumed. The resurrection of the body is what makes a man's dissolution to be a blessing. Thus is his body by death as seed sown in the ground that brings forth a harvest. This Christ has promised; this therefore we may and must pray for.

8. Absolution at the day of judgment. When our bodies are raised they, together with our souls, shall be presented before Christ's tribunal seat. There to be condemned for our sins is a far greater evil than any that in this world can befall us. And it

were better that our bodies should never be raised than to be raised to condemnation. Often therefore the apostle prays for the saints that they may be kept blameless unto the coming of Christ.

ANSWER 9. Eternal glory in heaven. They who are advanced thereunto are fully delivered from all evil, and from all fear of all evil. In which respect it is said that God shall wipe away all tears from their eyes, that is, He shall take away all occasions of mourning. Therefore by way of explication it is added, "There shall be no more death, neither sorrow, nor crying." This was it that the penitent thief prayed for in these words, "Lord, remember me when Thou comest into Thy kingdom." Thus we see how this prayer directs us to pray for al things that are needful for us, from that corruptible bread whereby our mortal bodies are nourished to that glory of soul and body that endures forever. For when we say, "Deliver us from evil," there remains nothing further for us to ask.

The Things for Which We Ought to Give Thanks in the Last Petition

QUESTION. What are the things for which thanks is to be given by virtue of the last petition?

ANSWER. Every sanctifying grace and freedom from the power of darkness.

For both these we have the expressed pattern of the apostle. In regard of the former he says, "I thank my God for the grace of God." Under this indefinite word "grace" he comprises every particular sanctifying grace. Wherefore he adds, "In every thing (that is, in every grace) ye are enriched. And ye are not destitute of any gift." In regard of the latter he also says, "I give thanks to the Father, who hath delivered us from the power of darkness." We heard before that sanctification was the sum of this petition. But particular sanctifying graces (whereof nine are reckoned up together in Galatians 5:22–23) are the parts and members that make up that sum. Of these therefore we must take notice, and for these we must give thanks. Now because that sum is implied under the negative, we are answerably to give thanks for freedom from the contrary, which the apostle calls the power of darkness. Under darkness he comprises sin, death, devil, and damnation. While we are under the power of these we are their vassals. It is therefore a blessing worthy of all praise to be freed from them.

Other particulars severally concern the distinct parts of this petition.

The Particulars for Which Thanks Is to Be Given by Virtue of the First Part of the Last Petition

QUESTION. What are the particulars for which the first part of the sixth petition requires thanks to be given?

ANSWER 1. Understanding of the law, whereby we know what sin is when we are tempted thereto, how fearful a thing it is to yield to such temptations, how wretched their case is that are left to the power of temptation. By the law is the knowledge of sin. That therefore which gives us notice of so great danger is a thing that is praise-worthy, especially if we have understanding thereof. In way of thankfulness David often acknowledges this.

ANSWER 2. Wisdom to discern our enemies and their assaults. This proceeds from the former and goes a degree further; and in that respect it binds us to more thankfulness. With thankfulness, says the psalmist to God, "Thou through Thy commandments hast made me wiser than mine enemies."

ANSWER 3. The victory that Christ has gotten over our spiritual enemies. It is in praise of Christ that the psalmist says to Him, "Thou hast led captivity captive." By captivity he means the world, the flesh, sin, death, the Devil and all other enemies of our soul. Were not these by Christ made captives, and so chained, restrained, and kept in, we could not stand against them; they would soon lead us captive. For our sakes Christ entered into combat with them and got victory over them. We reap the benefit thereof; we therefore must give the thanks to Christ and say (as the heavenly spirits do), "We give Thee thanks because Thou hast taken to Thee Thy great power, and hast reigned and destroyed them that destroy the earth."

ANSWER 4. Strength to withstand our enemies. As Christ Himself has overcome them, so by His Spirit He gives us power to overcome, in which respect it is said, "He hath given to us the Spirit of power." On which ground the apostle says, "I thank Him who hath enabled me."

ANSWER 5. Resolution to yield to no allurements whether they come from the flesh or the world. A true, settled resolution is a great means to keep us safe. This comes from God. For by nature our disposition is wholly inclined to the world and to the flesh. Wherefore as David blessed God for assuaging his passion and keeping him from shedding blood, so we must praise God (whenever our mind is alienated from the world and flesh) for that alteration of our disposition.

ANSWER 6. Patience to bear out all burdens. Afflictions to our weak flesh are sore temptations, but by patience we are kept from being swallowed up by them. In which respect the apostle saw great cause to thank God for the patience of the Thessalonians.

ANSWER 7. Power in all conflicts to overcome. Such, though they are led *unto* temptation, are not led *into* temptation. It is expressly noted of them who had gotten victory that they sang a song of praise.

The Particulars for Which Thanks Is to Be Given by Virtue of the Last Part of the Last Petition

QUESTION. What are the things for which the second part of the last petition requires thanks?

ANSWER 1. Repentance after sin committed. This is a sure evidence of deliverance from a great evil. Therefore the church glorified God because He had granted repentance.

ANSWER 2. Rescue out of Satan's clutches. If Satan has at any time gotten any advantage against us, as he gets great advantage against witches and sorcerers, yea, and against other impudent and audacious sinners whom he has fast in his clutches, to be rescued and recovered out of his hands affords just cause of much thanks. This Mary Magdalene, out of whom went seven devils, well knew to be most due, and therefore in testimony of thankfulness she followed Christ and ministered to Him of her substance.

ANSWER 3. Recovery out of the world. The apostle ascribed glory to Christ for delivering us from this present evil world.

ANSWER 4. Conquest of the Spirit over the flesh. For by the Spirit's conquest we are freed from the dominion of the flesh. For this therefore the apostle gives express thanks.

ANSWER 5. Removal of judgments. Judgments and all manner of crosses are in their kind evils, and removal of them is a deliverance from those evils. Whereupon the saints have been thankful for such deliverances. The Israelites gave thanks to God for freeing them from the Egyptian bondage, David for causing the plague to cease, Hezekiah for taking away a deadly disease, and the church for returning her from captivity.

ANSWER 6. Victory over death. Death in itself is a dreadful evil, the very entrance into damnation. But by Christ the sting of it is pulled out and the nature of it is altered. It is made a gate into eternal glory. This is that victory for which St. Paul gives thanks.

ANSWER 7. Hope of resurrection to life.

ANSWER 8. Hope of eternal glory. These are full and final deliverances from all evil. God's promise of these to such as believe is as a performance of them. Our hope therefore resting on God's promise for these affords just occasion of rejoicing and praising God, as St. Peter does and St. Paul also.

Duties Required in the Last Petition

QUESTION. What duties are we to endeavor after by virtue of the last petition?

ANSWER 1. To abstain from all sin. For this is the main thing here prayed against. This is what makes temptation so hurtful as it is. The more we forbear sin the less damage we shall receive from any temptations. Many, many therefore are the dissuasions of Scripture against sin.

ANSWER 2. To perfect holiness. For under the avoiding of any evil, an endeavoring after the contrary good is always in Scripture implied. Yea, they are very often joined together. Now holiness is perfected both by adding one grace to another and also by continual growth in every grace.

These two duties arise from the general sum of the last petition.

ANSWER 3. To be jealous over ourselves, fearing lest at any time we should be overcome by any temptation. For we are not only weak, easy to be overtaken, and overthrown by every temptation, but also very prone to yield to Satan's temptations because they are either agreeable to our corrupt humor or else we are so fearful as to think we shall never stand out against them. This Christian jealousy will make us the more instantly and constantly to seek help of God.

ANSWER 4. To avoid all occasions of evil. Occasions of evil are temptations to evil. Should not they then who pray against temptations avoid them as much as possibly they can?

ANSWER 5. To withstand beginnings. So did the apostle when he would not give place to false brethren (who were dangerous tempters), no, not for an hour. Thus much also he intends in this exhortation, "Give no place to the Devil," which is as if he had said, "If Satan at any time tempts you, do not yield an inch to him; let him get no advantage at all, which he cannot but get if at the beginning you yield any whit at all to him. Much good is gotten by a due observation of this duty, and much wisdom is manifested thereby. For that evil that in the beginning is easily prevented can hardly, if at all, without very much damage be redressed after it has found some entrance. Imagine poisonous and pestiferous diseases, fretting and festering sores, fires, breaches of water, and enemies entering within the walls of a city.

ANSWER 6. To watch continually. This is a duty whereunto in Scripture we are much exhorted, and that not without cause. For our spiritual enemies are always ready to tempt us, narrowly prying where to get any advantage against us. And soon they will get too great advantage if we are not the more watchful. To show that this duty is fitly inferred out of this petition, Christ expressly joins it with prayer against temptation, saying, "Watch and pray that ye enter not into temptation."

ANSWER 7. To be sober and temperate. Where these are not, every tempter will rule as he wishes. For intemperance and all excess blind the understanding and open a passage to all manner of evil desires and filthy lusts, and make us unfit to pray, to watch, to fight, and to defend ourselves against our spiritual enemies.

ANSWER 8. To cast off every burden. By burdens are meant not only such things as are simply evil in themselves, but such also as being in their nature good and may lawfully be used, yet through our weakness and inability to use them well, prove impediments to us in our spiritual combat, as the riches of that ruler whom Christ advised to sell all that he had and to give it to the poor. Thus if honors, offices, recreations, company that we frequent, or any worldly thing wherein we delight prove a burden to us and make us unfit to resist temptations, yea, rather make us yield to temptations, we are to cast them off, to avoid and forsake them.

ANSWER 9. To mortify our members of the earth. The flesh, that is our corrupt nature, which contains in it the mass of all sin, is called a body. This body is made up of several particular lusts and evil motions as a body of members. And as a body exercises all functions by the members, so the flesh executes all mischiefs by particular lusts; and one lust helps another as one member helps another. And as dear are these lusts to the natural man as the members of his body. Those particular lusts are therefore fitly called members, and they are said to be members on the earth in opposition to the spirit, and the graces thereof that come from heaven and bring men to heaven; in their own condition, which is as the earth, base, filthy, corrupt, and vain; in their operation whereby they make men grovel and dote on the earth and the things therein. By mortifying these the foresaid body (which is a dangerous tempter) will in time be deprived of all strength, and we freed from the danger of the temptations thereof. Be diligent therefore in searching them out, and having found them do not spare them as Saul did the fat beasts; but deal with them as Samuel did with Agag and Joshua with the kings of Canaan.

ANSWER 10. To beat down our body. This is done by forbearing to pamper ourselves and to satisfy our carnal desires, so that the flesh may not wax wanton and like a pampered jade become unruly; but that we may live within the compass prescribed and limited by God's Word.

ANSWER 11. To renounce the world. The world is such a tempter as the friendship of it is enmity with God. "If any man love the world, the love of the Father is not in him." Demas, that old disciple, by embracing the world was brought to renounce his Christian profession. It is therefore most meet that the world be crucified to us and we to the world; that our hearts be cleanly alienated one from another, and that we have no more to do one with another than the living with the dead.

Thus shall we be sure not to be overtaken by the temptations of the world.

ANSWER 12. To resist the Devil. This is the only way to escape his temptations. He is like a wolf that fiercely pursues and never leaves such as fearfully fly from him, but flies from such as manfully stand against him. So the apostle says, "Resist the Devil and he will flee from you."

ANSWER 13. To put our trust in God. To what end do we else pray unto God?

ANSWER 14. To suffer afflictions patiently. All crosses and afflictions are temptations. By a patient enduring of them we keep ourselves from being overcome by them. Let patience therefore have her perfect work.

These last twelve duties arise from the first part of the last petition.

ANSWER 15. To avoid that which is in any way evil. This we praying against must carefully avoid. The apostle exhorts us to abstain from all appearance of evil.

ANSWER 16. To return from that evil whereinto we are fallen. For they who pray to be delivered from evil must not lie in evil. All the exhortations in the Scripture to repent tend to this purpose.

ANSWER 17. To take heed of relapse. A relapse in bodily diseases is dangerous, much more in the soul's disease. It is a doggish trick to turn to his own vomit again.

ANSWER 18. To keep the enemy from returning after he is cast out. He will seek to reenter. If he gets what he seeks our last estate will be worse than our first.

ANSWER 19. To stand always armed. While we live we shall be tempted. Though the tempter is repulsed never so often, he will still be prying where to get an advantage. Therefore the apostle says, "Having done all, stand."

ANSWER 20. Be faithful unto death. Death brings a final end to all assaults. It is the last enemy. He who is faithful unto death by death receives full deliverance from all evil. Perseverance gives evidence of election to life for it is proper to the elect.

These last six duties arise from the last part of the last petition.

Duties Required in the Last Petition in Regard of Others

QUESTION. What duties does the last petition teach us in the behalf of others?

ANSWER 1. To consider one another. We ought to take notice of one another's spiritual estate so that we may better know how to do good mutually for one another. This is a general duty whereby way is made unto other duties.

ANSWER 2. To keep others from sin. Thus will they be kept from being hurt by any temptation. The captains of Ephraim who stood up against them who came from the war with sundry captives of Judah, and suffered them not to carry their captives away, render this reason: "Ye intend to add more to our sins, and to our trespass." Their intent therefore was to keep their brethren from sin.

ANSWER 3. To edify others. They who are well built up in grace are well armed against all temptations. This is a special fruit of love. For love edifies, and that by instruction, exhortation, admonition, and other like duties.

ANSWER 4. To encourage others against their enemies. What a notable encouragement is this of the apostle, "Watch you, stand fast in the faith, quit you like men, be strong." Another like, but more large encouragement is set down in Ephesians 6:10–13. By good encouragement life and spirit is put into men and they are emboldened like lions to stand against their enemies. For this the true grounds of good encouragement must be laid down, which are God's presence, God's promises, God's properties, the necessity of standing out and fighting valiantly, the glory of the conquest, the damages of yielding, the misery of being overcome, with the like.

ANSWER 5. To strengthen the weak. This Christ expressly gave in His charge to Peter. And this is done not only by encouragement, but also by bearing their infirmities and burdens. Thus they who through their own weakness might have been made a prey to tempters may be kept safe from them.

ANSWER 6. To keep others from falling from the grace of God. The apostle advises to look diligently hereunto. There is no place of standing between God's grace and Satan's snare; he who falls from that falls into this.

ANSWER 7. To restore such as fall. We may not leave such as are fallen for we pray that they may be delivered. The law teaches us to help up a beast being fallen. Does God take care for beasts? Or did He say it altogether for our sakes? For our sakes, no doubt, this is written.

ANSWER 8. To save the obstinate with fear. Though men blinded in mind and hardened in heart willfully give themselves over to Satan, yet we ought not to suffer them to abide in his clutches. But as we would snatch, and with violence pull men out of the fire, so ought we to pull such out of the temptation wherein they lie. Thus dealt St. Paul with the incestuous Corinthian. He delivered him unto Satan for the destruction of the flesh that the spirit might be saved. Was not this to save him with fear?

ANSWER 9. To receive the penitent. If a man has been overtaken with a temptation, and by his repentance manifests a recovery from the same, we ought so to account of him as if he had not fallen at all. So St. Paul required the Corinthians to receive the forenamed incestuous person and to forgive him and comfort him. This is a special means to make his deliverance firm and stable.

ANSWER 10. To pray for others. This is the main duty here intended. This I reserve to the last place because it is a duty that may be performed when no other can be, even to such as will not accept any other duty; of all the rest it is the most effectual.

The Matter of Humiliation Gathered Out of the Last Petition

QUESTION. What are the things to be bewailed by reason of the sixth petition?

ANSWER 1. Our first parents yielding to the devil. This is the original ground of all that spiritual slavery wherein we are, and of that need we have so earnestly to pray against temptation.

ANSWER 2. The power, malice, subtlety, and diligence of Satan. For Satan is the chief tempter who has a finger in all temptations in which respect the more powerful, malicious, subtle, and diligent he is, the more dangerous is temptation. Not without cause therefore did the divine voice cry, "Woe to the inhabitants of the earth, and of the sea, because the Devil is come down to you, having great wrath."

ANSWER 3. The many stumbling blocks in the world. In regard of these Christ cries, "Woe to the world." These are so much the more to be bewailed by reason of the deceitfulness of the world that so bewitches many that it draws them to those stumbling blocks and makes them to stumble and fall thereat, as Demas did. Yea, on this ground our love, even our too inordinate love, of this world is to be bewailed.

ANSWER 4. The depravity of our nature. God Himself much complains hereof. This is what makes all manner of temptations much more dangerous than otherwise they would be.

ANSWER 5. Our spiritual blindness. By reason hereof we cannot discern the temptations wherewith we are assaulted, but are easily led into the midst of them as the Aramites were into the midst of Samaria.

ANSWER 6. Our foolish proneness to yield to every temptation, as the fish is to snatch at every bait. Thus are we often taken.

ANSWER 7. The rebellions of our flesh. This makes us refuse all the means that are sanctified to keep us from temptation and to take part with the tempters, and so to become captives and slaves unto them. This rebellion, and this thraldom, the apostle greatly bewails.

ANSWER 8. Presumption in our strength. This is bewailed in the church of Laodicea, and not without cause. For it is the cause of many one's fall. Instance Peter and the other disciples.

ANSWER 9. Inability to stand against temptations. Of this weakness of the flesh Christ complained where He willed His disciples to pray against temptation.

ANSWER 10. Timidity, or an immoderate fear of man. This is the cause that by persecution, yea, by threats and reproaches many are drawn from their holy profession.

ANSWER 11. Impatience. Many crosses that might easily be borne by a patient spirit through impatience prove to be very hurtful temptations.

ANSWER 12. Provocations of God's wrath. Our only hope and confidence of being freed from temptations, or so helped against them as they shall not overcome us, is in God. If God then is provoked to wrath, and so moved to deny us His assistance, and to give us over to the power of tempters, how can we stand? Under this heading, as all manner of sins, so abusing His mercies, grieving His Spirit, despising His messengers, and such like, are comprised.

These last twelve are most directly against the first part of the last petition. The others that follow are against the other part.

ANSWER 13. Loss of first love.

ANSWER 14. Backsliding from the truth.

These two, and others like these, are directly contrary to the main intent of adding the latter clause of the last petition to the former, which is recovery from evil. If recovery from evil is to be prayed for, is it not a matter much to be bewailed that such as are recovered should relapse and make their last estate worse than the first?

ANSWER 15. Hardness of heart.

ANSWER 16. Infidelity.

ANSWER 17. Impenitence.

These last three, and others like them, make men incapable of recovery. These are so much the more therefore to be bewailed.

QUESTION. What other particulars are to be bewailed under the last petition in relation to others?

ANSWER 1. Enticing others to sin.

ANSWER 2. Encouraging them in sin.

ANSWER 3. Discouraging the weak.

ANSWER 4. Scoffing at grace.

By these and such like means men are sorely tempted. Now if we ought to pray for others that they are not led into temptation, to lead others into temptation gives just and great cause of humiliation.

ANSWER 5. Leaving them that are fallen.

ANSWER 6. Rejecting the penitent.

These two branches of failure to show mercy are contrary to the desire and duty of recovering others, intimated in the last branch of the last petition, and on that ground are to be bewailed.

QUESTION. What does the inference of this sixth petition upon the fifth show to be bewailed?

ANSWER 1. A dead and naked faith. In the former petition faith in Christ for pardon of sin is professed. In this petition a manifestation of the truth of that faith by forsaking sin, and by performing all duties of righteousness, is intimated. To profess faith and not to declare it by the fruits thereof is much to be lamented as a thing that is dishonoring to God, disgraceful to the gospel of Christ, advantageous to Satan, and damaging to the souls of such vain professors. St. Jude greatly bewailed them.

ANSWER 2. A vainglorious conceit of perfection. Christ often upbraided this to the Pharisees. This petition is in vain prescribed to such.

ANSWER 3. Ingratitude, when they who daily seek mercy of God take part with the enemies of God, like Israel of whom the prophet Hosea complained much.

Hitherto the first part of the substance of prayer, which is petition, in the six branches thereof has been handled. The second follows, which is praise.

8

The Second Part of the Prayer, Praise

Pressing Prayer with Weighty Reasons

QUESTION. Which is the form of praise?

ANSWER. "For Thine is the kingdom, and the power, and the glory forever."

QUESTION. How are these words to be considered?

ANSWER. In relation to the petitions and singly by themselves.

In relation to the petitions this clause respects him who makes the petitions to strengthen his faith and to enlarge his desire. But singly considered by itself it respects God to whom the petitions are directed to set out the glory of His name.

QUESTION. How is the forenamed relation manifested?

ANSWER. By this particle of connection, "for" or "because," which implies a reason of all the petitions, but not as if God were drawn by reasons to yield to that which otherwise He would not yield to. For what God does He does of Himself, simply because He will do it. "I will be gracious to whom I will be gracious; and I will show mercy on whom I will show mercy." He works all things after the counsel of His own will. For our sakes therefore this reason is added to the petitions, and that partly to put an edge unto our prayers and to sharpen them, and partly to put strength unto our faith and to make us without doubting to expect a gracious grant of them.

QUESTION. What doctrine may be raised from the addition of this reason?

ANSWER. Prayer is to be pressed with reasons. Take a view of the prayers of saints recorded in Scripture and you shall find this abundantly proven. For example, read the prayers of Moses, Joshua, Asa, Jehoshaphat, Hezekiah, and others.

Grounds and reasons of prayer being rightly ordered demonstrate a necessity of making the prayer and great equity for obtaining the things prayed for; and in that respect they put life, vigor, and fervency into the spirit of him who prays, whereby the prayer comes to be much more acceptable and available.

We learn hereby to ponder our prayers before we pour them forth, and duly to consider what we ask, why we ask what we ask, what grounds we have of obtaining our desire, so that we may with greater fervency of desire and steadfastness of faith, yea and importunity and constancy hold out, even if God seems at first not to hear or regard our prayer. They who know that their prayers are grounded on good, just, and weighty reasons will cry day and night unto Him and will not hold their peace nor will they rest. They will not let the Lord alone, but will hold Him until He blesses them.

Taking Grounds for Faith in Prayer from God Himself

QUESTION. Whence is the reason used in the Lord's Prayer taken?

ANSWER. From God Himself. For the sum of it is a declaration of such things as pertain to God and show Him to be both able and willing to grant such suits as are rightly made unto Him.

QUESTION. What doctrine does the kind of reason import?

ANSWER. In prayer the main ground of our pleading must be fetched from God. Well consider the forenamed prayers of Moses, Joshua, Asa, Jehoshaphat, Hezekiah, and others like them and in them all you shall find God's covenant, truth, mercy, power, and other like motives pleaded. In particular take for this purpose special notice of Daniel's powerful prayer thus expressed, "O my God, incline Thine ear and hear, open Thine eyes and behold our desolations, and the city which is called by Thy name. For we do not present our supplications before Thee for our righteousness, but for Thy great mercies. O Lord, hear. O Lord, forgive. O Lord, hearken and do. Defer not for Thine own sake, O my God; for Thy city and Thy people are called by Thy name." Here protestation is made against any worth in themselves, and the name and mercies of God only are pleaded. And that for good reason, for:

1. In ourselves there can be nothing to plead before God whereby He should be moved to grant our desire. For who does not see just cause to say of himself as Jacob once did, "I am less than all Thy mercies," that is, "I am not worthy of the least of all Thy mercies," yea, and to cry as the psalmist did, "Enter not into judgment with Thy servant, for in Thy sight shall no man living be justified."

2. Outside of God there can be nothing to move Him. For who has anything that He has not received of God? Of Him and through Him are all things. Whatever therefore is in prayer pleaded before God must be fetched from God Himself.

OBJECTION. Moses in his prayer pleaded Abraham, Isaac, and Israel desiring God to remember them. The psalmist pleads David, his afflictions, his oath, and his vow. Hezekiah pleads his uprightness and integrity. The desolations of God's people and the insults of their enemies are also often pleaded, and other like reasons taken from men.

ANSWER. The main force of all these reasons rests in God. For where Abraham, Isaac, Israel, and David are named God's covenant made to them is intended so as no worth in their persons, but God's truth in keeping His covenant made with them, is pleaded. Where mention is made of His servants' oath and vow, the honor and glory that by their oath and vow was covenanted to God is meant, so that not the worth of the oath and vow as man's work, but the matter thereof that tended to God's glory is pleaded. The praise of God is in this form of the Lord's Prayer chiefly intended, and often by the saints expressed and pleaded in their prayers to enforce the same. Where the integrity and uprightness of any of God's saints is produced in prayer it is to be considered as an effectual work of God's Spirit and an undoubted evidence of God's favor, so that no desert of man, but the stamp of God's own work, and pledge or seal of His own favor and grace, is pleaded. Besides, respect hereby may be had to the truth of God's covenant, as in Hezekiah's case. For God had made a covenant with David, and confirmed it by oath, that his children, even the fruit of his body, if they kept God's covenant, would sit upon his throne forevermore. Now Hezekiah, being lineally descended from David, and having endeavored in all sincerity to keep God's covenant, was so sick that he received the sentence of death before he had a child to succeed him on the throne of David. Wherefore, for sparing his life, at least till he might have issue, and God's covenant thereby be verified, he pleaded his integrity, which was the condition required of God. He pleaded it, I say, not as a matter of merit, but as evidence that the God of truth would make good His own word. God's truth and faithfulness therefore is the ground of Hezekiah's plea. Where the miseries, afflictions, and desolations of God's people are urged in prayer, there God's pity is especially aimed at. For misery is the object of mercy and pity. That object is laid forth to give assurance that the God of pity will afford succor where so fit an object for succor is presented before him. Yea in this kind of plea God's truth and power is also aimed at. For the greater the distress is, the more evidently is God's power manifested in giving deliverance. And God, having promised to deliver His saints out of all their troubles, by mentioning any troubles of His saints unto Him, His own promise and His truth in keeping promise is pleaded. Where the insults of enemies are pressed as a reason, the ground of that reason must be the honor of God because such insults make to the dishonor of His great name. Thus, by answering these objections distinctly, the truth of the doctrine is made clearer, that the only true ground of a sufficient plea in prayer is in God.

The grounds of plea that papists teach and practice must be false because they are not taken from God. They are these: intercession of saints, blood of martyrs, works of supererogation by extraordinary persons, merit of a man's own works, and others like these. What strength can these add to faith in prayer? What assurance can they give of being heard when they depend on man and have no warrant out of God's Word?

We who are better instructed ought to take notice of the things whereby God has made Himself known to us, being comprised under this title "the name of God." And when we come to prayer, meditate thereon seriously that our faith, being grounded on so sure a Rock as God is, and on His promises and properties, we may with comfort and patience expect a gracious answer and blessed grant of our petitions.

The reason added to the petitions being generally touched, it is further more distinctly in the several branches thereof to be handled.

Appropriating God's Attributes to Himself

QUESTION. How is God in this reason set out?

ANSWER. By His attributes, for these words, "kingdom," "power," "glory," and "forever" point out four distinct attributes of God:

1. Sovereignty, kingdom.
2. Omnipotence, power.
3. Excellence, glory.
4. Eternity, forever.

QUESTION. How are these attributes applied to God?

ANSWER. By a special property and excellence. So much does this particle "Thine" and the article "the" import. It is as if He had said, "Thine and Thine only are these. Thine they are originally of Thyself, and that in an infinite measure and degree." In the same manner that the apostle applies immortality may these and all other divine attributes be applied to God, who alone has kingdom, power, and glory forever.

Though this particle "Thine" is but once expressed, yet by virtue of the copulative particle "and" it is particularly to be applied to every one of the other properties.

As for the fourth attribute, eternity, intimated in this clause, "forever," it is so expressed as pertaining to all and each of the other three. For God's kingdom is forever. His power is forever. His glory is forever; and whatever else is in God is, as God Himself, forever. Well therefore may this be considered in relation to other attributes as an attribute of them, and simply in itself as a distinct attribute.

God's Having All things at His Command

QUESTION. What kind of kingdom is here meant?

ANSWER. God's universal kingdom, by virtue whereof He has a supreme and absolute sovereignty in all places, over all things. So as this kind of kingdom comprises all kinds under it, even His peculiar kingdom also, the church of Christ. In this extent it is said that His kingdom rules over all.

QUESTION. What does this application of kingdom to God import?

ANSWER. God has all things at His command. Where David applied this absolute sovereignty to God in the very words that Christ does, saying, "Thine is the kingdom, O Lord," he adds by way of explication, "All that is in heaven and in earth is Thine. Both riches and honor come of Thee and in Thine hand it is to make great, and to give strength unto all."

It is God who first made all things, and who still upholds, preserves, and governs all things. Of Him, and through Him, and to Him are all things. He is the Possessor of heaven and earth. All things therefore must be at His command.

On this ground we see what just cause we have to make all the forenamed petitions unto God, and of Him to ask whatever is to be asked in rayer. For all are at His disposing. The psalmist, upon his acknowledgement of God's sovereignty, makes this inference, "Command deliverance for Jacob."

The Absolute Supremacy of God's Sovereignty

QUESTION. What does the emphatic manner of attributing kingdom to God import?

ANSWER. God is the most supreme and absolute Sovereignty. The kingdom, that is, that Sovereignty that may indeed and properly be called a kingdom, which is over all and under none is God's. Wherefore God is called a great King, a King of kings and Lord of lords, a great King above all gods, the King and Lord of Hosts, a King who has the heavens for His throne and the earth for His footstool.

God was before all, even eternal. Though the creatures over which He reigns were not from eternity, yet the eternal God had an eternal right of reigning by virtue whereof He was King over all things that are so soon as ever they were. And this right He must have of Himself and by Himself. For He being an eternal King, who could be before Him from whom He might receive a right of sovereignty? As He is God of Himself, so He is Lord of Himself, a supreme and absolute Monarch.

This supremacy of God's sovereignty teaches such as have any sovereignty to cast their crowns down at the feet of this high Sovereign. However there are some who in their dominions are in all causes, and over all persons supreme governors, yet with this limitation, under God. That sovereignty that they have is God's image, by virtue whereof they are called gods.

Yet because they are what they are of God and under God, they are also called children of the Most High, anointed of the Lord, ministers of God.

ANSWER 2. It teaches us all to advance God above all and to prefer Him before all, to fear Him, love Him, trust in Him, and in every way respect Him more than all others, and to obey Him rather than any other king or governor. This is such a ruled case, so clear and evident, as the apostles made their enemies judges thereof. If a king in his dominions is to be preferred and obeyed before all subordinate magistrates, much more God before all kings and other governors throughout the whole world.

God Alone Is King

QUESTION. What does the appropriating of kingdom to God import?

ANSWER. God's is the only kingdom. This particle "Thine" (Thine is the kingdom) imports a property. All other kingdoms are but parts of His. There is no power but of God. The powers that be are ordained of God. Nebuchadnezzar was forced to acknowledge as much.

This is to be known and acknowledged both to keep us from all base and slavish obedience to earthly governors in things against God's will, and also to provoke us readily and willingly to obey them in all lawful things for conscience's sake, for the Lord's sake. If earthly kingdoms are, as they are, within the limits of God's kingdom, parts thereof, subordinate thereto, then no obedience must be yielded to the governors of them but that which may stand with the laws of God's kingdom so as God the only King may be obeyed therein and thereby. But in everything that may stand with the laws of God's kingdom obedience is to be yielded to governors on earth because their kingdoms are parts of God's, and they are God's deputies and ministers. Whoever therefore resists the power resists the ordinance of God; and they who resist shall receive to themselves damnation. These are the grounds that bind us to obey magistrates for conscience's sake. Not that one man has power over another's conscience; this power is God's prerogative. But that God to whom all men's consciences are and ought to be subject has ordained the powers and requires subjection to them. So that which is done for conscience's sake is done for the Lord's sake.

The Duties Due to God by Reason of His Kingdom, and Comfort Thence Arising

QUESTION. What are the duties that the Holy Ghost, by virtue of God's kingdom and sovereignty, requires of us?

ANSWER 1. To allow God to enter in and abide among us.

ANSWER 2. To be willing that He reign and rule over us.

ANSWER 3. To be humbled and to tremble at His presence.

ANSWER 4. To fear and reverence His majesty.

ANSWER 5. To worship Him.

ANSWER 6. To praise and glorify Him.

ANSWER 7. To serve and obey Him.

ANSWER 8. To offer Him the best that we have.

ANSWER 9. To take heed of profaning or abusing anything that is His.

ANSWER 10. To testify our love to Him by rejoicing in Him.

ANSWER 11. To seek help of Him.

ANSWER 12. To rest and rely upon Him.

QUESTION. What is the comfort that arises from God's sovereignty?

ANSWER. Assurance of supply of all things needful and protection from all things hurtful. Assurance, I say, to such as take Him for their King, and in testimony thereof are ready to perform all the forenamed duties. Though God is a King over all, yet all do not take Him for their King. Some being sons of Belial, without yoke, say, "Let us break His bonds asunder and cast His cords away from us. We will not have Him to rule over us." Yet they will say that God is their King. And because they do not yield willingly to Him, by force He keeps them under. To these more terror than comfort arises from God's sovereignty. But to His loyal subjects much comfort must arise. For their King having all things at His command, will He allow them to want what He knows to be beneficial for them or to be annoyed with any hurtful thing? All the properties of a good king are in God. But to provide for his subjects and to protect them are properties set down by the Holy Ghost in the description of a good king. Shall not God, the best and chief King, the only true King, whose this kingdom is, do those things for His subjects?

This much of God's kingdom. The next property is His power in these words, "and the power."

God's Power, What it Is and How Far it Extends

QUESTION. What is meant by God's power?

ANSWER. His ability to do anything. Power attributed to a creature implies that ability that it has; so it does also when applied to the Creator. Now as other attributes applied to God are His very essence, and as His essence is infinite, so also is His power, which extends itself to everything that by power may be done. You can see this according to these Scripture phrases: Is anything too hard for the Lord? With God nothing is impossible. With God all things are possible. In this respect He is called God Almighty.

QUESTION. Are all things, without exception, within the compass of God's power?

ANSWER. Not such things as import impotence or imperfection. God's power would not be omnipotent, but rather impotent, if those were within the circuit thereof. Such phrases therefore as "cannot" and "impossible" are, in relation to those things, applied to God.

Some of the particulars that by reason of omnipotence God cannot do are these:

1. Matters of contradiction, as one thing at the same time to be and not to be, or one and the same thing to be infinite and finite. Such things are in their nature impossible. And God cannot establish them because they are against truth and imply impotence. For whatever is, it is by the power of the Creator, and by His power it is as it is. If withal it is not when it is, or is contrary to what the Creator makes it, where is the power of the Creator? If He Himself should be supposed to establish such contradictions, He cannot be supposed to establish them by His power. The one part is by power, the other therefore must be, if it could be, by that which is contrary to power, even by impotence.

2. Matters of iniquity, all sinful matters. As these are contrary to the will, purity, and perfection of God, so they arise from impotence of understanding, will, memory, conscience, affection, and actions. It is by power that any either do not or cannot sin. It is by weakness therefore that any fall into sin. These emphatic phrases ("shall not the Judge of all the earth do right? Are not the ways of the Lord equal? Is God unrighteous? Is there unrighteousness with God?") all imply an impossibility. So far is God from sin as He cannot be tempted with evil, neither does He tempt any man.

3. Matters of inconstancy and variableness. By power it is that one remains firm, stable, constant, inviolable, and unchangeable. Weakness therefore causes the contrary. Of the Almighty it is said, "With Him is no variableness, neither shadow of turning." Where it is said, "He will not repent," He is called "the strength of Israel," whereby is implied that it is of strength that He does not change. On this ground it is also

said, "God cannot deny Himself. God cannot lie. It is impossible that God should lie."

4. Matters of passion or suffering, as to be mocked, deceived, oppressed, put to death, with the like. These imply a subjection to a superior power, and in that respect an impotence. Wherefore it is said of God, He is not mocked. He cannot be tempted. The Son of God, to make Himself capable of suffering, which for man's redemption was necessary, assumed flesh, in which He was put to death. For in His divine nature He could not die nor in any way suffer.

The Difference between God's Absolute and Actual Power

QUESTION. Does God's power actually extend itself to all things that by power may be done?

ANSWER. No, not to bring them into act or to effect them. There are many, many things that God is able to do that He does not, nor ever will do. He could have sent His angels to have rescued Christ out of the Jews' hands. He could out of stones have raised children to Abraham. He could have made more worlds. He could have sent more floods to destroy the world again and again. He could have redeemed the devils. Infinite are the things that He could do but will not do. Well, therefore, is God's power distinguished into His absolute and actual power.

God's absolute power is that whereby He is able to do whatever by power may be done, as is evident by these phrases, "With God nothing is impossible. With God all things are possible."

God's actual power is that whereby He does all things that in His counsel He determines to do. As it is written, "He hath done whatsoever He pleased."

Herein lies the difference between God's absolute and actual power. His absolute power extends itself beyond His will, as the forenamed instances show. But His actual power is bound within the compass of His will. In this limitation He was well instructed who said to Christ, "If Thou wilt Thou canst make me clean." And note they who said of God, "Our God whom we serve is able to deliver us." Thereupon they all so trusted to God's power that they subjected themselves to His will.

How Power Is Proper to God

QUESTION. Why is power by a property with emphasis applied to God thus, "And the power?"

ANSWER 1. Power, truly and properly, is God's alone. It is therefore called a might of power. So all power compared to His is as no power, but very weakness. His is the power. That which is worthy to be called power is God's. Power belongs unto God.

2. God's power is beyond all limits. It is an exceeding greatness of power. To it nothing is impossible. By it all things were made and are upheld and preserved. By it may all things be destroyed and brought to naught. The most stable and inviolable course that is set to any creature by it may be altered. By it the sun can be made to stand still or to run back, the sea to be divided, and the rock to send forth water.

3. All power is derived from God's. "Hast thou given the horse strength?" says God to man, implying thereby that God has done it, and none but God. "Thou couldst have no power at all (says Christ to Pilate) except it were given thee from above." Power and might are in God's hand. In His hand it is to give strength to all.

4. All power is subordinate to God's. This Asa acknowledges where he says, "It is nothing with Thee to help, whether with many, or with them that have no power." So, "If God be for us, who can be against us? It is better to trust in the Lord

than to put confidence in man." On these and other like grounds well may it be said to God, "Thine is the Power."

The Duties Due to God by Reason of His Power

QUESTION. What duties are required by virtue of God's power?

ANSWER 1. To put difference between God and all creatures. In regard of the power of God the psalmist says, "O Lord God of hosts, who is a strong Lord like unto Thee?" And to prove that none is like God he sets out many evidences of God's power.

ANSWER 2. To fly to God in all time of need and to seek help of Him, as that leper did of Christ who said, "If Thou wilt Thou canst make me clean."

ANSWER 3. To believe God's Word, for He is able to make it good. Abraham was strong in faith, being fully persuaded that what God had promised He was able to perform.

ANSWER 4. To be strong in God. His power is a power of might. He can give strength to us.

ANSWER 5. To abide contentedly in the state wherein God sets us. So did he who said, "I can do all things through Christ that strengtheneth me."

ANSWER 6. To endure patiently all afflictions. So did the same apostle who said, "I suffer these things, for I am persuaded that He is able to keep that which I have committed to Him."

ANSWER 7. To carry ourselves humbly before God. Humble yourselves under the mighty hand of God. God's is a mighty hand; we must therefore be humble under it.

ANSWER 8. To fear God. "Fear Him who is able to destroy both soul and body in hell."

ANSWER 9. To fear no creature. "The Lord is on my side. I will not fear. What can man do unto me?" On this ground three of the captives of the King of Babel, faithful servants of the Lord of heaven, thus answered that king, "We are not careful to answer thee; our God whom we serve is able to deliver us."

ANSWER 10. To praise God. "Praise Him for His mighty acts. Unto Him that is able to do exceeding abundantly be glory."

ANSWER 11. To hope well of such as are weak. God is able to make them stand.

ANSWER 12. To be bountiful to such as need. God is able to make all graces abound.

The Comfort Arising from God's Power

QUESTION. What comfort arises from the consideration of God's power?

ANSWER. Assurance of the accomplishment of God's promises. To strengthen the prophet's faith in the promise that God had made of returning the captivity of the Jews, God gives him this answer, "Behold, I am the Lord, the God of all flesh; is there anything too hard for Me?"

To exemplify this the Holy Ghost puts us in mind of God's power to strengthen our faith in these promises that follow:

1. The alteration of our corrupt nature. Though to man it is as easy to make a camel to go through the eye of a needle as a rich man to enter into heaven, yet to God that is not impossible. For with God all things are possible.

2. The vocation of the Jews. For God is able to graft them in again.

3. All needful grace. God is able to make all grace abound.

4. Perseverance to the end. No man shall pluck Christ's sheep out of His hand. For His Father who gave them to Him is greater than all.

5. Supply of all necessities. God who is able will supply them.

6. Assistance in all trouble. Upon this ground that God has a mighty arm and a strong hand, assurance is given to David of sufficient protection.

7. Deliverance out of all evil. For assurance hereof, with great emphasis, the prophet presses the power of God.

8. The resurrection of our bodies. For assurance hereof the apostle greatly amplifies the power of God.

9. Eternal glorification. Christ shall change our vile body so that it may be fashioned like His glorious body, according to the working whereby He is able even to subdue all things to Himself.

Hitherto we have dealt with God's kingdom and power. The third property is His glory, set down in these words, "and the glory."

God's Glory, What it Is

QUESTION. What is meant by God's glory?

ANSWER. That excellence that is in Him. For the excellence of a thing, that which causes it to be in high esteem, and procures a name, fame, and renown unto it, is the glory of it. The Hebrew word signifies that which is weighty and of worth. The Greek word signifies both fame and glory, for glory causes fame. In Scripture, glory and excellence are put for one and the same thing, and that in relation both to creatures and to the Creator, such as where the prophet, speaking of the glory of the church, says, "The glory of Lebanon shall be given unto it, the excellence of Carmel and Sharon. They shall see the glory of the Lord, and the excellence of our God." On this ground, where the excellence of our God is set forth, glory is attributed to Him and He is called "God of glory, King of glory, and Father of glory." And His name, habitation, throne, and gospel, because of the excellence of them, are called "a name of glory," "a habitation of glory," "a throne of glory," and "a gospel of glory." Yea, for the same end glory is also prefixed before the things of God, such as glory of majesty, glory of kingdom, glory of grace, and glory of power.

The Incomprehensibility of God's Glory

QUESTION. May God's glory be comprehended by man?

ANSWER. No, it is incomprehensible. It is a light that no man can approach unto. For as all other properties of God are His very essence, so is His glory, which is the excellence of all. When Moses desired God to show him His glory the Lord answered, "Thou canst not see My face, for there shall no man see Me and live." By this answer it appears that God's glory is His face, and His face is Himself. For these three words applied to God, "glory," "face," and "Me," are all put for one and the same thing. And that all these are incomprehensible this phrase shows, "Thou canst not see My face." Yet God, being willing to gratify him so far as he was able, showed him His back parts, some glimpse of His glory.

The Means of Manifesting God's Glory

QUESTION. How is God's glory manifested?

ANSWER. By such means as it pleases Him to afford, for He has afforded means in all ages to that purpose.

These means have been of several sorts, some extraordinary, others ordinary, some more obscure, others brighter.

Extraordinary means were such particular representations of God's glory as at sundry times were shown to sons of men, as a brightness in that cloud wherein God was wont to manifest His presence, and that apparition or vision that was shown to Ezekiel.

Ordinary means were the tabernacle and the ark. Other more clear and brighter means are His Word, His works, and His image.

Both parts of God's Word, the law and gospel, clearly set out the glory of God. The law sets out the glory of His justice, the gospel the glory of His mercy. Glory therefore is attributed to them both. Where the apostle calls the law a ministration of condemnation, he attributes glory to it But the gospel, which he calls a ministration of righteousness, he affirms to exceed in glory. This is that glass wherein with open face we behold the glory of God.

All God's works declare His glory, as His works of creation and preservation or providence. But among the works of God, they that are more than ordinary works of wonder include all manner of miracles, extraordinary judgments on the wicked, extraordinary deliverances of His people, and other mercies. And most principally that exceeding greatness of His power that He wrought in Christ when He raised Him from the dead.

The image of God, which is in sundry ways planted in creatures, in every way sets out the glory of God as that image after which man was first created and after which man is renewed; that whereby such as are in authority have superiority, dignity, and excellence above others and that which was set in Christ as He was made man. The most bright and perspicuous representation of God's glory that ever was given was Christ, the true, natural, only begotten Son of God, the brightness of His glory and the expressed image of His person. Of Christ, St. John says, "We beheld His glory, the glory as of the only begotten of the Father." And Christ says of Himself, "He that hath seen Me hath seen the Father." For Christ is God manifested in the flesh.

Of all places, heaven is the place where God's glory is most conspicuously seen. There the forenamed Son of God abides in His greatest glory; and there are other means of manifesting the divine glory so far as the creature may be made capable of enduring the brightness thereof. There it is said that Stephen saw the glory of God. There shall all the saints be presented before the glory of God. Now we see through a glass darkly, but there face to face. There the angels always behold the face of God. And there we shall be as the angels of God.

How Glory Is Proper to God

QUESTION. Why is glory by a property with emphasis applied to God thus, "and the glory"?

ANSWER 1. The Fountain of all glory is in God. That which the psalmist says of life may fitly be applied to glory: "With God is the Fountain of glory." All excellencies are in God, excellence of majesty, excellence of sovereignty, excellence of purity, excellence of power, excellence of wisdom, excellence of truth, excellence of justice, and excellence of mercy. He has them all in Himself, through Himself, and for Himself, and that without measure, above comprehension, even infinitely. Whatever excellence is in any creature, it issues out of this Fountain. The creature has all the excellence that in any kind it has from this Fountain by participation and communication. All glory therefore is God's. The glory that is in Himself and the glory that is in any creature is His.

ANSWER 2. The brightness of God's glory obscures all other glory. Behold the moon and it does not shine; yea, the stars are not pure in His sight. The glorious angels are said to have wings to cover their faces because the brightness of God's glory would otherwise dazzle them. If Aaron and the children of Israel were afraid to come nigh to Moses by reason of the shining of his face, how much more may the creature be afraid to come to God by reason of the incomprehensible shining of His glorious face? Where God's glory shines in His brightness, no other glory can any more be seen than the light of a candle in the midst of clear and bright sunshine. As the light of the sun is to the light of stars, so is the glory of the Creator to the glory of creatures. None of the stars have light in themselves, but receive all their light from the sun. And so bright is the light of the sun that when it shines the stars are not seen. On these grounds there is great and just cause to say unto God, "Thine is the glory."

Man's Giving Glory to God and Taking Glory from God

QUESTION. How is the creature said to give glory to God or to take it from Him?

ANSWER. Not properly, but respectively, namely in respect of the creature's mind and the Creator's account. As for giving glory to God, it is truly said, "Can a man be profitable to God as he that is wise may be profitable to himself? If thou be righteous what givest thou to Him? Or what receiveth He of thine hand?" But he who does those things that are pleasing and acceptable to God has a mind, will, and desire, if it were in his power, to give glory to God. And God does account such a mind, will, and desire where there is an answerable endeavor, as if indeed actually and properly glory were given to Him. This mind to glorify and praise God is manifested by an acknowledgement of God and of all his excellences by making them known and by an answerable respect and carriage. Where we are exhorted to give glory to God these directions are added, "Declare His glory among the nations. Worship the Lord. Fear before Him. Say, 'The Lord reigneth.' "

On the contrary side, as for taking glory from God, it is truly said, "If thou sinnest, what dost thou against God?" But the sinner, especially the willful sinner, whose sins are committed directly against the divine Majesty, has a mind, will, and desire, if it were in his power, to rob God of His glory and take it from Him. And God so accounts of him as if by him He were indeed actually and properly deprived of glory. To such He says, "Ye have robbed Me." In these respects glory is taken from God when He is denied to be or not glorified as God, or when that which is due to God is given to others or assumed to one's self. In these and other like respects God is said to be blasphemed.

To blaspheme, according to the notation of the original word, is to hurt one's fame; and in the law a blasphemer is said to strike through the name of the Lord. Not that any hurt is properly done to God, or to His glorious Name, but that, if it could be hurt, they do what they can to hurt it, or that they hinder the brightness of God's glory from shining forth to others as a man, who cannot take away any whit of light from the sun, may, notwithstanding by sundry means hinder the sunshine from others.

The Duties Due to God by Reason of His Glory

QUESTION. What duties does the appropriating of glory to God import?

ANSWER 1. To account Him the only true God. It is His chief glory to be a God, yea, to be the only true God. This glory He will not give to another. It is therefore to be reserved entirely to Him.

ANSWER 2. To advance Him above all. The Lord is high above all nations and His glory above the heavens. Accordingly He must be advanced.

ANSWER 3. To acknowledge His infinite perfection, and that in all His attributes. Herein His glory consists. Such praises as these—His wisdom is infinite. There is no searching thereof. The exceeding greatness of His power. His mercy is great above the heavens and His truth reaches unto the clouds. His righteousness is like the mountains, His judgments a great deep—imply an infinite perfection in God's properties.

ANSWER 4. To admire His excellence. Glory and excellence are the only true causes of admiration. The consideration of God's surpassing glory even ravished David's heart with a holy admiration thereof.

ANSWER 5. To adore His majesty. Adoration is properly due to glory, majesty, and excellence. When the prophet saw the appearance of the glory of God he fell down upon his face, which was the proper gesture of adoration.

ANSWER 6. To ascribe the glory of all glory to Him. If there is any glory in us—glory of dignity, glory of wealth, glory of strength, glory of any virtue—we ought to ascribe it to Him who is the Fountain of all glory, from whom we have all the glory that we have, and not to ourselves.

ANSWE 7. To seek the glory that comes from God alone, even that glory that warrants, approves, and gives. For glory being God's, God being the Fountain of all true glory, that which does not comes from him is but a show and shadow of true glory.

ANSWER 8. To abase and cast down ourselves at the glorious presence of God as Isaiah did. Thus is God's glory magnified.

ANSWER 9. To justify God and condemn ourselves in His proceedings against us, that God may be glorified. So Daniel did in the name of all his people. This was what Joshua intended when he said to Achan, "Give glory to the Lord, and make confession to Him."

ANSWER 10. To praise God in all things. "Whoso offereth praise glorifieth God." The nine lepers who, being healed of Christ, went away without giving thanks are said not to return to give glory to God.

ANSWER 11. To do all things to the glory of God. God's glory ought to be the mark whereat we aim in everything that we do.

ANSWER 12. To cause others to glorify God. For this end Christ charges us to let our light shine before men.

The Ways Whereby Others Are Brought to Glorify God

QUESTION. How may others be brought to glorify God?

ANSWER. 1. By declaring the glory and excellence of God. Thus may others come to knowledge of God and so to glorify Him. The psalmist having exhorted to set forth the glory of God's name, and to make His name glorious, adds as an effect thereof, "All the earth shall sing to Thy name."

ANSWER 2. By inciting and provoking men to glorify God. This David was very diligent to do. For it puts a kind of life into men and quickens them up the more to do a duty.

ANSWER 3. By furthering the Word of God and causing it to have a free passage. The Word is a powerful means to make men glorify God.

ANSWER 4. By showing forth the virtue of God in us. Christ by this means drew on multitudes to glorify God.

ANSWER 5. By shining as lights in darkness. Thus they who speak evil of us may by this light be brought to glorify God.

ANSWER 6. By converting sinners. When the Gentiles so heard the Word as thereby faith was wrought in them they glorified God. On this ground David vowed to teach sinners God's ways.

ANSWER 7. By our own repentance. When the believing Jews heard that God had granted repentance to the Gentiles they glorified God.

ANSWER 8. By manifest evidences of entire repentance. They who heard that Paul preached the faith that once he destroyed (a clear demonstration of his sound conversion) glorified God.

ANSWER 9. By works of mercy. St. Paul was hereby stirred up to give thanks to God and said of such works that they are abundant by many thanksgivings to God, and that many glorify God for liberal contribution unto them.

ANSWER 10. By fruits of righteousness. Of these it is expressly said, they are to the glory and praise of God. Men are made trees of righteousness, the planting of the Lord that He might be glorified.

ANSWER 11. By all manner of good works. They who see them will glorify God.

ANSWER 12. By the measure of grace answerable to the means. "Herein is My Father glorified, if ye bear much fruit," says Christ of such as were trained up under His powerful ministry.

13. By suffering for the truth of God. For God on the part of those who suffer is glorified.

Those Who Are to Set Forth God's Glory

QUESTION. Who are bound to set forth the glory of God?

ANSWER 1. Angels in heaven. They have the best ability to do it.

ANSWER 2. Members of the church. They on earth have the best means to do it. Such are comprised under these titles "Jerusalem" and "Zion," who are often incited to glorify God.

ANSWER 3. Ministers of the Word. Their proper and peculiar calling is to glorify God, and to teach others so to do.

ANSWER 4. Magistrates. They bear God's image and on earth are gods.

ANSWER 5. All sorts of people. Young men, maidens, old men, children, and others; for all have just cause so to do.

ANSWER 6. All living creatures. Their life is of God.

ANSWER. Senseless creatures also, such as fire, hail, snow, vaports, etc. Their being is of God.

To conclude, God's tender mercies are over all His works. Therefore all His works should praise Him.

The Chief Enemies of God's Glory

QUESTION. Who among men are greatest enemies of God's glory?

ANSWER. 1. Atheists, who say in their heart that there is no God.

ANSWER 2. Idolaters, who change the glory of the corruptible God into an image made like corruptible things.

ANSWER 3. Blasphemers, who strike through the name of God.

ANSWER 4. Sacrilegious persons, who rob God.

ANSWER 5. Profane persons, who despise God.

ANSWER 6. Proud persons, who arrogate God's due to themselves.

ANSWER 7. Unbelievers, who make God a liar.

ANSWER 8. Lewd professors, who cause others to blaspheme the name of God.

ANSWER 9. All impenitent sinners. Of such it is said, "They repented not to give God glory." For by repentance God is much glorified, and that both by the penitents themselves and others.

Hitherto we have treated the three expressed attributes of God—kingdom, power, and glory. The amplification of them follows in this clause, "forever."

Eternity, to What Things It Is Applied

QUESTION. How are the kingdom, power, and glory of God amplified?

ANSWER. By their unchangeable continuance. This phrase "forever" implies both eternity and immutability. The phrase in the original, to translate it word for word, is "for ages." The original root properly signifies that which is forever. Now because an age is the longest usual distinction of time, the same word that signifies eternity is put for an age. And when there is no end of that which is spoken of, the plural number indefinitely without any limitation thus, "for ages" is used to set out the everlasting nature of it. But everlastingness, or eternity, is diversely used in Scripture. For such things are said to be forever, everlasting, or eternal, that have both beginning and end, that have a beginning but no end, that have no beginning yet an end, or that have neither beginning nor end.

1. The things that have both beginning and end also that are said to be eternal and forever are such as have no set and determinate date. Thus, because there was no date set for that heap that was made of the ruins of Ai, neither was any time of the rebuilding of it known, it is said to be a heap forever. The like is noted of that heap that was to be made of that city where idolaters were harbored.

This applies also to such as are immutable while their date lasts. Thus the things that remained unalterable for the time of a man's life are said to be forever, as the service of him whose ear was bored through with a nail by his master, the things that endured all the time of the Jews' pedagogy and polity until the first coming of Christ, such as the Passover, and other like legal rites; and the things that are to endure until the end of the world, such as the covenant whereof the rainbow is a sign, and the earth. All these had their beginning; and they have had or shall have their end. Yet are they said to be forever because no abrogation or alteration was to be of them until their date and end was come.

2. The things that, having a beginning have no end, are more properly said to be forever or everlasting because these phrases have special respect to future continuance. Such are...

Good angels, who never die, who always behold the face of God.

Evil angels, who are reserved in everlasting chains.

The human nature of Christ, whose flesh saw no corruption and who, even as man, continues forever.

The souls of men, which return to God when the body which is but dust returns to the earth.

Men's bodies after the resurrection, when this corruptible must put on incorruption, and this mortal must put on immortality, and when we shall be ever with the Lord.

The highest heaven, that place where Christ now abides in His human nature, and which is the blessed habitation of the glorious angels and glorified saints. This is called an eternal house, "an inheritance incorruptible, that fadeth not away."

Hell, the place of the damned, "where their worm dieth not, and the fire is not quenched" (Mark 9:44), where their punishment is everlasting (Matthew 25:46).

All things that remain after the Day of Judgment, when there shall be no more death (Revelation 21:4).

3. Things that have no beginning but an end are such decrees of God as were in time accomplished. The decree was in the purpose of God before all times, but performed in an appointed time. Thus grace is said to be given before the world began. The decree of giving it was before the world, yet the decree had its date and was accomplished; grace is actually given in the time of this world.

4. Things that have neither beginning nor end are most properly eternal. For herein lies a difference between eternity and sempiternity, or everlastingness. Eternity looks backward and forward. It never saw beginning, nor ever shall see end. Everlastingness looks only forward to that which is to come. That which is properly eternal has its being of and in itself, being supported and sustained by none, and in that respect is immutable. Thus the phrases that set out true and proper eternity also by just consequence imply immutability. Wherefore under this phrase "forever" here in the Lord's Prayer both eternity and immutability are comprised. The things thus properly eternal are only God Himself and such things as are essential to Him, such as His Son, His Spirit, and His properties.

God says of Himself, "Before Me there was no God formed, neither shall there be after Me" (Isaiah 43:10). Fitly therefore does the man of God say unto Him, "From everlasting to everlasting Thou art God" (Psalm 90:2). The proper name of God, Jehovah, fully sets out this property and immutable eternity for it comprises under it all times past, present, and future.

The Son of God is called Father of Eternity in that He is eternal Himself and the Author of such things as endure forever.

The Spirit of God in the beginning moved upon the face of the waters (Genesis 1:2). He was therefore in the beginning; and if He was in the beginning He had no beginning. For it was He who formed the things that had a beginning, in which respect He is said to move, or (as the Jewish expositors interpret the word) to sit as a hen upon her eggs till her chicks are hatched.

All the properties of God are, as these three (kingdom, power, and glory) forever.

His dominion is an everlasting dominion (Daniel 7:14), even from generation to generation (Daniel 4:34).

His glory is eternal (1 Peter 5:10).

His righteousness is an everlasting righteousness (Psalm 119:142).

His truth is forever (Psalm 117:2).

His mercy is forever (Psalm 136:1).

And so also are His counsel, His law, His oath, His covenant, and the like.

Thus we see that eternity, properly taken, is proper to God. However other things are also called eternal, yet there is a manifest difference between that which is proper to God and that which is common to creatures.

God's eternity is without beginning. So is no creature's. For by Him were all things created that are in heaven and those that are in earth, visible and invisible.

God's is without alteration. So is no creature's as we shall afterwards show.

God's is independent. He ever was and ever remains to be of Himself and by Himself. Creatures have their continuance of God and by God. "In Him we live, and move, and have our being. Of Him, and through Him, and to Him are all things."

The Duties That Arise from God's Eternity

QUESTION. What duties does that eternity which is proper to God teach us?

ANSWER. 1. To acknowledge Him to be the only Creator. By the eternity of Christ St. John proves that He is God, and that all things were made by Him.

ANSWER 2. To seek preservation of Him. On this ground the psalmist thus prays, "O my God, take me not away in the midst of my days. Thy years are throughout all generations."

ANSWER 3. To give the praise of continuance of all good to Him. It was usual with the psalmist to give thanks to God because His mercy endures forever.

ANSWER 4. To ascribe eternal glory to Him who is eternal. This phrase is frequent among the saints, "To God be glory forever and ever."

ANSWER 5. In our time to serve Him. Thus we do what lies in our power to continue service to the Eternal One forever. If all generations were careful, everyone in their time to serve God, the mortality of man would be no hindrance to the perpetuity of God's service. Abraham called upon the name of the everlasting God. Because the Lord was an everlasting God Abraham was careful in his time to worship Him.

ANSWER 6. To make Him known to posterity. This is a further means of procuring an everlasting name to the everlasting God. For our posterity, being instructed by us, may declare God's name to their posterity, and so posterity to posterity throughout all generations. Mark these things (says the psalmist) that ye may tell it to the generations following. For this God is our God forever and ever."

ANSWER 7. To depend on Him for our posterity. We are mortal and shall not live forever to provide for our posterity. But God, remaining forever, we may well commend such as survive us to His providence, and depend on Him for His care over them. The psalmist having made acknowledgement of God's everlasting continuance, saying thus to Him, "Thou art the same and Thy years shall have no end," He makes this inference, "The children of Thy servants shall continue and their seed shall be established before Thee."

ANSWER 8. To fear Him more than creatures. Creatures, though never so mighty and malicious, may die and we are freed from fear of them. But God ever lives. "Thou, Lord, art most high forevermore, but Thine enemies shall perish."

ANSWER 9. To prefer Him before all. To show what just cause there is to prefer God before all, thus says the Lord of Himself, "Before Me there was no God formed, neither shall there be after Me."

ANSWER 10. To follow after righteousness.

ANSWER 11. To turn others to righteousness.

For both these shall shine, the one as the firmament, the other as the stars, in the kingdom of God forever and ever.

ANSWER 12. To hope in death.

ANSWER 13. To be comforted for those who die in the Lord. For the eternal God will raise up both us and others believing in Him to eternal life.

So much for God's eternity plainly expressed under this phrase, "for ever." His immutability is also implied thereby.

To What Things Eternity May Be Applied

QUESTION. What, besides eternity, is implied under this word "forever"?

ANSWER. Immutability. That which ever remains the same without any alteration is most properly said to be forever. Wherefore of God it is said, "Thou art the same, and Thy years shall have no end." His immutability and eternity are both joined together.

As eternity, so also immutability is diversely taken in Scripture.

Many things are said to be unchangeable because by voluntary appointment they are so ordered, such as...

1. Sundry laws and statutes. The law of the Medes and Persians was that no decree or statute that the king established may be altered.

2. Last Wills and Testaments. No man annuls a testament or adds thereto if it is confirmed.

3. Sacred vows of such as have power to make them. Indeed a husband had power in sundry cases and with due cautions to annul his wife's vow and a father his daughter's vow. But otherwise the law is strict in this case: "When thou shalt vow a vow unto the Lord thy God, thou shalt not be slack to pay it."

4. Things that are consecrated. It is a snare to a man to devour that which is consecrated. The first fruits of the Lord might not be sold, exchanged or alienated because they were holy to the Lord, consecrated to Him.

5. Lawful oaths. These must be kept though they are made to a man's hurt.

6. The bond of marriage. Hereof it is said, "What God hath joined together let no man put asunder."

Other things by custom become immutable:

1. Evil practices. "Can the Ethiopian change his skin, or the leopard his spots? Then may ye also do good that are accustomed to do evil."

2. Civil ordinances. At the Passover the governor was wont to release unto the people a prisoner whom they would. Thereupon it is said, "Of necessity he must deliver one to them."

Sundry things are made immutable by special support:

1. Celestial spirits. These are the things in heaven that are said to be gathered together in Christ, by whom they are confirmed and established.

2. The church militant. "For the gates of hell shall not prevail against it."

3. Particular saints. "They that trust in the Lord shall be as mount Zion which cannot be removed, but abideth forever."

4. The gifts and calling of God. These are without repentance, such as God never repents the bestowing of them. On this ground the apostle thus says of such as were called and made partakers of the gift of God, "I am confident of this very thing, that He which hath begun a good work in you will perform it until the day of Jesus Christ."

There are many things that have an immutable nature given them so that according to that course which God has appointed they cannot be altered:

1. Sundry native properties. "Can the Ethiopian change his skin, or the leopard his spots?" You cannot make one hair white or black.

2. The earth and the mountains thereon. These abide forever.

3. Seasons and intercourse of times. While the earth remains, seedtime, harvest, cold and heat, summer and winter, and day and night shall not cease. "Thus saith the Lord, If ye can break My covenant of the day, and My covenant of the night, and that there should not be day or night in their

season.' " Here the immutable intercourse of those seasons is set down as an undeniable principle.

4. The visible heavens and the host thereof. The Lord gives the sun for a light by day, and the ordinances of the moon and of the stars for a light by night, namely so to abide without alteration.

5. The highest heaven and all therein. There neither moth nor rust corrupt, nor thieves break through or steal.

Some things are essentially in themselves immutable, and so immutable as it is impossible they should be changed:

1. God Himself (Malachi 3:6; James 1:17).
2. God's counsel (Psalm 33:11; Hebrews 6:17).
3. God's law (Luke 16:17).
4. God's oath (Psalm 110:4; Isaiah 45:23).
5. God's covenants (Jeremiah 33:20–21).
6. God's promises (Hebrews 6:13, 18).
7. Every word of God (Numbers 23:19).
8. God's love (Jeremiah 31:3).

As God Himself is, so are the things that are essential to Him and come out of Him, as those that were before mentioned and others like them, immutable and inviolable.

The Difference Between the Immutability of the Creator and the Creatures

QUESTION. Wherein lies the difference between the immutability of the Creator and of the creatures?

ANSWER 1. God has His stability of Himself, which is evident by this title that God gives to Himself, "I AM THAT I AM." Creatures have all the stability that they have from God. The Lord gives the ordinances of the moon and of the stars. He has appointed them the courses that they keep so constantly. He has founded the earth and established the heavens.

ANSWER 2. It is simply and absolutely impossible that God's stability could be altered. But the most steadfast stability of the creatures may be altered. Some of the angels did not keep their first estate. The Lord removes the mountains and overturns them in His anger. He shakes the earth out of her place and makes the pillars thereof tremble. He commands the sun and it does not rise, etc. In Joshua's time the sun stood still. In Hezekiah's time it ran backward. Though many creatures never were or shall be changed, as the good angel, yet is it not simply impossible that they could be changed. He who made them can destroy them. If God in Christ had not confirmed them, but should leave them to themselves, there might be fear of their falling.

ANSWER 3. God remains immutable by Himself. "I am Jehovah," says the Lord. "I change not." Because He is Jehovah, of Himself and by Himself, therefore He does not change. But the creatures are supported by God and are kept stable and unchangeable by His providence. As the Lord first appointed them their firm and stable course so that they may the better keep it, He puts the hand of His divine providence under them to support them. By Him all things consist. The immutability therefore that is in any creature is wholly at God's disposal, either to confirm or alter it. So that immutability, properly taken, is proper to God.

The Duties That Arise from God's Immutability

QUESTION. To what duties are we bound by reason of God's immutability?

ANSWER 1. To put difference between the Creator and creatures, as the psalmist did where, in opposition between the Creator and creatures, he says, "They shall perish, but Thou shalt endure."

ANSWER 2. To respect God as saints in former times have done. He is the same God now that ever He was. Why then should He not be accordingly esteemed? This argument taken from God's immutability God Himself uses to provoke men to piety and to reclaim them from all impiety. True saints have also hereby been moved to carry themselves towards God as their fathers of old have done.

ANSWER 3. To trust in the Lord. As the mountains round about Jerusalem stand unmovable for the defense and safety thereof, so the Lord is round about His people forever.

ANSWER 4. To believe God's Word and promise. Sarah believed God's Word even against the ordinary course of nature because she judged Him faithful who had promised.

ANSWER 5. Confidently to wait for salvation. For this end God has shown to the heirs of promise the immutability of His counsel that we might have a strong consolation.

ANSWER 6. To hold close to God's Word and not to alter it in any way. Who shall dare to change the inviolable Word of the immutable God?

ANSWER 7. To yield to the counsel of God that has been made known. God in His counsel is unchangeable. It shall stand whether we yield unto it or repine against it. On this ground the saints, where the purpose of God was manifested, humbly submitted themselves thereto.

ANSWER 8. To be steadfast, constant, and immoveable in every good work. This is one special point wherein we must be perfect as our heavenly Father is perfect.

Some of those particulars wherein we must be immoveable and immutable are these.

1. In our promises (2 Corinthians 1:17).
2. In our oaths (Psalm 15:4).
3. In our vows (Ecclesiastes 5:4).
4. In our faith and hope (Colossians 1:23).
5. In our profession (Hebrews 3:12 and 13:9).
6. In all good duties (Galatians 6:9).

Hitherto we have dealt with the attributes here appropriated to God singly and severally considered by themselves. The relation that they have to the petitions is further to be declared.

How God's Kingdom Works Confidence in Prayer

QUESTION. What relation do the forenamed properties of God have to the petitions of this prayer?

ANSWER. As reasons to enforce them, which they do by giving us assurance of obtaining them, which will more clearly appear by a distinct application of every particular property to the petitions and of every particular petition to the several properties.

QUESTION. How does God's sovereignty give us assurance of obtaining our petitions?

ANSWER. It imports God's willingness to hear us. This is a great encouragement to move us to come to God, and to expect a gracious answer from Him. Upon this title given to God, "O Thou that hearest prayer," this inference is made, "unto Thee shall all flesh come." Now God's willingness and readiness to hear may well be gathered from this clause, "Thine is the kingdom," because it is the property of good kings readily to open their ears to their subjects' suits, as is excellently set down in the description of that king who was a type of Jesus Christ the King of kings. But God has all the properties of a good king in Him. Yea, they are all originally in Him as in the Head, Fountain, and Well-spring. The properties that are in other good kings are derived from Him. He has them infinitely above all measure. We may well therefore be assured that, the kingdom being God's, and He being our King and Sovereign, we may boldly present our suits to Him and confidently expect the accomplishment of our desires. Well did he know this who usually in his petitions to God, called Him "King," saying, "Hearken unto the voice of my cry, my King. Thou art my King, O God; command deliverance for Jacob." God is my King of old working salvation. Wherefore take due and true notice of your estate, whether you are indeed one of God's subjects, so that you may with the more steadfast faith present your petitions to God as to your King, and plead and press this argument, "Thine is the kingdom."

How God's Power Strengthens Faith in Prayer

QUESTION. How does God's power enforce our desire?

ANSWER. It shows how able God is to grant whatever we desire of Him. A king may be ready and willing to hear his subjects' suits, but if withal he is not able to grant their petitions and to effect their desires, what confidence can they have in calling upon him? When a poor subject thus cried to a mortal king, "Help, O Lord, my king," he answered, "If the Lord does not help you, how shall I help you?" What heart can a subject have to go to such a sovereign? There may be more hope of help from him who is unwilling than from him who is unable. Often therefore is God's power alleged to strengthen our faith in prayer, and saints themselves were wont to plead it.

QUESTION. May we confidently expect to obtain by prayer whatever God is able to grant?

ANSWER. No, we have before shown that God is able to do many things that He will not do. Though Christ knew that His Father could have sent more than twelve legions of angels to rescue Him, yet because He also knew that it was the will of His Father at that time to deliver Him into the hands of His enemies, He would not pray for those legions to be sent. Though God is able at any time to preserve any people from any judgment, yet when His will is not to deliver them even the prayers of Noah, Daniel, and Job, or of Moses and Samuel shall not be of force for them. Samuel prayed for Saul, but was not heard.

QUESTION. How then is God's power a ground of faith?

ANSWER. In that it is joined with His willingness. Therefore it is here added to His kingdom, which we have shown to set out His readiness to hear. They who place their confidence in God's power aright are not ignorant thereof. Instance the leper who thus frames his petition, "Lord, if Thou wilt, Thou canst make me clean." In those things whereof we have evidence for God's willingness we may with confidence rest upon God's power for obtaining them. Wherefore, well acquaint yourself with God's Word, and with His promises therein, that thereby you may be well instructed in the things that God is willing to grant, and so with greater confidence trust His power.

How God's Glory Settles the Soul for Obtaining Its Desire

QUESTION. How does God's glory encourage us with confidence to call on God?

ANSWER. It implies a concurring of His will and power together. God's glory is the main end that He aims at in all things. The Lord has made all things for Himself, namely to set out His glory. The things therefore that tend to His glory He will assuredly grant for they are none of those things that were before noted to import impotence or imperfection and in that regard are within the compass of His power. But they are the things that God aims at and that He has ordained to be done; in that regard no doubt can be made of God's willingness to grant them. Seeing then that God is able to do whatever He is willing to do, and seeing that whatever God is able and willing to do shall be done; and seeing that the things that tend to God's glory God is both able and willing to do, will not this conclusion necessarily follow from those premises: The things that are asked of God for the glory of God shall assuredly be granted? How fitly therefore does Christ, having prescribed sundry petitions that all tend to the glory of God, teach us to put God in mind of His glory for strengthening our faith in obtaining them. That this motive taken from God's glory may rightly be used in prayer, and your faith be strengthened thereby, be sure that all the petitions that you offer to God make for

God's glory. Do not let them be to satisfy your lusts. If so, you may ask and not receive.

How God's Unchangeable Eternity Makes Us Rest on God for Obtaining Our Desires

QUESTION. How does God's unchangeable eternity embolden us in faith to call upon God?

ANSWER. It makes us confidently to expect what God has formerly granted and to do for us that which He has always done for them who have called on Him and believed in Him. On this ground the psalmist thus pleads, "Our fathers trusted in Thee; they trusted, and Thou didst deliver them. They cried unto Thee and were delivered. They trusted in Thee and were not confounded." This pleading of God's former dealings implies faith in God's unchangeable continuing to be the same God, the same God in our time that He was of old in our fathers' time, the same God to us that He was to our fathers. On this ground it has been usual with saints to call to mind and to make mention of God's former dealings with others before their time when they called upon God to strengthen their faith and to call on others to remember the same. The prophet renders this reason of declaring God's former dealings to posterity, "That they might set their hope in God." Were not the kingdom, power, and glory God's forever, were not God ever the same God, this argument taken from God's former favors and God's former works would be of little force to make succeeding ages to trust in Him. Wherefore, that all ages might in faith call upon God, and with confidence depend on Him to be heard and helped, yea, that they who have once been heard and helped might hold on in calling upon God and seeking help of Him every day, even all the days of their life, fitly does the Lord add this clause "forever" to set out the immutable eternity of God Himself, and of all His properties, such as His sovereignty, omnipotence, and excellence. Often meditate hereon that you may with as strong confidence call on God as Abraham, David, the prophets, apostles, and other saints have done. But do it with this proviso, that you endeavor to be such as they were, and so to call on Him as they did; for God forever remains the same and casts His gracious eye upon the same kind of persons.

So much for the application of the particular properties of God to all the petitions in general. Each petition shall further be applied to each property.

The Special Relation that the Several Petitions Have to the Kingdom of God

QUESTION. What particular respect do every one of the petitions have to God's kingdom?

ANSWER 1. It pertains to a king to have his honor advanced. The Lord forbids to swear by Jerusalem because it is the city of the great King. So the things of the great King must not be profaned; the King is dishonored thereby, which He will not tolerate. "The Lord will give strength to His King, and exalt the horn of His anointed." It is fitting for a king to be exalted and have his name hallowed. There is good ground therefore to make this petition, "Hallowed be Thy name," to Him whose the kingdom is.

ANSWER 2. It cannot be doubted but that a king will maintain his kingdom. It belongs to him so to do. Who should do it if not he? Hereupon the prophet exhorts Zion to rejoice in the coming of her King, for coming to His own kingdom He comes with salvation. Well therefore may we say to Him whose the kingdom is, "Thy kingdom come."

ANSWER 3. Obedience is most due to a king. Of Christ, the King of the church, it is foretold that all kings shall fall down before Him and all nations shall serve Him. Yea, we are commanded to serve Him because He is a King. Ought we not then to make to Him, whose the kingdom is, this petition, "Thy will be done?"

ANSWER 4. A king provides all needful things for his subjects. So much is noted in the description of a good king: "He shall come down like rain upon the mown grass, and as showers that water the earth. In his days shall be abundance of peace." May we not now pray thus, "Give us this day our daily bread," to Him whose the kingdom is?

ANSWER 5. It is in the power of the highest to forgive. If the king grants a pardon to a traitor, who can condemn him? Christ, sitting in judgment, to show what authority He had to absolve and condemn, calls himself King. The King shall say, "Come, ye blessed," and He shall say, "Depart, ye cursed." There is therefore great reason thus to pray, "Forgive us our debts," to Him whose the kingdom is.

ANSWER 6. It is a king's office to deliver his subjects from their enemies, and from the evils that may befall them. Fitly to this purpose the prophet says, "The Lord hath taken away thy judgments. He hath cast out thine enemies. The King of Israel, even the Lord is in the midst of thee; thou shalt not see evil anymore." We have therefore just cause to say, "Lead us not into temptation, but deliver us from evil," to Him whose the kingdom is.

The Special Relation that the several Petitions Have to God's Power

QUESTION. What particular respect does every one of the petitions have to God's power?

ANSWER 1. To have God's name rightly and duly hallowed requires a divine power. The Lord, strong and mighty, is the King of Glory. Wherefore to hallow God's name must be desired and expected of Him whose the power is.

ANSWER 2. God's kingdom cannot be perfected but by almighty power for many and mighty are the enemies thereof.

Few and weak are the true members and friends thereof. They therefore who speak of the glory of God's kingdom talk of His power. So that this petition, "Thy kingdom come," is to be made to Him whose the power is.

ANSWER 3. It is by a strong hand that mortal, sinful men are brought to do God's will. With men it is impossible. To Him, therefore, whose the power is, it is requisite thus to pray, "Thy will be done on earth."

ANSWER 4. All our necessities cannot be supplied but by a divine power. A king was forced to say, "If the Lord help thee not, whence shall I help thee? Out of the barn floor, or out of the wine press?" But "God is able to make all grace abound towards you, that ye always, having all sufficiency in all things, may abound to every good work." As therefore we would have our desire granted, so let us say, "Give us this day our daily bread," to Him whose the power is.

ANSWER 5. Is it easier to say to the sick of the palsy, "Thy sins are forgiven thee," or to say, "Arise, and take up thy bed and walk"? Both are done by the same power, which is divine and omnipotent. Therefore, to Him whose the power is, make this petition, "Forgive us our debts."

ANSWER 6. To be able to stand against the assaults of Satan is above the ability of flesh and blood. To Him therefore whose the power is we must pray, "Lead us not into temptation, but deliver us from evil."

The Special Relation that the Several Petitions Have to God's Glory

QUESTION. What particular respect do every one of the petitions have to God's glory?

ANSWER 1. The hallowing of God's name is the chief part of His glory. "I will be sanctified in them that come nigh to Me, and before all the people I will be glorified." By being sanctified, or hallowed, God is glorified. In faith therefore we may thus pray, "Hallowed be Thy name," to Him whose the glory is.

ANSWER 2. God's kingdom is the prime place of His glory. It is the place where His honor dwells. To the church, the peculiar kingdom of God, it is said, "The glory of the Lord is risen upon thee. His glory shall be seen upon thee." Confidently therefore to Him whose the glory is we may make this appeal, "Thy kingdom come."

ANSWER 3. The creature cannot better glorify God than by obeying His will. "Herein is My Father glorified, that ye bear much fruit." To obey is better than sacrifice. He therefore who prays, "Thy will be done," to Him whose the glory is may be sure to have his prayer granted.

ANSWER 4. The divine providence in temporal blessings greatly amplifies God's glory. By giving bread to His people in the wilderness God showed His glory. Where the prophet says, "They shall speak of Thy glory," by way of explication he reckoned up many evidences of God's providence in temporal blessings thus, "The eyes of all wait upon Thee. Thou givest them their meat in due season." His glory therefore whose the glory is will move Him to grant this petition, "Give us this day our daily bread."

ANSWER 5. The glory of God is exceedingly commended by pardoning sin. To the praise of the glory of His grace we have forgiveness of sin. In much confidence therefore you may say, "Forgive us our debts," to Him whose the glory is.

ANSWER 6. Preservation and deliverance of saints from evil much magnifies and sets forth the glory of God. Where the prophet reckons up the many deliverances that God gave to His people, he infers thereupon, "They shall fear the name of the Lord from the West, and His glory from the rising of the sun." And on the same ground God Himself says, "I will set My glory among the heathen." This petition, "Lead us not into temptation, but deliver us from evil," may in faith be made to Him whose the glory is.

The Special Relation That the Several Petitions Have to God's Unchangeable Eternity

QUESTION. What particular respect do every one of the petitions have to God's immutable eternity?

ANSWER 1. God's name is forever and His memorial endures throughout all generations.

ANSWER 2. His kingdom is an everlasting kingdom.

ANSWER 3. God's will is to be done throughout all ages by us, by our sons, and by our sons' sons. We may therefore well make these petitions, "Hallowed be Thy name, Thy kingdom come, Thy will be done," though they are of everlasting and immutable matters, to the eternal God whose the kingdom is, and the power, and the glory forever.

ANSWER 4. We want bread every day, and so shall we do as long as we live. As our fathers from the beginning of the world have stood in need thereof, so do we, and so shall our posterity also. For whoever drinks of this water shall thirst again.

ANSWER 5. Our fathers of old up to our time have sinned; so do we all our days, and so will our posterity forever.

ANSWER 6. The devil has been a murderer from the beginning, and ever will be. There is perpetual enmity between the woman's seed and his seed. We and ours shall be forever in this world subject to many evils. We therefore who make these petitions, "Give us this day our daily bread, and forgive us our debts, and lead us not into temptation, but deliver us from evil," have need to be well instructed in God's eternity and immutability. For in faith we may make the forenamed petitions concerning our perpetual needs to Him whose kingdom, power, and glory are forever.

Hitherto we have treated the acknowledgement of God's properties as they have relation to the petitions, and are reasons to enforce them. The said acknowledgement is further to be considered singly and simply by itself.

The Necessary Use of This Clause, "Thine is the Kingdom, and the Power, and the Glory Forever"

QUESTION. What does the acknowledgement of God's properties singly considered import?

ANSWER. A form of praise. For where mention is made of David's blessing God, it is set down in this form, "Thine, O Lord, is the greatness, and the power, and the glory." Thus is this clause ("Thine is the kingdom and the power and the glory forever") the second part of the Lord's Prayer, whereby the perfection of that prayer is set out. For prayer consists of these two parts, petition and praise. They therefore who wholly omit this clause and cast it out of this pattern of prayer make it an imperfect pattern, as papists who throughout their whole liturgy have omitted it. Yea, the vulgar Latin translation has left it out of the text in that place where it is expressed by St. Matthew. The Rhemists' English translation does so also. And the great champion of the papists, Robert Bellarmine, where he purposely undertakes to expound the Lord's Prayer, clean omits this clause and declares that it is certain that those words are not of the evangelical text, but were inserted by the Greeks. But other diligent searchers into all sorts of Greek copies, as he, have found it not only in the expositions and commentaries of Greek fathers, but also in most of the Greek copies of the New Testament. And the ancient Syriac translator, who was none of the Greek expositors, has it. Yea, many of the Latin fathers also make mention thereof as of a part of the Lord's Prayer, though some of them sometimes in their expositions have omitted it.

OBJECTION. St. Luke left out this clause (Luke 11:1ff).

ANSWER. The history that St. Luke records as an occasion of setting down the Lord's Prayer is not the same that St. Matthew recorded, but another.

The occasion mentioned by St. Matthew was this: The hypocritical Pharisees got the name of devout persons by their frequent and much praying. But Christ, observing their devotion to be but plain superstition revealed sundry of their aberrations both in the manner and also in the matter of their prayers; and to give His disciples and others a pattern whereunto, if they held close, they might sufficiently be directed in the matter and manner of prayer, He prescribed that form that is thereupon called the Lord's Prayer. It was therefore necessary that this pattern of prayer should be perfect, without deficiency or superfluity.

The occasion mentioned by St. Luke was this: John the Baptist had declared to his disciples what things especially they should by prayer ask of God. Thereupon Christ's disciples entreated their Master to do the like for them. On this occasion, therefore, it was sufficient for Christ to note out such principal points as were most beneficial to be asked of God, though He did not prescribe so perfect a form as that which is recorded in His Sermon on the Mount. Let it now be well considered whether they who use the Lord's Prayer as a perfect pattern have sufficient cause from Luke's not mentioning this form of praise to clean omit it.

Surely as St. Matthew has recoded this prayer Christ uttered it, and so is it to be used of us when it is used as a form or pattern of prayer.

Adding Praise to Petition

QUESTION. What does the adding of this last part of the Lord's Prayer to the former import?

ANSWER. Praise must be added to petition. If expressed precepts, approved practices, precious promises, gracious approbations, and plentiful remunerations are motives to stir us up to perform a duty, motives are not wanting to provoke us to praise God, especially to provoke such as have the Spirit of supplication bestowed upon them and have a ready mind and forward will to present petitions unto God according to their needs. For…

1. Praise is the end of petitions. We call upon God for such and such blessings that we may praise and bless God for the same. Thus are we taught to pray, "Save us, O God of our salvation, that we may give thanks to Thy holy name and glory in Thy praise."

2. Praise makes petition powerful, for God is most willing and ready to grant their petitions whose heart He knows to be ready and willing to praise Him. To give praise for former benefits is an effectual means to obtain further benefits. The tradesman who deals with a merchant that is careful to pay for wares formerly received will be ready to trust him with more, according to his need. On this direction, "Offer unto God thanksgiving," this invitation is made, "Call upon Me in the day of trouble and I will deliver thee."

3. Praise is a due debt that petitioners are bound to pay. He who invites you to call on Him, and promises to deliver you, requires and expects this recompense, "Thou shalt glorify Me."

4. Praise is all that we can return unto God for all His benefits to us. Where this question was made, "What shall I render to the Lord for all His benefits toward me", this answer was given, "I will take the cup of salvation," that is, I will offer a solemn sacrifice wherein and whereby I will show the deliverances and preservations that God has afforded to me. For by way of exposition he adds a little after, "I will offer the sacrifice of thanksgiving."

5. Praise is an evidence of that good respect we bear to God. By petition we show the respect that we bear to ourselves. The ten lepers who came to Jesus and cried, "Have mercy on

us" showed a care of their own welfare. Only the one who returned to give glory to God showed his care of God's honor.

6. Praise moves God to show good respect to man. For He who thus said, "Them that honor Me will I honor," will perform what He has said.

7. Praise is the greatest honor that we can give to God. For thus says the Lord Himself, "Whoso offereth praise glorifieth Me."

8. To praise God is the most heavenly exercise that in this world can be performed. The celestial spirits spend their time therein (Revelation 5:13 and 7:11–12 and 19:1).

9. A setting forth of God's praise is a special means to quicken the spirit and make the heart the more ready to prayer and the more cheerful therein. When the psalmist's heart was set to praise the Lord, then he says to his tongue and instruments, "Awake up my glory, awake psaltery and harp. I myself will awake early." When the spirit of a man is so dull and heavy that he cannot pray, let him meditate on God's mercies and other excellences and set himself to praise God, and he shall find a spiritual vigor thereby put into him.

10. Ingratitude is one of the most odious vices that can be, detestable to God and man. The apostle reckoned it up among those notorious vices that could be in the world in the last and worst times thereof. The prophet herein makes such as bear the name of God's people to be more brutish than the most brute beasts, the ox and the ass. Nothing more provokes God to take away His blessing, as He threatened Israel. The things that God used to bestow upon grateful persons He used to take away from the ungrateful. The most memorable judgments that are recorded in the Scriptures were caused by ungratefulness. When God had culled a church out of the world, who in that respect were called sons of God, they unmindful of God's gracious calling and mixed themselves with daughters of men. This made God repent that He had made man, and thereupon

He brought upon the world that general deluge wherewith He swept away all but eight persons. After God, by His servant Abraham, had rescued Sodom and the neighboring cities from the hand of their enemies, they were not careful to render praise to God, but continued in their beastly abominations. They were therefore all burned with fire and brimstone from heaven. Israel's ungratefulness was the cause of her captivity. This was what provoked God to give the Gentiles over to a reprobate sense, and to give Christians over to antiChristianism. This was what caused Nebuchadnezzar to be made like a beast, and Herod to be eaten with worms. This I hope may be sufficient to work some care and conscience to perform this duty of praise.

How Praising God Is Done

QUESTION. What is it to praise God?

ANSWER 1. To acknowledge God to be what He is. Thus Moses in his psalm of thanksgiving praises God saying, "The Lord is a man of war. Jehovah is His name."

ANSWER 2. To attribute to God that which is His as Christ does in this form, and David too, saying, "Thine, O Lord, is the greatness, and the power, and the glory."

ANSWER 3. To ascribe to God that which is done by Him. Thus Moses praises God by ascribing to Him the overthrow of Pharaoh and his host. So does the psalmist in most of his psalms of praise.

ANSWER 4. To profess that which God gives to be given of Him, as David in his form of praise thus does, "All things come of Thee, and of Thine own have we given Thee."

ANSWER 5. To declare to others all the forenamed points concerning God. To this purpose David says, "Give thanks unto the Lord, make known His deeds among the people. Sing unto Him; sing psalms unto Him; talk ye of all His wondrous works." And again, "I will declare Thy name unto my brethren. In the midst of the congregation will I praise Thee."

ANSWER 6. To worship God in testimony of all the said points, as is evident by this exhortation, "Give unto the Lord the glory due to His name. Bring an offering and come before Him. Worship the Lord."

By all these particular branches of praising God gathered out of the Scriptures it is most clear that by praising and glorifying God we give nothing at all to God. Rather what He is, what is His, and what is done or given by Him, are acknowledged and declared, and God with due respect is reverenced and adored. This, as it directs us how to praise God, so it sets out God's goodness in accepting that which is His own as given to Him by us. And also it discovers the perverse disposition of ungrateful persons who do as much as in them lies to withhold from God that which is His own and most due unto Him.

The Things for Which God Is to Be Praised

QUESTION. What are the principal grounds for which God is to be praised?

ANSWER. His excellence in Himself, His sovereignty above us, and His mercy towards us. All these show that God is most worthy of all praise.

1. Excellence in anything is praiseworthy, such as excellence of knowledge, excellence of wisdom, excellence of power and strength, excellence of any virtue, yea excellence of eloquence, excellence of beauty and every other excellence. It is said of the woman whose excellences were many, "She shall be praised," and, "Let her own works praise her." But we have shown that all excellences are in God. Yea, the excellences that are in creatures are God's because they all come from God. If therefore praise is due to any, much more is it due to God. That very praise that in any respect may lawfully be given to any creature is most properly due to Him. Where David blesses

Abigail for her wise advice, he first blesses God who sent her, saying, "Blessed be the Lord which sent thee this day to meet me; and blessed be thy advice, and blessed be thou." But because Herod did not give God the glory that was given to him he was eaten of worms. Besides, there are such infinitely surpassing excellences in God as no creature is capable of, such as self-existence, eternity, all-sufficiency, immutability, omnipotence, omnipresence, etc. That praise therefore is due to God that may be ascribed to no other. "For who is like unto Thee, O Lord, amongst the gods? Who is like Thee, glorious in holiness, fearful in praises? There is none holy as the Lord; for there is none beside Thee: neither is there any rock like our God. Great is the Lord, and greatly to be praised." Thus we see how God's excellence ministers just and great cause of praising God. If when we are about to praise God our hearts were deeply fixed on a due meditation and serious consideration of God's excellences, they would be much quickened unto this heavenly duty of praising God.

2. Sovereignty makes one to be greatly praised. Who are more praised than kings? They are praised for the things that are praiseworthy in their own persons, and praiseworthy in their subjects. If in a kingdom there are learned divines, faithful ministers, just magistrates, wise counselors, valiant soldiers, victorious captains, skillful artists, industrious husbandmen, and obedient subjects, the king is much praised for them all; and it is supposed that his wise and good government is the cause of all. Besides, praise tends to be proportioned according to the dignity wherein men are. The higher a man's place is, the more praise tends to be given to him. Kings therefore, being the highest in their dominions, greatest praise tends to be given to them. But God has been proven to be the most supreme and absolute Sovereign over all. He is the King of kings. On this ground we are thus incited to praise God. "Sing praises to God, sing praises, sing praises to our King, sing praises; for God is

the King of all the earth." This reason is given of the heavenly Hallelujah, "For the Lord God omnipotent reigneth." As God by His sovereignty is the highest of all, so by virtue of His prudent government all good things that are in any way praiseworthy are indeed done. They who have knowledge hereof, and can in truth of heart acknowledge as much, will assuredly be ready on all occasions to praise God.

3. Kindness, goodness, and mercy are the things that most of all enflame the heart to give praise. They are the most principal objects of praise, for which thanks tends to be given. "I will praise Thy name," says the psalmist to God, "for Thy loving kindness." And he exhorts all nations to praise the Lord on this ground, "His merciful kindness is great towards us." After he had thus set out the goodness of God, "The Lord is gracious and full of compassion, slow to anger and of great mercy. The Lord is good to all, and His tender mercies are over all His works," he makes this inference, "All Thy works shall praise Thee, O Lord, and Thy saints shall bless Thee." God's mercies therefore, the main matter of praise, are to be called to mind, and to be set in order, when we go about to praise God. These are they that are of greatest power to rouse up our dull spirits, to put a spiritual life into us, and to provoke us to praise the Lord. I have distinctly laid down these in *The Whole Armor of God*, Treatise 3, Part 2.

]Editor's Note: Gouge is referring to his work on Ephesians 6, first published in 1616. The third treatise is "Of the Means to Use Spiritual Armour Aright." The first part of that third treatise is "Of Prayer in General."]

Now in that the forenamed grounds of praise are only in God, praise is due to Him alone. For…

1. His alone is true excellence, as was before proven.
2. His sovereignty only is absolute.

3. He alone is good, and every good thing comes from Him.

Idolaters, who give praise to false gods (as Belshazzar did), and flatterers who unduly praise men (as Herod's people did) deprive God of that glory that is due to Him. Let such duly weigh the fearful issue that befell both Belshazzar and Herod.

How far praise may be given to men is declared in *The Whole Armor of God,* Treatise 3, Part 2.

Hitherto we have spoken of the substance of the Lord's Prayer. The circumstance following it remains to be handled.

The Meaning and Use of "Amen" Being Prefixed Before a Speech

QUESTION. What is the circumstance following prayer?

ANSWER. The ratification of all. This is expressed in this one word "amen." That "amen" imports a confirmation of that which is said is evident by Benaiah's answer to David's direction concerning Solomon's crowning. For Benaiah, desiring from his heart that David's said direction might be accomplished and ratified, he answered thereto, "Amen." And to explain his mind and meaning more fully he adds, "The Lord God of my Lord the King say so too," that is, as other translators turn it, "ratify it." The Greek translators thus turn it, "Be it done." The root from whence the word comes signifies as much, as is evident by this phrase in Solomon's prayer, "O God of Israel, let Thy word, I pray Thee, be ratified, which Thou spakest unto David."

This particle in Scripture is diversely used. Sometimes it is prefixed before that which is uttered, and sometimes it is inferred after it. It is prefixed before speeches to show both the certainty and the necessity of that which is delivered. When Christ instructed Nicodemus in the mystery of regeneration, to declare unto him the necessity thereof, He thus expresses it, "Amen, Amen, I say to thee, except a man be born again he cannot see the kingdom of God." And, because Nicodemus made question thereof in the same manner, He again repeats it saying, "Amen, Amen, I say to thee, except a man be born of water and of the Spirit he cannot enter into the kingdom of God," to show that it was a true, certain, sure, infallible point that did not fall from his mouth unawares, but such a one as He dared stand behind, yea, and pawned His credit thereupon.

QUESTION. What duties does "amen" import when it is prefixed before a speech?

ANSWER. Two especially, attention and belief.

1. Where the Holy Ghost by any note or sign sets out the excellence, necessity, utility, or any other like commendation of a point, He requires us to give more than ordinary attention thereunto. When the disciples showed Christ the glorious building of the temple, that they might the better mark what He foretold of the destruction thereof, He expresses it thus, "Amen, I say unto you, there shall not be left here one stone upon another that shall not be thrown down."

2. Where the Holy Ghost knows us to be backward and hard to believe such principles as are of an infallible verity, He uses declarations and supplications to draw us on to give the more credence thereunto. Answerably therefore we must mix faith with our hearing of such points. To this purpose when Christ observed unbelief and doubting in His disciples He used this note of declaration, "Amen," to move them the more steadfastly to believe what He said.

The Use of "Amen" Being Added to a Speech

QUESTION. How is "amen" added to a speech?

ANSWER. By him who utters a speech and by him or them who hear it.

It was usual with the apostles, when they made a prayer, gave thanks, or pronounced a blessing, to add thereunto "Amen." And it was usual with the people of God who heard like speeches uttered by others to say "Amen," whether it was only one or many together.

Many are the kinds and forms of speeches whereunto "amen" is in Scripture noted to be added:

1. Petitions.
2. Benedictions and praises.
3. Imprecations and curses.
4. Exhortations to duties.
5. Declarations of promises.
6. Denunciations of judgments.

There are three special things "amen" imports when it is pronounced after any of the forenamed speeches.

1. True assent. This the apostle implies where he directs the church to pray, read, and preach in a known tongue for this end, that even the unlearned hearer may say, "Amen," that is, understanding what he hears give assent thereto.

2. Earnest desire. When the prophet Jeremiah heard the prophesy of Hananiah concerning the return of the King of Judah to his kingdom, and the other captives to their land, and of the vessels that were taken away to the temple, though he knew that to be a false prophesy, yet to show how earnestly he desired that it might be so he says thereto, "Amen." And to fully declare what he meant thereby he adds, "The Lord do so; the Lord perform thy words."

Steadfast faith. Where Christ makes a promise of His second coming, saying, "Surely I come quickly," the church, to show her steadfast faith in that promise, says, "Amen," which imports this much, "Lord, I believe what Thou hast said. Even so, come Lord Jesus."

These being the proper ends of saying "Amen"—to manifest assent, desire and faith—it is without contradiction true that whoever says "Amen" must understand that whereunto he says "Amen." In this case two things are necessarily to be understood—the words that are uttered and the meaning of those words.

If the words spoken are not understood, they are as spoken into the air, altogether in vain; and the speaker and hearer are as barbarians one to another. No more benefit can be received by the words of a man who is not understood than by the indistinct voice of an unreasonable creature. But suppose the words are such as in themselves are intelligible, being English words to an English man; yet if the sense and meaning of them are not conceived they are to no better purpose than words of a strange and unknown language. Words have sometimes a figurative sense and meaning, which if it is not understood the proper and true use and benefit of them is lost. If Christ had not made His disciples to understand the sense and meaning of this direction, "Take heed and beware of the leaven of the Pharisees and of the Sadducees," they would have gotten no good at all thereby. It is therefore necessary that as the words themselves, so the proper sense of them must be well understood.

OBJECTION. "Amen" is a Hebrew word. That language is understood by very few. Why, then, is it used of all nations, of all people in all nations, learned and unlearned?

ANSWER 1. The apostles, though they did not speak and write in Hebrew, but in Greek, yet they used this Hebrew word. So we have an expressed warrant for retaining this word in another language.

ANSWER 2. Continual use has made it familiar to all persons of all languages and in all nations. So that it is everywhere a proper, common, mother word. Thus these two titles "Jesus" and "Christ," though the one is Hebrew and the other Greek, are made so familiar as in all languages they are retained.

ANSWER 3. No other one word so fit for the purpose can in any other language be invented as "amen" is. Not without reason therefore, and just cause is it, that it has been made a word of all languages. It comprises under it whatever is expressed or understood in and by the speech whereunto it is added. These words ("Cursed be he that confirmeth not all the words of this Law to do them") had a large extent; yet the "amen" that the people were to say thereto extended itself as far.

The Duties That "Amen" Added to a Speech Imply

QUESTION. What duties are implied by the use of "Amen" after a speech ended?

ANSWER. Such as concern the speaker, such as concern the hearer, and such as concern both speaker and hearer.

Three duties especially are required of him who utters the speech whereunto "Amen" is added.

1. To speak intelligibly in a known tongue. This is a point much pressed in 1 Corinthians 14:2. See more hereof in *The Whole Armor of God* on Ephesians 6:18.

2. To speak audibly, so that they who are to say "Amen" may hear what is said. The Levites under the law were expressly enjoined to speak to the people with a loud voice. Accordingly the Levites who were the mouth of the people to God, and prayed in their presence, cried with a loud voice unto the Lord their God. Let a prayer be made as intelligibly as may be; if it be not heard of them that are present they cannot with assent, desire, and faith say "Amen."

3. To speak distinctly, that is, so that hearers may observe every petition and every particular point for which thanks is given. It is expressly noted of such as instructed the people of God that they did it distinctly, whereby the hearers better understood what was delivered. If prayer or thanksgiving is uttered by a voluble, swift tongue, too fast, hearers cannot advisedly observe the several branches thereof so that if they say "Amen," at the best it cannot be but to some parts; it cannot be to all the prayer or praise that is uttered.

Three duties also are required of them who say "Amen" to a speech uttered by others.

1. To attend diligently to that which is uttered. The people who said "Amen" to Ezra's blessing are said to stand up while he spoke. That gesture implied a diligent attention. If our minds are wandering, and not attentive to that which is uttered, what assent, what desire, what faith can there be? And if there is none of these, to what end is "Amen" said? Surely it is a plain mocking of God.

2. To give assent thereto. If with the mouth "amen" is uttered and no assent given with the heart, heart and tongue are repugnant; and no better censure can be given of such an "amen" than that it is the amen of a hypocrite, which is odious and detestable to God? The apostle under this phrase ("How shall we say, Amen"") implies assent; for a man may utter this word "amen" to that which he does not understand, but with assent of mind and heart he cannot say, "Amen."

3. To manifest that assent. The phrase of saying "Amen," often used in Scripture, imports a manifestation of assent. For that which is said and uttered is manifested. This manifestation of assent on the hearer's part must be as the uttering of the prayer on the speaker's part, audibly. Every hearer in an assembly must utter "Amen" as loudly as the minister utters the prayer. In many places it is put off only to the clerk. But herein all should be clerks. There is mention made of a celestial sound, which was, as it were, the voice of a great multitude, and as the voice of many waters, and as the voice of mighty thundering, saying, "Hallelujah." If full assemblies in our churches did all of them audibly after a prayer say "Amen" so audibly as the sound of everyone's voice there present might come at least to the minister's ears, it would be such a sound as is there mentioned, a heavenly sound, a sound well becoming a church. No echo like the echo that makes the walls of a church to ring again with "Amen." Such a sound would quicken a

minister's spirits and put a kind of heavenly life into the people themselves.

The duties that are required both of speaker and hearers by virtue of "Amen" to be added are these that follow.

1. To know the ground of all that is uttered, that that which is mentioned whereunto "Amen" is to be added, is grounded on God's Word and agreeable to His will. "For this is the confidence which we have in Him, that if we ask anything according to His will He heareth us."

2. To have the mind fixed thereon. The mind of the speaker as well as the hearer may be roving and wandering, especially when a set, prescribed, usual form of prayer is uttered or when a prayer is read. Now because the utterer of a prayer must say "Amen" to his own prayer as well as the hearers, he as well as they, and they as well as he, even all of them must hold their mind steady thereon; else will their heart be removed from God while they draw near to Him with their mouth, which is an abomination to Him.

3. To retain as well as they can in memory all that is uttered. For "Amen" must be applied to the whole speech, and to every part thereof. Matters well retained in memory make "Amen" to come from the heart and to be uttered with goodwill. "When I remember these things I pour out my soul in me," says the psalmist. That which is forgotten is as not heard, not understood, or not attended unto.

4. To be affected with the prayer. This will make men double their "Amen," as the Jews did when Ezra blessed the Lord. All the people answered, "Amen, Amen," with lifting up their hands. Did not their speech and gesture both declare much affection of heart? Without this inward affection "Amen" will be but coldly uttered.

5. To believe God's gracious acceptance of the prayer. It has been before proven that "Amen" is a ratification of all that is uttered before it. But with what heart can that which is not

before believed be after ratified? Expressly, therefore, Christ says, "What thing so ever ye desire, when ye pray, believe that ye receive it." And His apostle puts this in as a necessary proviso to prayer, "Let him ask in faith."

The Grounds of Faith Whereby We May Expect the Obtaining of What We Pray For

QUESTION. How may we believe the obtaining of those things that we pray for?

ANSWER. By praying for such things as we know to be promised. God's promises are the true and proper ground of a sound faith. Whatsoever is supposed to be believed without a promise is but supposed, or rather presumed; it is not rightly and truly believed. The psalmist having desired God to remember His promise made unto him thus says, "Upon it Thou hast caused me to hope," or to trust. The ground then of his confidence was God's promise. Now because God's promises are of divers kinds (some things being absolutely promised, others but conditionally), as God's promises are made so must our faith be ordered. Absolute promises must be believed absolutely; conditional promises, with submission to God's wisdom in granting or not granting what we pray for. St. Paul having prayed for the Philippians, and knowing that he prayed for such things as God had absolutely promised, thus manifests his steadfast faith, "I am confident of this very thing that He which hath begun a good work in you will perform it until the day of Jesus Christ." But when he desired to come to the Romans he referred that matter to the will of God, to be ordered therein as it should seem good to God. So did David in his desire of returning to his kingdom and to the tabernacle and ark of God, when by the treason of Absalom he was forced from all.

Concerning the petitions of the Lord's Prayer, they are, most of them, absolutely promised, even all of them but the fourth.

1. For hallowing God's name God Himself has said, "I have both glorified My name and will glorify it."

2. For the coming of His kingdom Christ has said, "The gates of hell shall not prevail against My church."

3. For doing His will, this is a branch of the new covenant that by Christ's death is made absolute: "I will put My law in their inward parts and write it in their hearts." And again, "I will put My Spirit within you, and cause you to walk in My statutes, and you shall keep My judgments and do them."

5. For pardoning sin, this is another branch of the foresaid new covenant: "I will forgive their iniquity, and I will remember their sin no more."

6. For not leading into temptation, but delivering from evil, the apostle says, "God will not suffer you to be tempted above that you are able, but will with the temptation make a way to escape."

4. For daily bread, God can instruct us both to be full and to be hungry, both to abound and to suffer need. Yea, He can so give and so take away as to minister thereby to His saints matter of blessing Him, as Job did.

Well therefore may we say "Amen" to all the petitions of the Lord's Prayer, to those five that are of blessings absolutely promised, with an assured faith of obtaining the very things that are prayed for. To that which is not so absolutely promised (which is the fourth), with such a submission of ourselves wholly to God's good pleasure as to believe that God will do that which He in His wisdom sees to be best for us; that He will give such temporal blessings as He knows to be good for us, or give us such grace as shall enable us to bear the want of such things as He denies us. What God denies to the prayers of His saints He knows that it is good for them to be without. He therefore who is well instructed in God's wisdom and assured of His love will without question think it much better to have that which

God knows to be hurtful or unfit for him to be denied rather than granted unto him.

If that which we pray for is not at first granted, we ought to persist and hold on in praying for it, as Jacob who said to the angel of the covenant, the Lord Jesus Christ (with whom by prayer he wrestled), "I will not let Thee go except Thou bless me." And in this perseverance in prayer we must also wait, and with patience expect a gracious answer of our humble and faithful supplications ordered according to the will of God. This is the expressed charge of the prophet, "Though it tarry, wait for it." This is the property of true faith. For He who believes will not make haste.

Setting "Amen" in the Last Place

QUESTION. Why is "Amen" set in the last place?

ANSWER. To show the extent of it and to show the use of it.

For the extent of "Amen," it must be applied to the whole prayer that goes before it, and to every part and particle thereof. Therefore in reciting the particular curses of the law, "Amen" was expressly added to every particular curse. Though so expressly by an audible voice it is not always added to every clause of every prayer, yet the mind giving assent, and the heart inclining a desire, and mind and heart yielding faith to the whole and to every part, "Amen," after all is uttered, is a testimony of as much. Thus then by saying "Amen" when all the Lord's Prayer is ended we show that our assent, desire, and faith is extended to praise as well as to petition and, among petitions, to such as tend to God's glory as our own good; and, of them that tend to His glory, to that which makes for the prosperous increase of His church as well as to that whereby His name is hallowed; yea, and to that which tends to the doing of His will, and that in the manner of doing it as it is done in heaven as well as in the matter thereof; and among the petitions that tend to our good as well to them that concern our spiritual welfare as to that which concerns our temporal welfare; and of those that promote our spiritual welfare as well to that whereby our sanctification is craved, as to that whereby we desire to be justified; and in that of our justification, to our profession of forgiving our debtors as well as to our supplication for God's discharge of our debts to Him; and in that of our sanctification, both to preservation from Satan's assaults, and also to recover out of his snares, and full delivery from all evil; yea, in every petition to others' good as well as to our own. Were "Amen" placed in any other place than in the very end of a prayer, even after all is finished, it could not have so large an extent.

For the use of "Amen," it is a recapitulation, or collection into a brief sum, of all that has gone before so that it being uttered when the prayer is finished it shows that when all particulars have been in special mentioned, we must as in a general view cast our mind upon them all again and review our desire of them, as Solomon did more amply and expressly. For after he had finished his long, pithy, powerful prayer that he made at the dedication of the temple, with a new and fresh desire he comprised the sum of all and thus commended it to God: "Let these my words wherewith I have made supplication before the Lord be nigh unto the Lord our God day and night, that He maintain the cause of His servant and the cause of His people Israel at all times, as the matter shall require." As the preface therefore prefixed before the Lord's Prayer teaches us not rashly but advisedly, with due preparation to come into God's presence and to pray to Him, so "Amen," being added after the prayer, teaches us, not abruptly but circumspectly, with due consideration of all that has been prayed, to depart out of God's presence and to break off prayer. Whenever we present any prayer to the divine Majesty let us so do. AMEN.